T0320069

New Growth Theory

To HIM
Whose Grace I feel all the time

New Growth Theory
An Applied Perspective

Jati K. Sengupta

Professor of Economics and Operations Research, University of California at Santa Barbara, USA

Edward Elgar

Cheltenham, UK • Northampton, MA, USA

Published by
Edward Elgar Publishing Limited
Glensanda House
Montpellier Parade
Cheltenham
Glos GL50 1UA
UK

Edward Elgar Publishing, Inc.
6 Market Street
Northampton
Massachusetts 01060
USA

A catalogue record for this book
is available from the British Library

Library of Congress Cataloguing in Publication Data

Sengupta, Jatikumar.
    New growth theory : an applied perspective / Jati K. Sengupta.
    Includes index.
     1. Economic development. 2. Economic policy. 3. Human capital.
    4. Information technology. I. Title.
    HD75.S46   1999
    338.9—dc21   98–42877
                                         CIP

ISBN 1 85898 875 6

Printed and bound in Great Britain by Bookcraft (Bath) Ltd.

Contents

List of Tables   ix
Preface   xi

1   Theory and Empiricism in Economic Growth   1

1.1   ELEMENTS OF NEW GROWTH THEORY   2
1.2   EMPIRICAL ANALYSIS AND ECONOMETRIC
       TESTS   6
1.3   POLICY ISSUES AND DECISION RULES   8
1.4   GROWTH AND EVOLUTIONARY DYNAMICS   8

**2   New Growth Theory: Empirical
        Perspectives   12**

2.1   MAJOR THEORETICAL DEVELOPMENTS   12
2.2   NONCONVEXITIES IN PRODUCTION AND
       TECHNOLOGY   22
2.3   STOCHASTIC GROWTH   34
2.4   MODELLING LEARNING AND ADAPTIVITY   38

3   Stochastic Aspects of Learning by Doing   40

3.1   SOURCES OF STOCHASTIC LEARNING   41
3.2   DYNAMIC ADJUSTMENTS AND SECTORAL
       SPILLOVERS   52
3.3   SOURCES OF DYNAMIC INSTABILITY   57
3.4   STOCHASTIC LEARNING ALONG THE
       EFFICIENCY FRONTIER   61

4   Recent Growth Episodes in NICs   66

4.1   OPENNESS IN TRADE, PRODUCTIVITY
       AND GROWTH   67
4.2   TIME-SERIES MODELS OF EXPORT
       EXTERNALITY   74
4.3   ECONOMIC FLUCTUATIONS AND GROWTH
       IN JAPAN (1965–90)   85
4.4   EXPORTS AND PRODUCTIVITY GROWTH
       IN KOREA AND OTHER NICs IN ASIA   95

**5   Growth Stabilization and Exchange Rate
       Instability**   116

5.1   STOCHASTIC MODELS OF VOLATILITY   119
5.2   NONLINEAR DYNAMICS IN EXCHANGE
       RATE FLUCTUATIONS   129
5.3   TESTS OF NONLINEARITY IN EXCHANGE
       MARKETS   149
5.4   EXCHANGE RATE IMBALANCE AND
       GROWTH   152

6   Growth and Development Policy   153

6.1   DYNAMICS OF ADJUSTMENT POLICIES   155
6.2   LEARNING AND GROWTH   159
6.3   TRADE AND FOREIGN EXCHANGE   168
6.4   POLICY IMPACT ANALYSIS   172

**7   Evolutionary Dynamics in Economic
       Growth**   182

7.1   SCHUMPETERIAN DYNAMICS   183

Contents

7.2 DIMENSIONS AND DIFFUSION OF NEW
    TECHNOLOGY   190
7.3 MODELS OF EVOLUTION AND DIVERSITY   197
7.4 CHAOTIC DYNAMICS IN ECONOMIC
    GROWTH   205

8   Infrastructure and Economic Growth   209

8.1 PRODUCTIVITY OF PUBLIC CAPITAL   210
8.2 SOCIAL OVERHEAD CAPITAL   214
8.3 HUMAN DEVELOPMENT AND GROWTH   216
8.4 INSTITUTIONAL CHANGE AND
    ORGANIZATIONAL DEVELOPMENT   218

    References   220

    Index   231

List of Tables

2.1 Sources of GNP Growth 23

2.2 Factors Influencing R&D Intensity 25

2.3 Estimates of the Speed of Adjustment (N_i) and the Weight Ratio (η_i) for the Two Input Models 32

2.4 Estimates of the Speed of Adjustment (N_L) and the Weight Ratio (η_L) for the Optimal Labor Demand Equation 33

2.5 Estimates of the Speed of Adjustment (N_i) and the Weight Ratio (η_i) for the Four Input Model (Backward-Looking Model) 33

3.1 Percentage Distribution of Exports to the US 53

4.1 TFP Growth Regression on the Trade Openness Variables 70

4.2 Rates of Growth of Output and Shares of TFP (1952–80) 72

4.3 Saving Investment Trend in the Asian Pacific Rim 73

4.4 Error Corrections Models of Export Externality 77

4.5 Error Corrections Models of Export Demand 77

4.6 Estimates of the Production Function Parameters in some Asian NICs 83

4.7 Sources of Output Growth 84

4.8 Sources of Output Growth Measured by Loglinear Production Functions 90

4.9 Estimates of Solow Residuals ($\Delta \ln R$) Adjusted for Exports 92

4.10 Estimates of the Speed of Adjustment Parameters (ϕ_i) and the Weight Ratio $\theta_i = \Lambda_i/\Psi_i$ (i = K,L) 93

4.11 Estimates of the Parameters of the Loglinear Production Frontier Implied by the Optimal Input Demands 94

4.12 Structural Change and Economic Growth in East Asia 97

4.13 Specialization in High-Technology Exports (HTX) in East Asia 98

4.14 Externality Effect of Exports on Growth 1967–86 101

4.15 Estimates of Cointegration Test Statistics 103

4.16 Regression and LP Estimates of the Dynamic Production Function (1961–86) in Korean Manufacturing 110

4.17 Regression and LP Estimates of the Dynamic Cost Function (1961–86) in Korean Manufacturing 111

4.18 Changes in Labor Productivity over Two Subperiods 111

5.1 Impact of Fundamentals on Real Exchange Rates 125

5.2 Impact of Interest Rate and Inflation 127

5.3 Estimates of the Linear Second-Order Variance Process 128

5.4 Impact of Interest Rate Inflation 139

5.5 Real Exchange Rate Fluctuations in Asia 140

5.6 Variance Process Model for Asia 141

5.7 Arch Model for Variance in Asia 142

5.8 Logistic Model for Variance in Asia 143

5.9 Real Exchange Rate Fluctuations in Latin America 144

5.10 Variance Process Model for Latin America 145

5.11 Arch Model for Variance in Latin America 146

5.12 Logistic Model for Variance in Latin America 147

5.13 Lorenz Logistic Model for Variance for Industrial Countries 148

5.14 Test of Near-Random Walk by a Cubic Regressor 150

5.15 Estimates of Feedback Loops 151

6.1 Indicators of Economic Performance of Selected Developing Countries 156

6.2 Distribution of Strategic Technology Alliances Between and Within Economic Blocs 158

6.3 Estimates of the Speed of Adjustment Parameters (ϕ_i), the Stable Characteristic Roots (ζ_i) and θ_i 163

6.4 Two-Step Estimation of the Labor Demand Equation in the Two-Input Model (Backward-Looking Model) 165

6.5 Evolution of Exports (E), Savings (S) and Investment (I) in Relation to GNP (Y) in % 170

6.6 Sources of Growth 177

6.7 Taxonomy of Innovative Business in Italy (1981–85) 178

7.1 Short-Run and Long-Run Spillover Effects 192

Preface

New growth theory attempts to explain the process of long run growth through endogenous forces such as human capital, knowledge spillover and information technology. It grew out of a challenge to the neoclassical theory, which explains steady state growth rate in terms of the exogenous rate of technological progress.

The challenge has now spread to other newer areas such as evolutionary and nonlinear dynamics, where nonstationarity and complexity in evolution play critical roles. Learning along the efficiency frontier in production and information technology has raised new research problems before the new growth theorists. One such problem involves the dynamic process of adjustment that goes on when one technology is replaced by a newer and more efficient technology. Schumpeter developed a model of 'creative destruction' to analyze this type of dynamics of adjustment. Taking cue from ecological theorists other new growth theorists have applied concepts of evolutionary stable strategies to the growth and evolution of new innovations. Once again the stochastic aspects of interaction between sectors or players have provided the main focus of this approach, where maximizing fitness of survival and growth has provided the main objective.

New growth theory takes a favorable view of the scope of economic policy. It shows that it is both feasible and optimal to influence the long run growth rates of an economy through both public and private measures, which may improve the quality of human capital and the adoption of the newer and more efficient technology. This emphasis on economic policy making provides an operational support to models of computable general equilibrium, where social overhead capital and investment in infrastructure can be optimally decided by a social planner. Also this suggests the need to broaden the economic growth concept to an overall social and human development. This monograph adopts this view.

Two distinctive features of this book are: emphasis on the empirical and econometric aspects of new growth theory, and the analysis of an overall view of growth in a global perspective. We hope this view will stimulate greater interest and awareness of the problems of economic growth and development.

Finally, I would like to record my deep appreciation to my wife for her abiding support and encouragement.

Jati K. Sengupta

xi

1. Theory and Empiricism in Economic Growth

Modern growth theory is an active field of research in economics today. Several reasons may be cited: availability of more empirical data, development of new techniques in time series analysis and the increased interdependence of countries through globalization of trade and transmission of new technologies of communication. Thus attention has shifted from theory to testing and sometimes from international comparison to specific growth experiences of individual countries. Notably the success stories of rapid growth episodes of some countries have drawn more attention and this has sometimes led to an active search for new answers that are not readily available from past theories.

This shift to empiricism in economic growth analysis is the focus of this monograph. It is our belief that this focus would provide not only a critical review of the applied perspective so far developed in new growth theory, which has evolved over the last decade and is still evolving, but also a challenge for the modern theorists to develop new insights into the dynamic forces of growth and development.

The object of the book is two-fold: to review the most significant applications of new growth theory and to introduce some of the newer models of nonlinear and evolutionary dynamics, which are likely to yield important testable hypotheses in the future.

The plan of the book is as follows. Chapter 2 deals with the major applied hypotheses of new growth theory, its endogenous and adaptivity aspects. Chapter 3 discusses both the deterministic and stochastic aspects of the learning phenomena in new growth theory. Learning and adaptivity play a key role in modern growth theory e.g., in the diffusion of knowledge and in the adjustment by innovators and entrepreneurs from the short run to a long run horizon. Dynamic instability associated with this process may sometimes lead to nonlinearities and chaotic fluctuations. Chapter 4 analyzes the historical growth experiences of the newly industrializing countries (NICs) of Asia, which have attracted considerable attention from the new growth theorists today. Chapter 5 discusses the sources of the recent instability in the financial markets in Asia, which has adversely affected the growth rate of the newly industrializing countries of Asia over the last six months of 1997. Chapter 6 analyzes three key areas of

1

economic policy under growth e.g., disequilibrium models, computable general equilibrium and trade and foreign exchange policies. Chapter 7 briefly reviews the testable propositions from the models of evolutionary dynamics. Schumpeterian dynamics and the recent nonlinear models of complexity and chaotic dynamics are also analyzed. Finally, Chapter 8 discusses the role of economic and social infrastructure investment in sustaining economic growth. The key role played by the human development index and the social indicator index in appraising the quality of overall development is analyzed here.

This chapter gives a brief overview of some of the key elements to be discussed in this monograph. Some of the major applied aspects of new growth theory are discussed first and since new growth theory developed first as a challenge to the neoclassical theory, its implications for neoclassical theory are analyzed in brief. This is followed by a brief discussion of the newer econometric methods of time series analysis which are frequently applied in empirical tests of the hypotheses generated by new growth theory. Finally, the historical and evolutionary dynamics of growth are briefly discussed.

1.1   ELEMENTS OF NEW GROWTH THEORY

Two major elements of new growth theory have received considerable attention from the applied economists and econometricians today. One is the endogenous sources of steady state growth in per capita output and consumption. This is often contrasted with the neoclassical approach which cannot provide any satisfactory explanation. The second key element is the externality associated with what is known as knowledge capital, which in various forms may combine with human capital in the form of skills and generate a potential source of self-sustained growth rate in the steady state.

Solow's model, which is closely related to the neoclassical model assumed technological progress to be exogenous and with constant returns to scale it derived the key result that the steady state growth rate equals the rate g of technical progress. Thus the growth rates of physical capital (K_t) and labor (L_t) have no effect on the growth rate of output and since technological progress is determined outside the model, the long run growth rate is not explained by any endogenous factors. McCallum (1996) has recently compared this framework with the endogenous growth theory in its three variants e.g., (i) one featuring externalities resulting from capital-and-knowledge accumulation, (ii) the second featuring human capital in the form of workplace skills and (iii) finally the continuing growth of existing productive 'designs' and its spillover in the flexible manufacturing system technology.

McCallum (1996) derived an optimal growth path from the neoclassical model by assuming that the households maximize a preference function

$$\text{Max} \int_0^\infty e^{-\rho t} u(c_t) dt \qquad (1.1)$$

subject to the budget constraint

$$f(\hat{k}_t) = c_t /(1+g)^t + (1+v)(1+g)\hat{k}_{t+1} - (1-\delta)\hat{k}_t$$

where v is the per capita value of government transfers, δ is the fixed rate of depreciation of capital and $f(\hat{k}_t)$ is the per capita production function in efficiency units i.e. $\hat{y}_t = f(\hat{k}_t)$, $\hat{k}_t = K_t /(1+g)^t L_t$. On assuming $u(c_t) = \log c_t$ and $\hat{y}_t = A\hat{k}_t^\alpha$ one can then easily derive from the solution of (1.1) the following equation of motion of $\hat{k}_t$:

$$\log \hat{k}_{t+1} - \log \hat{k}_t = (1-\alpha)\left[\log \hat{k}^* - \log \hat{k}_t\right] \qquad (1.2)$$

where $\log k^* = (1-\alpha)^{-1} \log[(\alpha\rho A)/(1+v)(1+g)]$. Since $(1-\alpha)$ is positive, this implies that $\hat{k}_t$ approaches the steady state value $\hat{k}^*$ as time goes to infinity, with $(1-\alpha)$ being the rate of convergence.

The human capital in the sense of workplace skills is added by the Lucas model (1988). On assuming a linear form of human capital (h_t) accumulation

$$h_{t+1} - h_t = B(1-n_t)h_t - \delta_h h_t \qquad (1.3)$$

where $(1-n_t)$ is the fraction of household's work time allocated to learning new skills and δ_h is the rate of depreciation of human capital, one would then obtain from above the following equation for testing convergence to the steady state:

$$\log k_{t+1} - \log k_t = (1-\alpha)\left[\log h_t - \log k_t\right]$$
$$+ \varepsilon \log h_t + \log A_0 \qquad (1.4)$$

where $\quad A_0 = \alpha\rho(1-\rho)^{1-\alpha} A /(1+v)$

Here the production function is Cobb–Douglas

$$y_t = Ak_t^\alpha \, \bar{k}_t^\varepsilon = Ak_t^{\alpha+\varepsilon}$$

where it is assumed as before that $u(c_t) = \log c_t$, and the parameter ε is the externality factor with $\bar{k}_t$ denoting the economy-wide average capital stock per capita. But since all households are alike we obtain $k_t = \bar{k}_t$. Clearly the equation of motion (1.4) for capital (k_t) reveals conditional convergence, since $\log k_t$ has a negative slope coefficient. Note however that $\log h_t$ has a positive feedback coefficient given by $(\varepsilon + 1 - \alpha)$.

Productivity growth has sometimes been estimated as a residual (e.g., Solow residual), after the contributions of the measured factor inputs such as physical and human capital and labor are subtracted from output growth. This residual is mostly attributed to technical progress. Recently Lau (1996) analyzed the contributions of long-term sources of growth for selected developed and developing countries as follows:

		Capital	Labor	Human Capital	Technical Progress
USA	1948–90	24%	31%	7%	36%
UK	1957–90	37%	4%	9%	49%
Japan	1957–90	45%	6%	4%	45%
South Korea	1960–90	61%	20%	19%	0%
Taiwan	1953–90	70%	14%	16%	0%

Two surprising conclusions emerged. Technical progress is practically of no importance in long-term growth for the developing NICs of East Asia, though it is of great importance for the developed industrial countries. Second, the NICs in Asia exhibited significant economies of scale, i.e. return to scale of up to 1.6 with 1.0 being constant returns to scale, but as these economies mature these increasing returns to scale tend to be exhausted. By contrast in the developed industrial countries the returns to scale reached their constant level close to 1.0 by 1990. However this contrasting scenario is most likely to change over the next two decades e.g., the NICs in Asia would invest more in R&D technology and innovation and the international spillover of knowledge would enhance the productivity growth in the newer technology-intensive industries such as microelectronics, semiconductors and the communications network.

One has to note however that the dimensions of new technology and its international transmission are not fully understood and hence inadequate model specifications are available here. Recently Mairesse and Sassenou (1991) surveyed the international econometric studies at the firm level relating R&D expenditure to productivity and found that there is a significant positive relationship between R&D expenditure and productivity but there are sharp disparities between the time-series and cross-section estimates. The time-series estimates of the output elasticity of research capital and physical capital (with standard errors in parenthesis) for US, France and Japan are as follows:

Country	Output Proxy	Research Capital	Physical Capital	R^2
USA (1966–67) 133 firms	sales	0.26 (0.03)	0.41 (0.02)	0.56
France (1972–73) 98 firms	value added	0.20 (0.06)	0.31 (0.06)	0.30
Japan (1973–81) 394 firms	value added	0.03 (0.01)	0.28 (0.03)	0.54

The results indicate that the size of the R&D elasticity is about half of the physical capital elasticity in the US and France but to merely 10 percent in Japan. However the results for recent periods, particularly for the microelectronics and semiconductor industries in the US are likely to be very different. These empirical aspects are discussed in some detail in later chapters.

The important point to note is that we have as yet no operational model of how an innovation takes place, interacts with others and finally spreads all over. Rosenberg (1996) has discussed in some detail the various aspects of uncertainty involved in the technological innovation processes relating to laser, to integrated circuits and to microprocessors. He noted two significant points in new technology developments. One is that the impact of an innovation has complementary impact on other innovations. Thus the telephone transmission technology was dramatically altered by the combination of two different innovations: laser and fiber optics. Secondly, the impact of the computer technology has spilled over from manufacturing industries to such industries as airlines and generated significant cost reductions in operation, distribution and other services.

An endogenous view of technological progress assumes that it is quite rational for economic agents to take the risk of new innovations through R&D investment, when they see prospects for reaping returns on their investments. Returns when realized usually come in the form of economic rents or royalty on patents in a world of imperfectly competitive product markets. As Grossman and Helpman (1991) have argued that most R&D investments generate two distinct types of output. One is the product-specific information yielding a new good. The other is the generation of more general technical information and know-how which may facilitate the undertaking or development of subsequent innovations. It is this second aspect which was emphasized by the Schumpeterian model of 'creative destruction'. The empirical studies of the linkage of R&D expenditure to productivity surveyed by Mairesse and Sassenou (1991) do not incorporate this externality effect of an innovation.

1.2   EMPIRICAL ANALYSIS AND ECONOMETRIC TESTS

Empirical applications of economic growth models have followed three phases, which are parallel to the development of growth theory itself. In the 1950's the post-Keynesian models of growth e.g., Harrod–Domar models featured very significantly in the large-scale econometric models built for several developed and underdeveloped countries. These models in some formulations incorporated the neoclassical production functions and their econometric estimation involved sophisticated estimation techniques involving three-stage least squares and full-information nonlinear maximum likelihood. This phase is followed by a phase characterized by modelling quantitative economic policy, involving short-run stabilization and long-run growth. For developing economies this led to the application of national planning models of different degrees of sophistication. Besides econometric

6

estimation of some of the behavioral equations of the model, these planning models invariably contained a set of policy variables which are potentially usable by the policy makers and an objective function which was intended to quantify the policy goals. A detailed survey of these models for a number of countries by Fox, Sengupta and Thorbecke (1973) shows that the optimization techniques of linear and quadratic programming are usually combined here with the standard econometric estimation techniques, particularly for the developing economies, where public sector investment has to be allocated among a set of competing sectors. The intersectoral input–output model is frequently applied in this framework and integrated with the econometric parts of the general equilibrium model. In recent times this has led to the development and application of computable general equilibrium models for developing economies.

The recent phase developed over the last two decades concentrates more on the econometric testing of specific hypotheses, e.g., convergence of growth rates across countries, output elasticity of R&D investment and the impact of openness in trade on the growth of output. International cross-section and time series data are frequently used, though there are significant problems of heterogeneity and lack of comparability. Two methods of dynamic time series modelling have found increasing applications in new growth theory. One is the treatment of nonstationarity in the time series data by incorporating the cointegration approach. The other is the Kalman filtering approach to reduce the noise variance from the data. The first has been found to be useful in eliminating or reducing the spuriousness of many regression relationships. The second has proved its significance in estimating the Euler equations for the optimal growth paths.

As an example of the cointegration approach consider a linear regression of output (y_t) to the inputs x_{it}, where $y_t = \alpha' x_t = \sum_i \alpha_i x_{it}$. A time series y_t is said to be integrated of order d, denoted I(d), if it must be differenced d times to make it stationary. Thus a time series y_t is I(0) if it is stationary, whereas if it is I(1), its first difference is stationary. Suppose now that we have a steady state relation $y_t = \alpha' x_t$, where $z_t = y_t - \alpha' x_t = 0$ measures the extent to which the system is out of equilibrium and can therefore be termed 'equilibrium error'. Hence if both y_t and $\hat{x}_t = \alpha' x_t$ are I(1), then the equilibrium error z_t will be I(0) and it will rarely drift far from its equilibrium value zero. In such circumstance $\hat{x}_t$ and y_t are said to be cointegrated and in this case meaningful statistical inference can be drawn by using the so-called error correction models to transform the original

7

regression problem in nonstationary variables. Engle and Granger (1987) have generalized this cointegration approach in order to derive more meaningful relationships among the permanent rather than transitory components of the time series variables y_t, x_{1t}, x_{2t}, ... This type of approach will be frequently applied in testing different specific hypotheses of new growth theory.

Kalman filtering methods have been applied more often in updating decision rules of economic agents, when they have to adjust short run behavior to attain the optimal or desired growth paths.

1.3   POLICY ISSUES AND DECISION RULES

In neoclassical growth models, the rate of growth of per capita output often peters out unless exogenous technical progress continues to sustain the investment for new technology. In the new growth theory, the process of knowledge accumulation and its spillover across sectors and national boundaries serve to sustain endogenously the continual productivity gains and hence the long run growth rate of economy. In turn these productivity gains may initiate further investment in newer and complementary activities. As we have noted that the computer technology and its recent innovations have had a dramatic effect on almost every aspect of manufacturing and communication activities, e.g., airlines, banking, flexible manufacturing systems and this impact is continually spreading.

The new growth theory allows an explicit role of public policy which can enhance the process of knowledge diffusion and therefore the endogenous process of technological change. At another level the human capital in the sense of skill, creativity and work experience can be augmented by deliberate public policies through monetary and fiscal measures. Promoting investment in social and economic infrastructure would perform the same role as the generation of increasing returns to scale. Likewise a deliberate public policy to promote R&D research through tax credits, direct subsidies or openness in trade and international diffusion of knowledge would be helpful in achieving a self-sustained growth process.

1.4   GROWTH AND EVOLUTIONARY DYNAMICS

Two premises of endogenous growth theory have been challenged by the modern theorists who model long run growth in terms of evolutionary dynamics. One is the endogeneous feature of technological innovations, where the notions of economic rationality and expected profit opportunities seem to guide the potential innovators. This premise is challenged by evolutionary dynamics which views innovation to be linked to evolution via technological competition. Technological competition initiates the process of selection by driving the less efficient firms out of the market (i.e. by accelerating 'the death rates' or the exit rate) and by ushering in newer and more efficient firms (i.e., by accelerating the birth rates or the rate of entry). Schumpeterian innovation produces growth because it creates new market conditions and new structural frameworks. This innovation is more pervasive than the technological competition viewed by the new growth theory. As Lombardini and Donati (1996) have argued this type of innovative activity is incompatible with the conventional notions of economic rationality through profit maximization as understood in the neoclassical approach. However, the Schumpeterian model of 'creative destruction' which offers a significant component of the theory of evolutionary dynamics has not been successfully formalized into a quantitative model, which can be readily tested by empirical data. Some attempts have of course been made to link rapid technological diffusion in an industry such as microelectronics with a high rate of exit of old firms and a high rate of entry of new firms.

The second premise of new growth theory is that the incentive structure of the competitive market system is sufficient to generate new and productive innovations. This view is in marked contrast with the evolutionary approach, which postulates that the most favorable context for innovation is oligopolistic competition. In fact one important feature of the Schumpeterian entrepreneur is his motivation to invest in new techniques and new markets with a view to acquire more *power*, both economic and social. Innovations certainly depend to some extent on the social infrastructure e.g., a good school system and universities where research is done and they occur in clusters due to several reasons e.g., any revolutionary discovery in information technology impacts on the other industries, some innovations open the way to a larger set of complementary innovations and so on. Due to the impact of clusters of innovative activities the aggregate pool of knowledge capital yields economies due to agglomeration and scale and also positive feedback among the intermediate activities that are closely linked with the initial innovative revolution.

One way to model the evolutionary dynamics of technological competition, which is the underlying concept behind Schumpeter's model of 'creative destruction' is to consider a stochastic process model of evolution of an economy, characterized by the Markovian birth and death processes.

Let x(t) be stream of innovations viewed as a discrete process taking the value x (x=1,2,...) at time t and let the probability $P_x(t) = \text{Prob}(x(t) = x)$ be characterized by a simple birth and death process. This yields the differential equations

$$\frac{dP_x(t)}{dt} = \lambda_{x-1}P_{x-1}(t) - (\lambda_x + \mu_x)P_x(t) + \mu_{x+1}P_{x+1}(t)$$

for x=1,2,3   (1.5)

$$\frac{dP_0(t)}{dt} = \mu_1 P_1(t) \qquad\qquad \text{for x=0}$$

where λ_x is the birth rate or the transition probability of a positive jump and μ_x is the death rate or the transition probability of a negative jump. If we assume that the birth and death rates are constants, then the above system can be explicitly solved and the mean M(t) and variance V(t) of the X(t) process can be explicitly computed as follows:

$$M(t) = x(0)e^{(\lambda-\mu)t}$$

$$V(t) = \frac{(\lambda+\mu)x_0}{\lambda-\mu}e^{(\lambda-\mu)t}\left[e^{(\lambda-\mu)t} - 1\right]$$

Clearly if the birth rate exceeds the death rate, then both M(t) and V(t) tend to infinity as $t \to \infty$. However if $\lambda = \mu$, then $M(t) = x_0$ and $V(t) = 2\lambda t\, x(0)$, where x(0) is the value of X(t) at initial time zero. When $\lambda < \mu$ the probability of extinction $P_0(t)$ takes the value unity when $t \to \infty$ and the mean level of innovations is zero. Thus for $\lambda > \mu$ we obtain long run growth that is self-sustained and nonstationary.

This model of self-sustained growth can be empirically tested when time-series data on innovative output are available for an industry. For example let p(t) be the proportion of innovative output to total industry output at time t and assume a first order Markov process for the transition probability. Then one could estimate the birth and death rate parameters λ and μ from the following regression model

$$p(t) = \lambda p^+(t-1) + \mu p^-(t-1) + \text{error} \qquad\qquad (1.6)$$

where

$$p^+(t-1) = p(t-1), \quad \text{if} \quad p(t-1) > p(t)$$
$$p^-(t-1) = p(t-1), \quad \text{if} \quad p(t-1) \le p(t)$$

If the estimated values satisfy $\lambda > \mu$, then we have creative destruction in that industry, but for $\mu > \lambda$ we have only destruction with no new creation thus leading to extinction of the technology. Another interesting case arises in this model, when λ_x and μ_x follow a logistic behavior. Thus assume $\lambda_x = (k - x)x$ and $\mu_x = (x - h)x$ with $k > h$. Then the mean solution $M(t)$ can be obtained as:

$$\frac{dM(t)}{dt} = M(t)\big[(k+h) - 2M(t) - 2V(t)/M(t)\big]$$

This shows that $M(t)$ declines over time and attains a steady state, till a new innovation shock enters into the industry changing the parameters k and h. The steady state variance $\overline{V}$ also declines as the steady state mean rises over time, since

$$\overline{V} = \overline{M}\left(\frac{k+h}{2} - M\right)$$

This type of evolutionary models is commonly applied in ecology and biological sciences to explain the patten of diversity and growth in evolution. Economic growth models can profitably adapt these evolutionary processes in order to study the phenomena of innovation shocks and knowledge spillover in the overall economy.

2. New Growth Theory: Empirical Perspectives

Endogenous growth theory developed over the last decade is often called new economic growth theory. It may be viewed in two different ways: theoretical and empirical. On the theoretical side it provides some basic modifications to the neoclassical growth model and its competitive market assumptions. The challenges posed by these basic modifications have several applied implications. On the empirical side new growth theory has generated much interest in econometric testing of several new hypotheses about the empirical growth process. For example the role of openness in trade, the dynamic pattern of knowledge spillover across countries and the dynamic role of scale economies in fast growing countries of southeast Asia have provided key issues before the new growth theorists.

Our objective here is two-fold. We examine some of the most important aspects of both the theoretical and the empirical developments of new growth theory and then appraise these developments in terms of the historical experiences of some countries like Japan and Korea, which belong to the group of successful countries known as NICs (newly industrial countries). In this framework we present some new hypotheses about the growth process, which are amenable to direct empirical testing. These hypotheses deal with the innovation processes and technological diffusion which generate increasing returns on a global scale.

We develop a model of stochastic growth with stochastic technological progress and discuss an intertemporal optimization model where the producers play an active role in deciding capital accumulation paths in the future.

2.1 MAJOR THEORETICAL DEVELOPMENTS

Recent developments in new growth theory have raised several new issues in understanding the empirical growth process, of which the following three will be briefly discussed. One is the technological change and its impact on the production function. The second is human capital and its spillover across countries and the third is the convergence of growth paths in an international cross-section framework. We discuss these three aspects briefly.

2.1.1 Technological Progress

Solow (1956) in his classic contribution analyzed economic growth by assuming a standard neoclassical production function with decreasing returns to capital. Taking the rate of saving, population growth and technological progress as exogenous, he showed that these variables determine the steady-state level of income per capita. Assume a Cobb–Douglas production function for output Y(t) at time t:

$$Y(t) = K(t)^{\alpha}(A(t)L(t))^{1-\alpha} \qquad 0 < \alpha < 1 \qquad (2.1)$$

where K and L are capital and labor and A is the level of technology. L and A are assumed to grow exogenously at rates n and g, i.e., $L(t) = L(0)$ exp (nt) and $A(t) = A(0)$ exp(gt). The model assumes that a constant fraction of output, s is invested. Defining k as the stock of capital per unit of effective or augmented labor, $k = K/AL$ and y as the level of output per effective unit of labor, $y = Y/AL$ the path of evolution of k(t) can then be specified by the following differential equation

$$\dot{k}(t) = sy(t) - (n + g + \delta)k(t)$$
$$= sk^{\alpha}(t) - (n + g + \delta)k(t) \qquad (2.2)$$

where dot denotes the time derivative and δ is the constant rate of depreciation. This is the fundamental equation of the Solow model, which implies that there is a steady state value k* defined by

$$k^{*} = \lceil s/(n + g + d)\rceil^{1/(1-\alpha)} \qquad (2.3)$$

On substituting (2.3) into the production function (2.1) and taking logs one finds that the steady state per capita income is given by

$$\ln(Y(t)/L(t)) = \ln A(0) + gt + \alpha(1 - \alpha)^{-1}$$
$$\ln s - \alpha(1 - \alpha)^{-1} \ln(n + g + \delta) \qquad (2.4)$$

This implies that in the long-run or the steady state equilibrium, total output and capital stock grow at a uniform rate equal to the growth of effective or augmented labor:

$$\dot{Y}/Y = \dot{K}/K = n + g \tag{2.5}$$

On writing the production function (2.1) in a slightly different form as

$$Y(t) = A(t)\, K^{\alpha}(t)\, L(t)^{1-\alpha} \tag{2.6}$$

and using the competitive market assumption that the two inputs are paid the value of their marginal products, one obtains the neutral technological progress function as

$$\dot{A}(t)/(A(t) = \dot{q}/q(t) - w_k(\dot{k}/k) \tag{2.7}$$

where $q(t) = Y(t)/L(t)$, $w_k = (\partial Y(t)/\partial K)(K/Y)$, i.e., the relative share of capital and $k = Y/L$. Here the term $A(t)$ in the production function (2.6) is called Hicks-neutral technical change, which indicates shifts in the production function which leave marginal rates of substitution unchanged. Solow estimated the rate of technological progress $(\dot{A}/A)$ per annum for the U.S. economy over the period 1909–1949 as follows:

$$\dot{A}/A \quad \frac{1909\text{–}29}{0.9\%} \quad \frac{1930\text{–}49}{2.25\%} \quad \frac{1909\text{–}49}{1.5\%} \; .$$

The term $\dot{A}/A$ is frequently interpreted as total factor productivity (TFP) growth and also as Solow residual. Recently a number of estimates have been attempted by researchers with slightly different versions of TFP growth. For example Norsworthy and Jang (1992) defined TFP growth as

$$\dot{A}/A = \dot{Y}/Y - w_k(\dot{K}/K) - w_L(\dot{L}/L) - w_M(\dot{M}/M)$$

where w_K, w_L and w_M are the share in the total cost of production of the three inputs, capital, labor and other materials. Their estimates for the US and Japan in respect of the manufacturing sector are as follows:

	TFP Growth (%)	
	US	Japan
1965–73	0.59	0.91
1973–77	0.38	1.64

Recently Hall (1990) developed a modified Solow residual by incorporating the presence of market power (degree of monopoly) and also increasing returns. But since the share of labor can be measured in relation to either total costs or total revenues, two concepts of modified Solow residuals are possible. By using μ, the ratio of price to marginal cost, i.e., mark-up ratio to denote market power and γ as the returns to scale index, i.e.,

$$\gamma = \frac{K}{Y}\frac{\partial Y}{\partial K} + \frac{L}{Y}\frac{\partial Y}{\partial L} = \text{the elasticity of output with respect to both inputs,}$$

the modified Solow residuals are defined as:

$$\dot{A}/A = \dot{Y}/Y - (1-\alpha)\dot{L}/L - \alpha \ln K - (\mu - 1)\alpha\left[\frac{\dot{L}}{L} - \frac{\dot{K}}{K}\right]$$

$$- (\gamma - 1)\dot{K}/K \text{ (revenue based)}$$

$$\dot{A}/A = \dot{Y}/Y - (1-\alpha)\dot{L}/L - \alpha\dot{K}/K - (\gamma - 1)$$

$$\left[(1-\alpha)\dot{L}/L + \alpha\frac{\dot{K}}{K}\right] \text{ (cost based)}$$

Hall's empirical estimates found important evidence for the existence of market power ($\mu > 1$) and also increasing returns ($\gamma > 1$) to scale in several sectors of the US economy. This raises the fundamental question whether the two basic assumptions of the Solow model (perfect competition and the constant returns to scale) are empirically tenable at all. Recently Basu (1996) raised two objections to Hall's empirical estimate of increasing returns to scale. One is that the final estimate of returns to scale while controlling for cyclical variations in factor utilization is almost exactly one. He exploits the intuition that materials inputs have none or less fixed utilization rates, hence materials growth can be taken as a good measure of unobserved changes in capital and labor utilization. Use of this measure shows that cyclical factor utilization of labor and capital are quite large and technology shocks very small and have low correlation with output growth. Secondly, Basu and Fernald (1995) used gross output data of 21 two-digit manufacturing industries in the US for the years 1953–85 and found that an increase in the output of one manufacturing sector has no significant spillover effect on the productivity of other sectors. However the use of value added data confirm the finding by Caballero and Lyons (1992) that output spillovers are very large. Basu and Fernald (1995) attribute this large productivity spillover to the misspecifications in the Divisia index of value added. Their results find essentially constant returns, no short-run spillovers and small markups of price over marginal cost.

The Solow model in its empirical applications to the US and other industrial countries identified technological progress as the most important factor determining long run growth. Here technological progress is viewed as neutral technical change, which is treated as exogenous. New growth theory has challenged this exogeneity assumption in several ways.

First of all, Romer (1990) proposed a model of *endogenous* technological change that arises from intentional investment decisions made by profit-maximizing agents. This new technology is not a public good but a nonrival input (i.e., complementary to all other inputs) that is only partially excludable. Due to nonconvexity introduced by this nonrival input the production function exhibits increasing returns to scale and hence the price-taking competitive equilibrium cannot be supported in this framework. Instead one has to seek an equilibrium in the framework of monopolistic competition. In Romer's model the four basic inputs are physical capital (K), labor (L), human capital (H) and the level of technology (A). Total capital is viewed as the cumulative output foregone and it evolves according to the rule

$$\dot{K}(t) = Y(t) - C(t)$$

where C(t) is aggregate consumption at time t. Final output Y in this model is expressed as a function of physical labor, human capital devoted to final output (H_Y) and physical capital. But the production technology assumed here assigns a special role to capital, i.e., it disaggregates capital into an infinite number of distinct types of producer durables. Thus K may be set equal to

$$K = \eta \sum_{i=1}^{\infty} x_i$$

where x_i is the input for durable good i. By assuming a Cobb–Douglas production function and the index i to be continuous one could write output Y as

$$Y(H_A, L, x) = H_Y^{\alpha} L^{\beta} \int_0^{\infty} x(i)^{1-\alpha-\beta} di$$
$$= H_Y^{\alpha} L^{\beta} A \bar{x}^{1-\alpha-\beta}$$

16

$$= (H_Y A)^{\alpha} (LA)^{\beta} K^{1-\alpha-\beta} \eta^{\alpha+\beta-1} \qquad (2.8)$$

where we have used the equation $K = \eta A \bar{x}$ in the production function with $\bar{x}$ denoting the optimal input demand for durable goods solved through a profit maximization model. This production function (2.8) behaves just like the neoclassical model with labor and human capital augmenting technological change. Thus if A grew at an exogenously specified exponential rate g, the economy would converge to a path on which K grows at the same exponential rate g. However this specification has two major differences from the Solow model. One is due to the nonconvexity introduced by the nonrival input A, where its growth by itself increases the productivity of human capital in the research sector H_A (i.e., $H = H_Y + H_A$).

By summing across all people engaged in research, the aggregate stock of designs, which is nothing but A in this formulation is then assumed to evolve according to the following path

$$\dot{A} = \phi H_A A \qquad (2.9)$$

where ϕ is a positive productivity parameter and H_A is human capital employed in research. Thus the research sector in this model exhibits increasing returns to scale. An increase in scale measured by total human capital H serves to speed up the rate of growth. Since $H_Y + H_A \leq H$, one may then show the existence of stagnation when the level of H is too small. For if H is too low, the nonnegativity constraint on H_A is binding and positive growth does not take place. On the other hand any policy which encourages research has the effect of increasing the productivity parameter ϕ in (2.9), which in its turn favorably affects the growth of output.

Thus this model suggests that an economy with a larger stock of human capital will experience faster growth. Also opening up through international trade can help to speed up growth.

A second important feature of the Romer model is that the price-taking competitive behavior cannot be supported when the production process is subject to nonconvexity, i.e., the knowledge capital as a nonrival good can be accumulated without bound on a per capita basis. Instead the framework is an equilibrium with monopolistic competition.

Much like the Romer model, Lucas (1988, 1993) argues that the externalities from a learning spillover technology gives those who are

17

operating near the current goods frontier a definite advantage in moving beyond it. This advantage may be persistent both myopically and in the long run. The production function is used here in the following form:

$$Y(t) = AK^{\alpha}(t)[u(t)h(t)L(t)]^{1-\alpha} h_a^{\gamma}(t) \qquad (2.10)$$

with the technology for the growth of human capital, $\dot{h}(t)$ specified as

$$\dot{h}(t) = h(t)\,\phi\,[1 - u(t)] \qquad (2.11)$$

Here h(t) is the skill level of human capital, with $h_a(t)$ denoting its external effect or learning spillover effect. The technology level A here is assumed to be constant. Also u(t) is the proportion of labor time devoted to current production, so that [1 − u(t)] is the proportion devoted to human capital accumulation and ϕ is a positive productivity parameter. For any allocation 0 < u(t) < 1, there exist no diminishing returns to the stock of human capital. Thus a constant returns learning spillover technology may be equally consistent with both fast and slow growth. Thus if the technology available to individual agents has constant returns, then some allocations may yield high external benefits and growth in production and wages, while others may not. Another feature of this learning spillover technology is that it yields a strong connection between rapid productivity growth and openness in trade. Thus countries opening up would take advantage of scale economies according to the learning spillover theory and this process will make their production grow more rapidly than those who are limited to producing traditional goods with no spillover effects. Also, the import-substitution policies will not succeed in stimulating growth at a sustained level, though initially it may offer a one-time stimulus.

2.1.2 Knowledge Spillover

From an applied perspective the spillover effects of knowledge capital help to improve labor productivity across the board. As Lucas pointed out, this may be the most significant factor explaining the large difference in marginal productivity of capital between an LDC (less developed country) and a developed economy, when the concept of capital is broadened to include human or knowledge capital. This may be seen in a better perspective by dividing the economy into two sectors: domestic and the export sector and then specifying the production functions for the two

sectors with outputs X and N for the export and the non-export sectors as
follows:

$$X = G(L_X, K_X, H_N)$$
$$N = F(L_N, K_N, H_X)$$

where $L = L_X + L_N$ and $K = K_N + K_X$ are labor and capital for the two
sectors and H_N, H_X are the knowledge capitals. Differentiating these
functions with respect to time one obtains:

$$\Delta X = G_L \Delta L_X + G_K \Delta K_X + G_{H_N} \Delta H_N$$
$$\Delta N = F_L \Delta L_N + F_K \Delta K_N + F_{H_X} \Delta H_X \qquad (2.12)$$

where the subscripts on F and G denote the marginal productivity of the
respective inputs in the two sectors. The intersectoral spillover effects are
captured by the two effects F_{H_X} and G_{H_N}. If this ratio F_{H_X} / G_{H_N} is
greater than one, then the dynamic externality effects of the knowledge
capital from the export to the non export sector is more dominant. For the
fast growing NICs in Asia this dominance has been empirically observed by
many researchers, e.g., Enos and Park (1988), Feder (1982) and Sengupta
(1993). This knowledge spillover effect through the export sector has been
empirically confirmed by Enos and Park (1988), who have studied the
pattern of adoption and diffusion of imported technology in four major
industries in South Korea, e.g., petrochemicals, synthetic fibers, machinery
and iron and steel and compared this experience with Japan. They found that
Korea's growth has stemmed more from increases in labor supply and the
associated skill factor than the advances in technology. Furthermore, as
Amsden (1989) has analyzed there is a basic difference between Japan and
Korea in this respect. In Korea at least until 1980, the government has been
the primary agent in technology transfer but in Japan it has been the large
private firms responding to the stimulus of export trade.

Two other dimensions of the knowledge spillover argument are useful
in analyzing the rapid growth of NICs in Asia. One emphasizes the role of
international trade through the external human capital in promoting high
productivity growth in initially poor countries as a result of the diffusion of
knowledge already available in industrial countries. Part of this growth in
productivity is facilitated by improved domestic absorptive capacity through
increased levels of human capital. Thus the NICs in Asia benefited greatly

from the rapid technology transfers and a growing skilled labor force able to adapt it to local needs. Grossman and Helpman (1991) have explored another related mechanism in this perspective. In their models, productivity growth is sustained by private sector R&D, resulting in new intermediate goods thus enhancing all around intersectoral productivity and also contributing to public knowledge.

The second dimension of the learning spillover technology, analyzed in some detail by the north–south trade model of Stokey (1991) and Young (1991) emphasizes the point that this technology gives those who operate near the current goods frontier a definite advantage in moving beyond it. This opens up the possibility that a forward-looking view on knowledge capital and the associated technology effects may provide a strong connection we observe between rapid productivity growth and trade or openness. The success of the NICs in Asia over the last two decades can be attributed in great part to the productivity improvements stemming from foreign R&D spillovers through trade.

Recently Nadiri and Kim (1996) employed a translog variable cost function with such inputs as labor, materials, physical and R&D capital with the physical and R&D capital treated as quasi-fixed subject to adjustment costs in order to compare the productivity growth in the manufacturing sector in US, Japan and Korea over the period 1975–1990. Their estimated results show that resource accumulation, not technical change has been the key factor in rapid output growth. Also both R&D capital and technical change have been the major contributors of TFP growth in the US and Japan but not in the Korean manufacturing sector. Their estimates are as follows: (1975–90):

	Labor productivity	Labor effect	Materials effect	Capital effect	R&D effect	Technical change
US	2.48	−0.08	1.54	0.49	0.24	0.34
Japan	3.68	0.04	2.22	0.85	0.30	0.38
Korea	7.89	0.56	5.54	1.65	0.13	0.45

But recently the contribution of R&D in Korean manufacturing is rising rapidly. The net rates of return to physical and R&D capital in Korean manufacturing has been very significant and it has offered strong incentives for a steady growth of investment in physical and R&D capital. Recent studies by Lin (1996) emphasized the strong role of government policies favoring R&D investment in the private sector.

2.1.3   Steady State Convergence

One of the important stylized aspects of new growth theory is the question of convergence of different countries to the steady state. The neoclassical models do seem to predict that economies with lower initial levels of per capita capital stock will converge more quickly to a steady state. Solow's growth model following this neoclassical framework predicts such convergence. New growth theory however argues that countries need not converge, even if they have the same preferences and technology. They found that in larger samples of world economies, absolute convergence does not hold, though in more restricted samples like the advanced industrial countries it has some validity. Recently Mankiew, Romer and Weil (1992) have used international cross-section data of 175 countries over the period 1960–85 to test the convergence hypothesis and the Solow model's performance. They argue that the Solow model does not predict uniform convergence in general, since the countries will converge to different steady states when they have different savings rates and different population growth rates. Thus the samples (e.g., OECD countries) where convergence is observed are precisely those where savings and population growth rates are very similar. On using the fundamental growth equation of the Solow model

$$\dot{k} = sf(k) - nk$$

with its growth rate of capital $g = \dot{k}/k$, it is clearly seen that the partial derivative of g with respect to the initial level of capital k is negative, e.g.,

$$\partial g / \partial k = (s/k)\left(\frac{\partial f}{\partial k} - \frac{f(k)}{k}\right) < 0$$

since the average product of capital f(k)/k is greater than the marginal product $\partial f/\partial k$. Thus Mankiew et al. (1992) go on to show that controlling for these variables the Solow model does a decent job of explaining the cross-country variation in income. Furthermore they show when a measure of human capital investment is added to augment the Solow model, it performs much better, e.g., nearly 80% of the variation in income is explained by the three variables (e.g., savings, population growth and human capital). Under this framework of *conditional convergence* how much does the initial level of per capita income in 1960 explain the subsequent growth in income? A great deal of empirical evidence is in favor. But when these controls are ignored, there exists no apparent strong relationship in the international sample. With more recent and improved data 1960–1990 these results hold in general, i.e., unconditional convergence is observable among very similar economies (e.g., OECD countries) but for diverse international samples there is no evidence of unconditional convergence. All these empirical regression studies suffer however from the shortcoming that the results are not statistically very robust to the choice of explanatory variables and the type of samples included in the international sample set. This has been strongly emphasized by Levine and Reinelt (1982) and more recently by Solow (1994).

2.2 NONCONVEXITIES IN PRODUCTION AND TECHNOLOGY

Nonconvexities in the production set have several important implications for firm and industry growth. One implication is the increasing returns effect due either to *economies of scale* or to *economies of scope*. Romer (1990) and others have characterized this effect in terms of the presence of nonrival inputs, where, e.g., doubling all nonrival inputs increases total output by more than double. The production function then takes the form

$$F(\lambda R, \lambda N) > F(\lambda R, N) = \lambda F(R, N)$$

where R is the set of rival inputs, N the set of nonrival inputs and λ is a positive integer for the output function $F(\cdot)$. This means that the elasticity of output with respect to all inputs, both rival and nonrival is greater than one and the resulting production function is not concave. To assess the empirical significance of this increasing returns effect we may consider the time series data on total factor productivity in Korean manufacturing sector over the 20 year period 1961–80 available from Kwon (1986). The least squares estimate of the loglinear production is as follows:

$$\ln Y = 4.92^{**} - 0.47 \ln R_1 + 0.16 \ln R_2 - 0.57 \ln R_3$$
$$+ 1.51^{**} \ln N; \ R^2 = 0.99$$

Here Y is output, R_1 through R_3 are three rival inputs, e.g., capital stock, energy consumed and raw material and N is a nonrival input proxied by labor employed in the export sector. The two asterisks denote significant coefficients at 1% level and R^2 is the squared multiple correlation indicating goodness of fit. Clearly the nonrival input (N) has a substantial increasing returns effect. An alternative way to test this hypothesis is to fit a cost function (ln C) over the same data set. This yields

$$\ln C = 0.168^* + 0.797^{**} \ln Y - 0.77 \ln z; \; R^2 = 0.92$$

which shows that the overall degree of increasing returns to scale is 1.25, which is the reciprocal of the output coefficient 0.797 in the cost function. Here the second independent variable ln z is a proxy for technical progress measured by output growth. Its negative coefficient implies the cost reducing impact of technical progress. More generally Enos and Park (1988) have estimated the following sources of growth of GNP:

Table 2.1 Sources of GNP Growth

Source	USA 1948–69 %	S. Korea 1963–82 %	Japan 1953–72 %
Labor	22.0	35.8	17.1
Capital	19.8	21.4	23.8
Scale economies	10.5	18.0	22.0
Technological progress	29.8	11.8	22.4
Miscellaneous	17.9	13.0	14.7
Total	100.0	100.0	100.0

A second aspect of nonconcavity in the production frontier underlying the rapid growth process of such countries as NICs in Asia is due to the *learning curve effect*. As Scherer (1996) points out the 'slope' of the typical semiconductor device learning curve is approximately 28 percent, which means that unit costs fall by 28 percent on average with each doubling or redoubling of cumulative output. The existence of this type of learning by doing economies leads companies to engage in a dynamic form of limit pricing, where the first firm to race down the learning curve gains a cost advantage over its slower rivals. Recognizing the gains of being the first down the learning curve, firms have an incentive to focus on continuing cost reduction and productivity improvement and thus build on capacity growing ahead of demand. The only exception to the learning curve effect is that as products mature, learning curves sooner or later flatten out when most of the opportunities for further improvement has been exploited.

A third aspect of nonconvexity in the production set which has gained rapid importance in recent years is due to the introduction of *flexible manufacturing systems* (FMS) in the technology-intensive industries such as telecommunications, service industries and microelectronics. FMS refers to automated computer-integrated manufacturing systems, which have grown tremendously over the last two decades due to globalization of markets and international trade and rapid innovations in communication involving shorter product life cycles and increased competition for more efficient technology. The objectives of FMS are to improve both flexibility and productivity. Recently Sengupta (1995) had discussed the two major implications of the FMS technology for economic systems. One is the fact that the traditional characterizations such as production frontiers become inadequate in this framework and secondly, the time span of technology and product cycles acquire strategic importance in this automated flexible production environments. The conventional costing techniques used by economists and accountants in the traditional setup of discrete production processes do not apply to an FMS environment. Three special features specific to this environment show the need for new procedures for manufacturing cost analysis, e.g., (a) *automation*, which substantially modifies the role of labor costs, (b) *flexibility*, which requires the plant manager to distribute the cost of allocating FMS resources among all the parts and modules, and (c) *integration*, among the various system resources so as to exploit the economies of scope. The relevance of this FMS-based cost efficiency analysis may be seen more directly in the recent empirical trends of R&D intensities in companies as measured by company-financed business unit R&D expenditures expressed as a percentage of unit sales and transfers. The study by Cohen and Levinthal (1989) uses the survey data over the period 1975–77 collected by Levine et al. (1987), which consists of 1302 R&D performing business units representing 297 firms in 151 lines of business as available from the US Federal Trade Commission's Line of Business Program. This empirical study estimates by regression coefficients the partial effects of various explanatory variables on R&D intensity. Some of the significant coefficients are detailed in Table 2.2. Appropriability of rents due to inventive activity is here measured as follows. The respondents were asked on a seven-point scale the effectiveness of six mechanisms used by firms to capture and protect the competitive advantages of new processes and new products. For a given line of business, 'appropriability' is then the maximum score received by any one of these mechanisms for either process or product innovations. Thus if appropriability increases, the inter-industry spillover level declines. Three methods of estimation, e.g., ordinary least squares (OLS), generalized least squares (GLS) and Tobit method of estimation are employed here. It is clear from above that the computer science research, which is closely related to FMS technology is as important as appropriability and university research. This suggests a dual role of R&D research as stressed by Cohen and Levinthal (1989). R&D not only generates new information but also enhances the firm's capacity to assimilate and exploit existing information. Also the demand factors, e.g., optimistic demand outlook for the future here represented by the income elasticity of demand play a very significant role in determining R&D intensities.

Table 2.2 Factors Influencing R&D Intensity

Source	Regression coefficient (standard error)		
	OLS	GLS	Tobit
1. Appropriability	0.396*	0.360**	0.260
	(0.156)	(0.104)	(0.161)
2. University research	0.346**	0.245**	0.321
	(0.128)	(0.089)	(0.147)
3. Basic research: physics	0.189	0.037	0.156
	(0.109)	(0.082)	(0.109)
4. Computer science research	0.336**	0.157	0.446**
	(0.123)	(0.093)	(0.121)
5. Income elasticity of demand	1.077**	0.587**	1.112**
	(0.170)	(0.131)	(0.188)

One of the most important implications of nonconvexities in the production set is that the firms have to adopt dynamic pricing strategies over time, where some of the parameters characterizing future demand and the state of the economy are either unknown or very imperfectly known. Two types of approaches have been adopted in the literature to handle this dynamic problem. One is the dynamic adjustment cost approach discussed by Treadway (1974) and Morrison and Berndt (1981), where the firm has to choose $x_i(t)$, the vector of quasi-fixed inputs and $v_j(t)$, the vector of variable inputs to minimize the present value of the cost $V(0)$ of producing a given flow of output $Y(t)$ subject to a production function constraint $Y(t) = F(v, x, \dot{x})$ where

$$V(0) = \int_0^\infty e^{-rt} \left[\sum_j \hat{w}_j v_j + \sum_i \hat{q}_i z_i \right] dt \qquad (2.13)$$

Here r is the firm's discount rate, $\hat{q}_i$ is the asset price of new quasi–fixed inputs and $z_i = \dot{x}_i + \delta_i x_i$, with δ_i being the fixed depreciation rate and z_i is then the gross addition to the stock of x_i where $\dot{x}_i$ denotes the time derivative of x_i. Treadway (1974) considered the production function in a separable form

$$Y(t) = F(v, x) - C(\dot{x})$$

where $C(\dot{x})$ is adjustment cost which is assumed to be strictly convex, implying that the quasi-fixed input is available at increasing unit costs. On assuming that factor prices are expected to increase at a constant exponential rate, Morrison and Berndt (1981) derived the optimal input demand equations for $x_i(t)$ and $v_j(t)$. For empirical results however they imposed the condition of long-run constant returns to scale; otherwise there may not be a convergence to the steady state solution.

A second approach is to distinguish between current output and cumulative output in the production function, where the latter may better reflect the cumulative research and development expenditure or even a learning curve effect. Norsworthy and Jang (1992) have empirically found for the microelectronics and semiconductor industries that the net effect of adding capital to reduce the variable cost of production is substantial for Japan and other NICs in Asia. Let $y(t)$ denote the cumulative output at time t where the sales rate is $s(t) = dy(t)/dt = \dot{y}$

$$\dot{y} = f(y(t), p(t), e(t))$$

where $p(t)$ is the output price and $e(t)$ is the set of all exogenous factors including random noise, where the slope of the demand curve $\partial f/\partial p$ is negative. Production cost $c = c(y(t), t)$ is assumed to be decreasing with cumulative output $y(t)$ and also with time t. Now the optimal growth path of output is modeled as a two-step optimization process decided by the representative producer who is assumed to compete in the world market. For all exporters monopolistically competing in the R&D intensive world markets, the two-tier framework is of central importance. On the domestic front the producer exploits all the scale economies so as to realize all the cost savings, whereas in the international front he acts much like a price taker. An earlier empirical study for Japan by Sengupta and Okamura (1996) found such a type of characterization very insightful for the growth of the manufacturing sector over the period 1965–90. Following this approach we assume that the representative producer decides in the first step the desired or target levels of output through an intertemporal profit-maximizing process as follows:

$$\text{Max}\,\pi = \int_0^\infty e^{-rt}(p(t) - c)s\,dt$$
$$\text{s.t.} \quad \dot{y} = s = f(y(t), p(t), e(t)) \tag{2.14}$$
$$y(0) = y_0$$

The second step minimizes an intertemporal loss function based on the deviation of outputs from their desired or target levels. Whereas the first step assumes a monopolistic competition framework in international trade and derives an optimal pricing rule consistent with demand expectations and cost economies, the second step allows the dynamic adjustments in disequilibrium, which specify the transitional dynamics of the system. On using the current value Hamiltonian

$$H = e^{-rt}(P - c + \lambda)s$$

and assuming the regularity conditions for the existence of an optimal trajectory, the Pontryagin maximum principle specifies the necessary conditions for optimality as follows:

$$\dot{\lambda} = r\lambda - \frac{\partial H}{\partial y}$$
$$\dot{y} = f(y, p, e) \tag{2.15}$$

$$\partial H / \partial p = 0, \text{ for all } t$$

and

$$\lim_{t\to\infty} e^{-rt}\lambda(t) = 0 \quad \text{(transversality)}$$

By using ε as the price elasticity of demand, the condition $\partial H/\partial p = 0$ implies the optimal pricing rule at each t.

$$p(t) = \varepsilon(1 + \varepsilon)^{-1} (c - \lambda) \tag{2.16}$$

That is, price is related to marginal cost after it is adjusted to the effect of additional unit on future profits λ. If λ is positive for any subperiod, then price is below the myopic level c and vice versa. If current demand has a positive effect on future profits, then the producer invests now by lowering price and giving up short run profits in return for future higher profits and likewise for learning cost.

It is clear from (2.16) that the optimal pricing rule depends very significantly on the sign and magnitude of optimal $\lambda(t)$. By using the first condition of (2.15) and some algebraic calculation one may derive the time path of $\lambda(t)$ in the future as follows:

$$\lambda(t) = \int_t^\infty [-c_y f(y, p, e) - (pf_y / \varepsilon)]e^{-r(\tau - t)}d\tau \tag{2.17}$$

where $\quad -c_y = -\partial c/\partial y = $ future cost decline (> 0)

$\quad\quad \varepsilon < 0$, since demand curve is negatively sloped

$\quad\quad f_y = \partial f/\partial y$.

Thus we see that $\lambda(t)$ is the accumulation of the future cost decline (the first term) plus the effect on revenues of that additional unit (the second term). The first term is positive since cost declines with experience but the second depends on future demand trends. On taking the time derivative of the optimal price equation in (2.16) and using the implicit function theorem $dp/dt = -(\partial^2 H/\partial p \partial t)/(\partial^2 H/\partial p^2)$ we may derive

$$\text{sign}(\dot{p}) = \text{sign}\left[-r\lambda - 2\frac{f_y f}{f_p} + \frac{f_{yp} f^2}{f_p^2} + c_t - p\frac{\partial}{\partial t}\left(\frac{1}{\varepsilon}\right) \right]$$

where the subscripts denote partial derivatives. The first term is the effect of the discount rate reflecting risk aversion, i.e., the higher it is, the more preferred is short run profits. In cases where λ is positive (i.e., learning curve effect and demand learning), it means investing less in the future and higher prices now. This obviously creates a pressure for declining prices. The second term is the effect of experience on demand, i.e., if it is positive ($f_y > 0$), then this means that price is lower now and increasing with the object of stimulating future demand. The third term is the second order effect of price change on demand. As a special case if the demand function is a function of price alone, then it follows

$$\sin g(\dot{p}) = \text{sign}(-r\lambda + c_t) \qquad (2.18)$$

where $c_t = \partial c/\partial t$ declines over time since unit cost declines ($c_y < 0$) with experience.

It follows from the transversality condition in (2.15) that the optimal price converges to the limit price determined by the unit cost. But since unit cost declines over time, there is a long run tendency for optimal prices to decline as e.g., in the semiconductor and R&D intensive industries. Given the optimal price trajectory the output demand $\dot{y}$ is determined from the equation of motion $\dot{y} = f(y, p, e)$, once the exogenous variables e are substituted. We denote the optimal output variables by $Q_t = \dot{y}(t)$ and then set up the second stage optimization problem in a quadratic form

$$\text{Min } J = E_t \sum_{t=0}^{\infty} \rho^t \Big[(X_t - X_t^*) \Lambda (X_t - X_t^*) \\ + (X_t - X_{t-1})' \psi (X_t - X_{t-1}) \Big]$$

where ρ^t is the exogenous discounting function, $E_t(\bullet)$ is the conditional expectation as of time t and the weight matrices Λ, ψ are assumed to be known. The input vector X_t is subject to the production function $Q_t = F(X_t)$ and the decision problem is here taken in discrete form, since it involves adjustment lags, one due to the deviation from the target level X_t^* and the other due to lagged input vector X_{t-1}. Assuming a Cobb–Douglas production technology

$$Q_t = B(A_t, V_t) K_t^a L_t^b$$

where the technical progress function $B(\bullet)$ is assumed to depend on knowledge spillover (A_t) and an external variable V_t proxied by exports, i.e., $B = A_t V_t^\gamma$, the optimal input paths for the export-oriented producer monopolistically competing in the international market can be explicitly derived as

$$\ln L_t = N_L \ln L_{t-1} + M_L d_t^L \qquad (2.19)$$
$$\ln K_t = N_K \ln K_{t-1} + M_K d_t^L$$

where

$$N_L = (1 - \mu_1), N_K = 1 - \theta_1, M_L = (1 - \mu_1)(1 - \rho\mu_1),$$
$$M_K = (1 - \theta_1)(1 - \rho\theta_1)$$
$$d_t^L = \sum_{s=0}^{\infty} \rho^s \mu_1^s \ln L_{t+s}^*, d_t^K = \sum_{s=0}^{\infty} \rho^s \theta_1^s \ln K_{t+s}^*$$

$\mu_1, \theta_1 = $ stable (nonexplosive) roots of the underlying characteristic
equation for each of the two inputs.

We applied these two linear decision rules (2.19) to explain the growth process in Japan over the period 1965–90 and tested the following hypothesis: which of the two forces, past history or future expectations plays a more dominant role? Note that both the equations of (2.19) are in the form of linear partial adjustment rules, which can be estimated by ordinary least squares if the additive error components are white noise and the terms d_t^L, d_t^K can be replaced by their consistent estimates. Both Kennan (1979) and more recently Gregory et al. (1993) have shown that one can estimate d_t^L, d_t^K consistently by the instrument variables method. In our empirical application we have used lagged logarithmic values of output (Q_{t-s}), the ratio of input prices (w_{t-s}/ϕ_{t-s}) and the exports (V_{t-s}) as the instrument variables to estimate d_t and have used up to third order lags, i.e., AR(-3) process approximation. This is called the backward looking approach, since the past values are used to build up the estimate. A second estimate, called the forward looking approach is also constructed when d_t is expressed as a linear function of current and future values of the three instrument variables mentioned above. Once again approximations up to the third order (i.e., AR(3) processes) have been retained, since the higher order did not improve R^2 value.

Note some interesting features of the linear estimating equations in (2.19). If the two inputs are each integrated of order one, then each optimal demand equation provides an error correction model interpretation, where the steady state has a long run structural interpretation. Secondly, the speed of adjustment parameter N_i (i = K,L) can be easily related to the weight ratio η_L defined as follows: $\eta_i = -N_i \rho + N_i (1 - N_i)^{-1}$, i = K,L. Finally, one has to invoke the rational expectations hypothesis that $E_t(L_{t+1}) = L_{t+1}$ and $E_t(\ln L_t^*) = \ln L_t^* = f(\ln Q_{t-s}, \ln(w_{t-s}/\phi_{t-s}), \ln V_{t-s})$. This hypothesis implies that future expectations are realized in terms of the observed variables. Under perfect foresight conditions this assumption appears reasonable and it has been frequently applied in modern growth theory.

For estimating the dynamic input demand functions in (2.19) the aggregate data for Japan (1965–90) are utilized for labor (L), capital (K) and their prices. For the case of heterogenous labor three categories are used: female labor (F) and male labor divided into two types: unskilled (U) and skilled (S), where U_t denotes manhours for male labor with education up to the secondary school and S_t with higher education level. The output Y_t is defined as GNP deflated by the GNP deflator and the export variable V_t is exports deflated by the official export price index. These statistical data are obtained from the Statistical Yearbook of Japan for various years. The data for capital stock are used as a proxy for capital service and obtained from the official publication: Gross Capital Stock of Private Enterprises for various years. The details of the data set are discussed in Sengupta and Okamura (1996).

The estimated results of the dynamic adjustment models are presented in Table 2.3. Whereas the first two tables present the case of homogeneous labor (L), the third table specifies the speeds of adjustment of three categories of labor: female labor and two types of male labor, unskilled and skilled. Of the two inputs, capital (K) and labor (L), the dynamic adjustment process for labor is much faster than capital, i.e., $N_L > N_K$, thus implying that labor converges to the steady state much sooner than capital. This difference in speeds of convergence is reduced somewhat in the forward looking case compared to the backward looking view. The detailed estimates of the optimal labor demand equations for the forward looking case appears as follows:

GNP without exports

$$\Delta \ln L_t = 16.6 - \underset{(0.18)}{0.811} \ln L_{t-1} + \underset{(0.50)}{1.117} \ln Y_t - \underset{(0.55)}{1.028} \ln Y_{t+2}$$
$$+ \underset{(0.21)}{0.447} \ln RW_t - \underset{(0.202)}{0.368} \ln RW(t+1)$$
$$R^2 = 0.635; DW = 2.18; \hat{N}_L = 3.489$$

GNP with exports

$$\Delta \ln L_t = 15.7 - \underset{(0.123)}{0.837} \ln L_{t-1} + \underset{(0.476)}{1.081} \ln Y_t$$
$$\underset{(0.714)}{-2.460} \ln Y_{t+2} + \underset{(0.550)}{1.502} \ln Y_{t+3} + \underset{(0.151)}{0.457} \ln RW_t$$
$$\underset{(0.147)}{-0.783} \ln V_t + \underset{(0.175)}{0.484} \ln V_{t+1} + \underset{(0.135)}{0.405} \ln V_{t+3}$$
$$R^2 = 0.877; DW = 1.824; \hat{N}_L = 4.281$$

Table 2.3 Estimates of the Speed of Adjustment (N_i) *and the Weight Ratio* (η_i) *for the Two Input Models*

Output ($\ln Y_t$)	Inputs ($\ln X_{it}$)	Backward-looking model	
		N_i	η_i
1. GNP (without exports used as an instrument variable)	K	0.055*	0.003
	L	0.937*	13.944
2. GNP (with exports as an instrument variable)	K	0.118*	0.016
	L	0.898*	7.873
		Forward-looking model	
1. GNP (without exports as an instrument variable)	K	0.132*	0.020
	L	0.811*	3.489
2. GNP (with exports)	K	0.082*	0.007
	L	0.837*	4.281

Note: The estimates of N_i are all significant at 5% level of t-test.

Table 2.4 Estimates of the Speed of Adjustment (N_L) and the Weight Ratio (η_L) for the Optimal Labor Demand Equation

Dependent variable	N_L		η_L	
	Forward	Backward	Forward	Backward
ln GNP without exports	0.811*	0.937*	3.489*	13.944*
ln GNP with exports	0.837*	0.898*	4.281*	7.873*
ln GDP without exports	0.888*	0.936	7.008*	13.687*

Table 2.5 Estimates of the Speed of Adjustment (N_i) and the Weight Ratio (η_i) for the Four Input Model (Backward-Looking Model)

Output (ln Y_t)	Input (ln X_{it})	N_i	η_i
GNP (without exports	K	0.702*	1.659
used as an instrument	F	0.335**	0.169
variable	U	1.071*	NA
	S	0.418*	0.299
GNP (with exports)	K	0.328*	0.162
	F	0.689*	1.524
	U	1.027*	NA
	S	0.826*	3.921

Notes:
1. One and two asterisks denote significant t-values at 5 and 10% respectively.
2. Labor is shown here in three groups: female (F) and two types of male labor: unskilled (U) and skilled (S).
3. NA denotes negative values

Here the standard errors are in parentheses and RW_t denotes the ratio of factor prices. Since learning by doing is more important for labor input, the optimal adjustment path for labor plays a more dynamic role in the growth frontier. Three points emerge here very distinctly. One is that the forward looking estimates are very different in magnitude compared to the backward looking estimates. Furthermore future or expected incomes have strong impact on the current demand for labor. When only the skilled component of the total labor demand equation is considered, this impact is reinforced more strongly. Secondly, the value of the weight ratio $\hat{\eta}_L = \Lambda_L / \psi_L$ is nearly half that of the backward-looking model thus suggesting an asymmetry in the adjustment process. If the GNP variable Y_t is replaced by GDP the estimate of the ratio $\hat{\eta}_L$ is still very high:

Variables	Value of $\hat{\eta}_L$	
	Forward-looking	Backward-looking
ln GNP without exports	3.489*	13.944*
ln GNP with exports	4.281*	7.873*
ln GDP without exports	7.008*	13.687*

*Significant at 5% level.

For the two industrial sectors: durable and nondurable manufacturing in U.S. over 1947–69 Kennan's two-step estimates consistently produced a value of $\hat{\eta}_L$ less than 0.14, i.e., 0.134 for the durable and 0.053 for the nondurable sector. This provides strong evidence that the U.S. producers place much more weight on smoothing out fluctuations in input demand, whereas their Japanese counterparts emphasize their long run goals of an optimal trend. This also explains in part the rationality of Japanese producers in building ahead of demand and concentrating on investment in technology-intensive industries. As Romer (1991) has pointed out, Japan now spends considerably more as a fraction of GDP on commercial nonbasic research that generates excludable benefits than does the United States and they are better off as a result. Finally, the export externality factor increases the speed of adjustment for labor from $\hat{N}_L = 0.811$ to $\hat{N}_L = 0.837$ with a corresponding increase in the weight ratio $\hat{\eta}_L$ from 3.489 to 4.281. This result is always upheld in the case of heterogeneous labor, in particular for female labor.

Thus it is clear that the future expectations play a stronger role than the past endowments and history in the long-term calculations of Japanese producers.

2.3   STOCHASTIC GROWTH

From an applied standpoint two types of stochastic issues have been recently discussed in the growth literature. One is the stochastic variability of the capital–output ratio in both Solow–Swan type exogenous growth models and AK-type endogenous growth models with general savings and production functions. Thus Binder and Pesaran (1996) have recently investigated empirically the degree to which stochastic technological progress and stochastic labor input can contribute to differences in steady state capital–output ratios across countries. They found that *ceteris parabus* countries with a higher volatility of the logarithm of the capital–output ratio tend to have a lower mean logarithmic capital–output ratio in the Solow–Swan growth model. This aspect is not observed in the deterministic version at all.

A second type of stochasticity is introduced in the Solow–Swan type growth model through an endogenous technological progress function, where various types of nonlinearity affect the stability or convergence of the growth process. This type of issues has been discussed by several authors such as Goodwin (1990), Medio (1992) and Lorenz (1993). Goodwin suggests that there is considerable agreement among economists and economic historians that the introduction of a successful technical innovation follows a logistic function, either

$$\dot{x} = bx(1 - x / \bar{x}) \qquad \text{(continuous time)} \qquad (2.20)$$

or $\qquad x_{t+1} = ax_t(1 - x_t / \bar{x}) \qquad \text{(discrete time)}$

where a, b are positive parameters and $\bar{x}$ is the maximum level for the innovation. On rescaling the first equation of (2.20) it may be simply written as

$$\dot{x} = x(t)(m - x(t)).$$

One equilibrium solution is $x^* = m$ and in the vicinity of this equilibrium point the characteristic equation has the single eigenvalue $(-m)$. This implies that in the local vicinity of x^* the innovation process has stability so long as $m > 0$. Now suppose the parameter m varies randomly, i.e.,

$$m = m_0 + \mu(t) \qquad (2.21)$$

where m_0 is a constant being the mean value of m and $\mu(t)$ is assumed to be white noise with mean zero and variance σ^2. The appropriate Fokker–Planck equation for the population probability distribution $p(X,t)$ of this system can then be specified and the steady-state equilibrium probability distribution when it exists can be shown to be a gamma distribution

$$p^*(X) = C(X)^{2(m_0/\sigma^2)-2} \exp[-(2X/\sigma^2)] \qquad (2.22)$$

provided $m_0 > \sigma^2/2$. There is no equilibrium solution otherwise. Here C is the normalization constant making the integrated probability density unity. On using this density the mean $\overline{X}$ and the volatility of the innovation process V can be easily derived as follows:

$$\overline{X} = m_0[1 - (\sigma^2/2m_0)]$$

$$V = \frac{\sqrt{E(X - \overline{X})^2}}{\overline{X}} = \left[\frac{\sigma^2/2m_0}{1 - (\sigma^2/2m_0)}\right]^{1/2} \qquad (2.23)$$

We note that the relative fluctuations measured by V become increasingly severe as σ^2 increases towards $2m_0$, beyond which no equilibrium solution exists.

A more direct way to introduce stochasticity into a Solow type model through an endogenous technical innovation is to assume that technical progress is proportional to the growth rate of aggregate cumulative output denoted by Y/Z where $Y = \dot{Z}$ and Z is cumulative output as the embodied form of all knowledge capital and cumulative experience. Thus we postulate

$$Y = \dot{Z} = Z^\theta L^{\alpha_1} K^{\alpha_2}; \quad \alpha_i > 0, \ 0 < \theta < 1$$
$$\dot{K} = s\,Y, \quad \dot{L} = n\,L$$

and derive the logistic equation in terms of the variable $u = \dot{Z}/Z$ as follows

$$\dot{u}/u = \alpha_1 n - u\left(1 - \theta - \frac{\alpha_2 sZ}{sZ + K_0}\right)$$

This yields $\qquad \dot{u}/u = (1 - \alpha_2 - \theta)[m - u] \qquad (2.24)$

where $\qquad m = n\alpha_1(1 - \theta - \alpha_2)^{-1}$

and $\qquad K_0$ is set to zero as a starting point.

Again by assuming that the parameter m follows a white noise process specified in (2.21), one can derive the steady state mean and volatility of the process, where the latter becomes explosive as σ^2 increases towards $2m_0$.

Consider now the stochasticity in the capital–output ratio k(t), which may be generated by stochastic technical progress and stochastic productivity of human capital, which has been discussed recently by Binder and Pesaran (1996). Assume that it follows a birth and death process model, which satisfies the Chapman–Kolmogorov equation in the time derivative of the probability density of k(t) taking a value k = 0,1,2,...,... at time t:

$$\dot{p}_k(t) = \lambda_{k-1} p_{k-1}(t) + \mu_{k+1} p_{k+1}(t) - (\lambda_k + \mu_k) p_k(t).$$

Assume that the birth λ_k and death rate μ_k parameters are $\lambda_k(t) = a(1-k(t))$ k(t), $\mu_1(t) = bk(t)$, a + b = 1. Then it yields a logistic equation for the mean $\bar{k}(t)$:

$$d\bar{k}(t)/dt = a\bar{k}(t) - \bar{k}^2(t) - v(t) \tag{2.25}$$

where v(t) is the variance of the process k(t). The deterministic model is obtained by dropping the variance term, i.e.,

$$\dot{k}(t) = ak(t) - k^2(t) = ak(t)\left[1 - \frac{k(t)}{a}\right] \tag{2.26}$$

It is clear from (2.25) and (2.26) that $\bar{k}(t)$ is not equal to k(t) so long as the variance function is positive for any t. Furthermore there is an asymmetrical relationship between the mean and the variance functions, e.g.,

$$\frac{\partial v(t)}{\partial \bar{k}(t)} \begin{array}{c} < \\ = \\ > \end{array} \text{zero, according as } \bar{k} \begin{array}{c} > \\ = \\ < \end{array} a/2$$

It is also clear from the variance function

$$v(t) = a\bar{k}(t) - \bar{k}^2 - \dot{\bar{k}}$$

that it may be explosive in a certain region of the phase space when there is chaotic instability.

37

An interesting extension of the logistic process model occurs when we consider a two-sector model of growth discussed in (2.12) before. Assume there are two sectors with outputs $y_1(t)$ and $y_2(t)$, where the first one is more dynamic in the export market and hence in international trade. The growth of output is assumed to follow a logistic process, i.e.,

$$\dot{x}_1(t) = [\lambda_1 - \mu_1 f(x_1, x_2)] x_1(t)$$
$$\dot{x}_2(t) = [\lambda_2 - \mu_2 g(x_2, x_1)] x_2(t)$$

where $f(\bullet)$ and $g(\bullet)$ are two interaction terms. If the interaction of the two sectors are linear, i.e., $f(x_1, x_2) = \alpha_1 x_1 + \alpha_2 x_2$, $g(x_2, x_1) = \beta_1 x_1 + \beta_2 x_2$ then the growth equations become

$$\dot{x}_1(t) = \lambda_1 x_1(t) - \mu_1 \alpha_1 x_1^2(t) - \mu_1 \alpha_2 x_1(t) x_2(t)$$
$$\dot{x}_2(t) = \lambda_2 x_2(t) - \mu_2 \beta_1 x_1(t) x_2(t) - \mu_2 \beta_2 x_2^2(t)$$

The stochastic analogue of this system is

$$\dot{m}_{11}(t) = \lambda_1 m_{11}(t) - \mu_{11} m_{12}(t) - \mu_{12} \overline{m}_{11}(t)$$
$$\dot{m}_{21}(t) = \lambda_2 m_{21}(t) - \mu_{21} \overline{m}_{11}(t) - \mu_{22} m_{22}(t)$$

where $m_{11}(t) = E(x_1(t))$, $m_{12}(t) = E(x^2(t))$, $m_{21}(t) = E(x_2(t))$, $m_{22}(t)$ $= E(x_2^2(t))$ and $\overline{m}_{11}(t) = E(x_1(t) x_2(t))$ and E is expectation. These derivations have been explicitly derived by Bharucha-Reid (1960) and Tintner and Sengupta (1972). Two points emerge from these sectoral applications. One is that for normal interaction functions the output volume of one sector would vary inversely with that of the other; also asymmetry in growth of the two sectors noted before in (2.12) can be easily expected, i.e., growth of the export sector pulls up the other sector but not vice versa. Secondly, the mean and variance function may be inversely related in some regions of the phase space, thus implying that the stochastic volatility or explosive behavior may be more endogenous than that implied by the deterministic model.

2.4   MODELLING LEARNING AND ADAPTIVITY

In diffusion of knowledge the learning and adaptivity play a critical role in industrial growth. Investments in R&D affect not only productivity growth within the industry, the spillover effects are also generated. Caves and Barton (1989) used empirical U.S. data over the period 1977–85 to estimate the impact of the following four variables: technical efficiency (TE), R&D expenditure as a ratio to sales (R&D), the ratio of gross capital expenditure per employee ($\Delta K/L$) and the ratio of imports to domestic supply (IM) on the real output per employee (PR) representing productivity changes:

$$PR = 0.013 + 0.004 TE + 0.004\ R\&D + 0.001\ \Delta K/L + 0.050\ IM$$
$$\ (1.74)\qquad (2.88)\qquad\quad (2.90)\qquad\quad (2.22)$$

$R^2 = 0.084$, t–values in parenthesis; $F = 5.22$. Here technical efficiency (TE) is measured by the estimates of a stochastic production frontier $y = f(x)$ exp $(v-u)$, where y is output and $f(x)$ exp(v) is the deterministic core of the frontier production function multiplied by some symmetrical error v. The one-sided error term $u > 0$ which captures technical efficiency is then estimated.

The estimates above imply a positive impact of both TE, R&D and IM on productivity. Although R^2 value is very low, the F-statistic value 5.22 indicates that it is significant overall. Also this model supports the hypothesis that international competition from imports, which may be taken as a proxy for openness in international trade raises productivity.

Recently Coe and Helpman (1995) have estimated for a panel of countries in which TFP is regressed on domestic R&D and foreign R&D measures as the sum of R&D capital stock of trade partners weighted by the bilateral import share. The results show significant impacts of both foreign and domestic R&D capital stocks on TFP. Furthermore those economies which are more open tend to derive larger productivity benefits from foreign R&D capital stocks. Clearly for some specific industries like microelectronics and communications these benefits are likely to be far greater. This provides a strong empirical support to the phenomenon of learning and spillover effects through technological competition and trade.

3. Stochastic Aspects of Learning by Doing

New growth theory refers to the recent developments in endogenous models of economic growth, which purport to explain the rate of sustained growth of per capita income in the long run. From an applied perspective three types of forces have played an active dynamic role in this growth process. One is the technology and innovation as the engine of sustained growth. The endogeneity of technological progress is mostly due to the direct and international investment by profit-seeking entrepreneurs, who hold a forward looking view of the state of the world. Schumpeter (1934), Solow (1994) and many others, e.g., Grossman and Helpman (1994) have emphasized this dynamic role of technology for future sustained growth. A second important factor is the dynamic externalities due to the international diffusion of *'knowledge capital'* and the rapid advance of information technology. According to Lucas (1993) this knowledge spillover effect may be the most significant factor explaining the large differences in marginal productivity of capital between a less developed and a fast developing or developed economy, when the concept of capital is broadened to include human capital. The third important source of endogenous growth, as evidenced by the rapid growth episodes of the newly industrializing countries (NICs) of southeast Asia is the openness in trade and its impact on sectoral growth of output. Thus Lucas (1993) has strongly emphasized that the diffusion of spillover research technology implies the strong connection we observe between rapid productivity growth and trade or openness. Consider for example two small economies like Korea and the Philippines in 1960. Suppose now as Lucas argues that Korea shifts its workforce into producing new goods intended for the world market, but Philippines continues to produce the traditional goods. Then according to a learning-based growth theory, Korean production would grow more rapidly. Thus a large volume of trade is essential for this type of growth episode.

Modeling the learning process in the framework of new growth theory and empirically applying it over time series data have posed several challenges before the researchers. Two basic reasons may be cited for this. One is that the learning process has a core component of stochasticity. This is evidenced both in the inception of R&D technology and its diffusion across industries and over international boundaries. The second is the adjustment process, linking future expectations and gradual policy adjustments in the short run. The gap between the myopic and the steady state optimal paths of the policy variables has several stochastic components, which are important in an applied empirical work.

The object of this chapter is to formulate the stochastic aspects of learning-based growth models and then analyze their empirical and policy relevance. The analysis of technical innovation processes is developed both in the framework of the Solow model and the recent endogenous models of growth, where 'the knowledge capital' plays a catalytic role along with physical capital. Stochastic aspects of the nonlinear dynamics and the possibility of chaotic behavior in the stochastic evolution process are emphasized in particular. We discuss in particular the learning by doing models generalized by Nordhaus (1967) and others, where the savings rate and the rate of technical change are endogenously determined by an optimizing choice mechanism. Chaotic dynamics are analyzed in this framework through the parameter changes in the technical progress function. Then we discuss the dynamic spillover effects of innovations originating in the export-intensive sector but spreading to other sectors, where the impact of the dynamic process of learning is generated by a monopolistically competitive research sector, as recently emphasized by Aghion and Howitt (1992) and Jovanovic (1997).

3.1 SOURCES OF STOCHASTIC LEARNING

The earliest form of learning by doing is due to Arrow (1962), who modeled the technical innovation process in terms of the experience of the airframe industry. Here the experience is measured by cumulated gross investment $K(t)$:

$$K(t) = \sum_{-\infty}^{t} I(v)dv \qquad (3.1)$$

and the production function is specified as

$$K(t) = F[K(t), A(t) L(t)] \qquad (3.2)$$

where the current efficiency of labor is measured by

$$A(t) = [K(t)]^{\gamma}, \quad 0 < \gamma < 1 \qquad (3.3)$$

Note that even if the production function F(K, AL) has constant returns to scale in the two inputs K and AL, as in the neoclassical model, the overall function exhibits homogeneity of degree greater than one, e.g., in the Cobb–Douglas case

$$F(K, AL) = K^\beta (AL)^{1-\beta} = K^{\beta+\gamma(1-\beta)} L^{1-\beta}, \quad 0 < \beta < 1 \qquad (3.4)$$

Assume a constant ratio (s) of savings to output. Then the ratio k(t) of output to augmented labor (k(t) = Y(t)/AL(t)) follows the differential equation

$$\dot{k} = s(1 - \gamma)f(k) - nk \qquad (3.5)$$

where $\dot{L}/L = n$ is the fixed growth rate of labor. Let k^0 be the capital–labor ratio defined by

$$f(k^0)/k^0 = n(s(1 - \gamma))^{-1} \qquad (3.6)$$

then by the property of the production function $f(k) > 0$, $f'(k) > 0$, $f''(k) < 0$ for all $0 < k < \infty$ it follows that starting from any arbitrary initial stock of capital k_0 the unique solution of (3.5) tends to k^0, i.e., $\lim_{t \to \infty} k(t) = k^0$, where k^0 is the balanced growth capital–labor ratio corresponding to a fixed savings rate.

It is clear that in a state of balanced growth with fixed k and a fixed level of savings per capita, the process of learning by doing follows the following path:

$$\dot{A}/A = \gamma(\dot{K}/K) = \frac{\gamma}{1-\gamma}\left(\frac{\dot{k}}{k} + n\right)$$

i.e.,

$$A(t) = [k(t)]^{\gamma/1-\lambda} \exp\left(t\left(\frac{\gamma n}{1-\lambda}\right)\right) \qquad (3.7)$$

Clearly the higher the level of γ, the higher is the learning curve effect in raising output. Also this effect is enhanced by increasing the level of k(t) itself, i.e., capital augmenting.

A second approach to learning by doing is to allow this effect through both labor and capital, i.e.,

$$Y = F(\gamma K, \mu L)$$

where the rates of factor augmentation are assumed to follow the rule

$$\dot{\gamma}/\gamma = g(\dot{\mu}/\mu) \tag{3.8}$$

where $g' < 0$ and $g'' < 0$.

This approach is due to Kennedy (1964), who has interpreted the $g(\bullet)$ function as an innovation possibility curve. With a fixed savings ratio s and the following per capita variables $y = Y/L$, $k = K/L$ and $x = \gamma K/\mu L$, Nordhaus (1967) has analyzed the time path of capital labor ratio as follows

$$\dot{k} = s\mu f(x) - nk \tag{3.9}$$

To determine the optimal trajectory of technical change, Nordhaus assumes a planning authority which controls the aggregate savings rate s and the direction of technical change $\tau = \dot{\mu}/\mu$. The objective is to maximize the discounted stream of per capita consumption, i.e.,

$$MaxJ = \int_0^\infty \exp(-\rho t)[(1-s)\mu f(x)]dt \ . \tag{3.10}$$

Forming the Hamiltonian

$$H = \exp(-\rho t)[(1-s)\mu f\left(\frac{\lambda k}{\mu}\right) + p_1\left\{s\mu f\left(\frac{\lambda k}{\mu}\right) - nk\right\}$$
$$+ p_2 e^{ht} g(\beta)\lambda + p_3 \tau \mu]$$

and applying Pontryagin principle, the optimal trajectories must satisfy the following conditions on the continuous adjoint variables $p_i(t)$ (I=1,2,3) as follows:

$$\dot{p}_1 = (\rho + n)p_1 - f'(x)\gamma\lambda$$
$$\dot{p}_2 = (\rho - h - g(\tau))p_2 - f'(x)k\gamma e^{-ht} \tag{3.11}$$
$$\dot{p}_3 = (\rho - \tau)p_3 - \gamma[f(x) - xf'(x)]$$

where $\gamma = 1-s+sp_1$, h is the solution to the equation $g(\tau) = 0$, prime denotes

43

derivatives and a dot over a variable denotes its time derivative. In addition, the optimal trajectories of s(t) and τ(t) must satisfy at each time point the conditions

s(t) maximizes $\{1 - s + sp_1(t)\}$

and
(3.12)

$$\partial H / \partial \tau = 0 = p_2(t)g'(\tau)\lambda e^{ht} + p_3(t)\mu$$
$$\partial^2 H / \partial \tau^2 \leq 0 \text{ and } g(\tau) \text{ is concave in } \tau.$$

It is clear that these optimizing conditions may be interpreted in two different ways. One is to view it as a central planner's problem, where knowledge capital is in the public domain and both the savings rate and the direction of the public innovation process are endogenously determined as an optimal choice problem. This is very different from the Solow model, where these two variables are more or less exogenous. Secondly, it may be viewed as a monopolistically competitive market equilibrium solution, where the private firms undertake research innovations in order to exploit the dynamic profits and rents over time until new entry occurs with improved innovations. Aghion and Howitt (1992) have analyzed this second aspect in a framework of vertical innovations, when the amount of research in any period depends upon the expected amount of research in the next period and furthermore the productivity of research or R&D investment is measured by a parameter indicating the effect of research on the Poisson arrival rate of innovation. We discuss in Section 3 an alternative formulation of a two-tier model of technical diffusion, where the productivity shock is reflected in terms of a stochastic parameter. Note that this model of optimal technical innovation has several features. First of all, the innovation possibility function (3.8) links capital augmentation to the efficiency of labor or human capital and this is very much in line with the modern theory of 'knowledge capital'. Secondly, the use of $\tau = \dot{\mu}/\mu$ as the control variable by the planning authority suggests that R&D expenditures have to be optimally allocated, since the ratio μ/λ must satisfy the optimality rule given in (3.12):

$$\mu / \lambda = (-e^{ht}g'(\tau))p_2 / p_3$$

where $-g'(\tau)$ is positive. However the condition $g''(\tau) < 0$ which is required for optimality may not hold if the production set is nonconvex and the competitive market equilibrium has to obtain. Thus there is a direct conflict between the planned economy setup and the competitive equilibrium. In endogenous growth theory this conflict is handled in two ways, e.g., either one replaces the competitive framework by monopolistic competition, or the objective function (3.10) is replaced by a discounted profit functional for a private producer. In the latter case a two–tier framework of directing technical innovation is of central importance. In the domestic front the producer acts jointly with the state support like a large quasi-monopoly firm, which exploits all the scale economies, whereas in the international front it acts more like a price taker. This aspect will be discussed later in Section 3. Finally, the steady state level of k determined by (3.9) yields

$$f(x^0)/x^0 = n(s\lambda) . \qquad (3.13)$$

This may be compared with the equation (3.6) when learning by doing occurs only through labor augmentation. Clearly when μ rises, τ falls and this leads to an increase in the output–capital ratio in efficiency units given by the left hand side variable in (3.13). For the labor augmenting variety of learning by doing, a rise in γ in (3.6) leads to an increase in output–capital ratio. Recently Binder and Pesaran (1996) have empirically investigated the degree to which stochasticity in technological progress and the labor input can contribute to differences in steady state capital output ratios across countries. In the framework of this model (3.8), the parameters λ and μ would be stochastic in character, which would affect the transient and the steady state behavior of the capital–output ratio in the extended Solow model. The sources of this stochasticity are two-fold. One is the uncertainty associated with the R&D investments, which not only generates new information embodied in new products or new services, but also enhances the firm's ability to exploit existing information. Recently Cohen and Levinthal (1989) have empirically analyzed R&D investment data of 1302 business units representing 151 lines of business from the FTC's data file and found that learning or absorptive capacity represents an important part of a firm's ability to create new knowledge or a new product. This explains why firms may conduct basic research, e.g., for reasons that they are more able to identify and exploit useful scientific and technical knowledge, whereby they may gain a first-mover advantage in exploiting new technologies. A second source of uncertainty involves adjusting labor and capital stocks to their desired levels. For example a firm which finds that its current stocks of capital and labor are inconsistent with the long run equilibrium implied by current factor prices and their expected changes in future, will generally spread the planned adjustment to long run equilibrium over time. This imparts a stochasticity to the changes in labor and capital. Treadway (1974), Kennan (1979) and Gregory et al. (1993) have analyzed such problems.

So far we have discussed learning by doing through the labor and capital inputs. A third type arises through the Hicksian technical progress function, where the production function is specified as

$$Y(t) = F[K(t), L(t), t].$$

Here t on the right hand side represents a time trend variable used as a proxy for neutral technological progress, e.g., a shift in production function. Recently Norsworthy and Jang (1992) have discussed the disadvantages of this type of specification and suggested other types of explanatory variables such as 'cumulative output' which has a learning curve effect of economies of scale. Assuming a Cobb–Douglas form, the production function here takes the form

$$Y = \dot{Z} = AZ^\theta L^{a_1} K^{a_2}; \quad \alpha_i > 0, \quad 0 < \theta < 1 \qquad (3.14)$$

where $Z(t) = \int_0^t Y(\tau)d\tau$ is cumulative output representing the embodied form of all knowledge capital and cumulative experience. With the other assumptions of the Solow model, i.e., a fixed savings ratio s and the growth of labor as $n = \dot{L}/L$, one could easily derive the logistic equation in terms of the variable $u = \dot{Z}/Z$ as follows

$$\dot{u}/u = n\alpha_1 \left(1 - \theta - \frac{s\alpha_2 Z}{sZ + K_0} \right)$$

This yields the reduced form

$$\dot{u}/u = r(m - u) \qquad (3.15)$$

where $r = 1 - \alpha_2 - \theta$, $m = n\alpha_1(1 - \theta - \alpha_2)^{-1}$ and K_0 is set to zero as a starting point. This can also be written in a convenient form as follows:

$$\dot{u}/u = b(1 - u/\bar{u}) \tag{3.16}$$

where b is a suitable positive parameter and $\bar{u}$ is the maximum level of u, e.g., $b = rm$ and $\bar{u} = 1/m$ in the case above. Now consider two types of stochasticity in the logistic process model (3.15) and (3.16). One arises through the variations in the random parameters m in (3.15) and b in (3.16). The sources of randomness may be due to the Hicksian technical progress function. A second type of stochasticity arises through interpreting u(t)dt as a stochastic process satisfying a birth and death process for example. Here we consider the probability that u(t) takes a particular value at time t, when the transitions to other states are Markovian.

Consider the first case and assume that the parameter m varies randomly, i.e., $m = m_0 + \gamma(t)$ around the mean value m_0 with $\gamma(t)$ as a white noise component with mean zero and variance σ^2. One can then derive the appropriate Fokker–Planck equation for the population probability distribution f(u,t) by following the methods outlined in Bharucha-Reid (1960). The steady state probability distribution f*(u) then takes the limiting form

$$f^*(u) = c \exp(-2\mu/\sigma^2)$$

where c is the normalization constant, making the integrated probability unity. The mean $M = E(u)$ and the root mean square measure of relative fluctuation R can be derived as

$$M = M_0[1 - (\sigma^2/2m_0)] \tag{3.17}$$

$$R = \frac{\sqrt{E(\mu - M)^2}}{M} = \left[\frac{\sigma^2/2m_0}{1 - (\sigma^2/2m_0)}\right]^{1/2}$$

Note that relative fluctuations become increasingly severe as σ^2 increases towards $2m_0$, beyond which no equilibrium or steady state solution exists. Thus the mean variance ratio m_0/σ^2 taking the value 0.50 provides a critical level of volatility measured by the relative fluctuations.

Consider now the second form of the logistic equation (3.16) and assume that the parameter $b = b_0 + \sigma\xi(t)$ fluctuates like a Gaussian variable around the mean value b_0 with a variance σ^2 where $\xi(t)$ represents white noise. This yields a Gaussian delta continuous process for $u(t)$, which satisfies the Fokker–Planck equation

$$\partial P / \partial t = -\frac{\partial}{\partial u}[a(u)P] + \frac{1}{2}\frac{\partial^2}{\partial u^2}[c(u)P] \qquad (3.18)$$

where $P = p[u \mid y,t]$ is the conditional probability that the random variable U will take the value u at time t given that it takes a value y at time zero and $a(u)$, $c(u)$ are defined as follows

$$a(u) = \sigma(u) + \frac{1}{4}\frac{\partial}{\partial u}(\beta(u)^2); \quad \alpha(u) = b_0 u\left(1 - \frac{u}{\bar{u}}\right)$$

$$c(u) = [\beta(u)]^2; \quad \beta(u) = \sigma u\left(1 - \frac{u}{\bar{u}}\right)$$

and $du/dt = \alpha(u) + \beta(u)\,\xi(t)$.

Again one can show that such stochastic processes, which are completely determined by the coefficients $a(u)$ and $c(u)$ of the Fokker–Planck equation have unlimited state spaces if $c(u) > 0$ and $a(u)$ is infinite. In such cases the relative fluctuations enter an explosive phase as in (3.17). For the normalized variable $z = \exp(\sigma u)$ the mean Ez and variance V(z) can be derived as follows

$$Ez = \exp\left(\frac{\sigma^2 t}{2}\right)\exp\left[\sigma\left(u_0 + \frac{b_0 t}{\sigma}\right)\right]; \quad u_0 = u(t) \text{ at } t = 0$$

$$\mathrm{Var}z = (Ez)^2\left[e^{t\sigma^2} - 1\right]$$

$$\sqrt{\mathrm{var}\,z}\,/\,Ez = \left(e^{t\sigma^2} - 1\right)^{1/2} \to \infty \text{ as } t \to \infty.$$

Note also that the deterministic model is

$$du / dt = b_0 u(1 - u / \bar{u})$$

which completely ignores the effects of $\beta(u) \, \xi(t)$, which combines the noise terms σ^2 and $\xi(t)$. Thus the effect of variance σ^2 may be stabilizing when it tends to reduce the mean level of u as t gets larger; or it may be destabilizing when it tends to make the u-process explosive. The zones of stability and chaotic instability are thus characterized by the stochastic interpretation of the growth model subject to the Hicksian type of neutral technological progress. The empirical estimation of Binder and Pesaran (1996) of the volatility of the capital–output ratio over 72 countries (1960–92) shows the importance of such issues for stochastic growth models. The steady state probability density function p(u) of the process defined by (3.18) is of the form

$$p(u) = Cu^{(2b_0 / \sigma^2) - 1}(1 - u / \bar{u})^{-(2u / \sigma^2) - 1} \tag{3.19}$$

which shows that if $2b_0 / \sigma^2$ is less than one, then the density function is U-shaped, indicating that it approaches zero or $\bar{u}$. But if $2b_0 > \sigma^2$ then the density is monotonically increasing in a J-shaped form; which suggests the existence of explosive regions where the steady state equilibrium may not exist at all.

There is an alternative way of looking at the deterministic growth equation (3.15) for u(t). One can rewrite it with an additive error term dε:

$$du = [gu - hu^2)dt] + d\varepsilon \tag{3.20}$$

where the first term under square bracket on the right hand side represents the systematic part of the stochastic changes du and the error term dε has a mean zero in the limit with a variance $(gu - hu^2)dt$. Note that the parameters g and h are functions of the parameters r and m defined before in (3.15), i.e., the learning and experience effects in the R&D processes. Let μ be the asymptotic mean of the u(t) process and $X(t) = u(t) - \mu$. Then

$$X(t + \Delta t) - X(t) = [g \, u(t) - h \, U^2(t)]dt + d\varepsilon(t) .$$

This implies

$$E\{X(t + \Delta t) - X(t)\} = [g \, E(u(t)) - h \, E(u^2(t))]dt + E(d\varepsilon) \, .$$

Letting $\Delta t \to 0$ this yields

$$(g/h)\mu - \mu^2 = \sigma_u^2 \tag{3.21}$$

where σ_u^2 is the asymptotic variance of u. This shows very clearly that

$$\partial\sigma_u^2/\partial\mu = (g/h) - \mu \overset{>}{\underset{<}{=}} 0, \text{ according as } \mu \overset{<}{\underset{>}{=}} \tfrac{1}{2}(g/h) \, .$$

Hence $\partial\mu/\partial\sigma_u^2 < 0$ if $\mu > g/h$. Thus as the mean income level μ increases above the level set by g/2h, higher variance of u leads to a lower mean level of u, i.e., higher volatility tends to have lower means. But for the other case when $\mu < g/2h$, the correlation between μ and σ_μ^2 is expected to be strongly positive.

Now we consider a stochastic birth and death process model for u(t) and assume that the transition probability $p_u(t) = \text{Prob}[u(t) = u]$ for u=0,1,2,... satisfies the standard Markovian assumptions, e.g., (i) assumption of stationary independent increments, i.e., the transition from u to u+1 is given by $\lambda_u\Delta t + 0(\Delta t)$ and from u to u − 1 by $\mu \, \Delta t + 0(\Delta t)$, where $0(\Delta t)$ denotes infinitesimals of order two or higher which can be neglected for $\Delta t \to 0$ and (ii) the probability of no transition is $(1 - \lambda_u - \mu_u)\Delta t + 0(\Delta t)$ and (iii) the probability of transition to a value other than the neighboring value is $0(\Delta t)$. Under these assumptions the transition probability $p_u(t)$ of u(t) taking a value u at time t satisfies the following Chapman–Kolmogorov equation (see, e.g., Tintner and Sengupta (1972):

$$dp_u/dt = \lambda_{u-1}p_{u-1}(t) + \mu_{u+1}p_{u+1}(t) - (\lambda_u + \mu_u)p_u(t) \tag{3.22}$$

where the parameters λ_u, μ_u which depend on the level of u are called birth and death rate parameters, since the former leads to positive growth (e.g., effect of experience) and the latter to decay (e.g., obsolescence due to the introduction of new technology). Now assume that the birth rate parameter λ_u declines with increasing u but the death rate parameter μ_u remains proportional to u^2, i.e.,

$$\lambda_u = ua_1(1-u), \mu = a_2 u^2$$

where a_1, a_2 are positive constants. Then the mean value function $m(t) = E[u(t)]$ would follow the trajectory as follows:

$$dm(t)/dt = (a_1 + a_2)\left[\frac{a_1}{a_1 + a_2}m(t) - m^2(t) - v(t)\right] \qquad (3.23)$$

where $v(t)$ is the variance function for the income process $u(t)$. For the deterministic growth model the differential equation (3.23) reduces to a simpler form

$$\dot{u}(t) = a_1 u(t) - u^2(t) \qquad (3.24)$$

if we normalize as $a_1 + a_2 = 1.0$. The stochastic case however is of the form

$$\dot{m}(t) = a_1 m(t) - m^2(t) - v(t) \qquad (3.25)$$

On comparing the deterministic and stochastic forms of the growth equations (3.24) and (3.25), one may derive some useful results. First of all, in the steady state one obtains

$$\partial m/\partial v > 0 \text{ if and only if } m < (1/2) a_1$$

whereas $\dot{u}(t)$ is zero at the level $u(t) = a_1$ and positive for $u(t) < a_1$. Otherwise the higher variance would tend to be associated with a larger mean. Clearly some countries would correspond with the latter case, as Goodwin (1990) has shown in his nonlinear model of economic growth. Secondly, the presence of a positive variance function in (32.5) implies that the deterministic trajectory $u(t)$ in (3.24) would tend to be shifted downward in the stochastic growth model. Due to this downward bias the steady state value of the mean m^0 would be less than the steady state deterministic value of u, $m^0 < a_1 = u^0$. Note that the shift in the mean value process $m(t)$ can be empirically analyzed through the econometric tests on the variance process $v(t)$, i.e., whether it follows random walk or other Arch processes.

Recently, Sengupta and Zheng (1995) have empirically estimated mean variance models to stock market volatility, where chaotic behavior could not be ruled out. Finally, one may consider a discrete time variant of the logistic model (3.24) as $u_t = f(u_{t-1})$ and analyze the stability of the map $f(\bullet)$ given an initial point u_0. The sequence of points u_0, $f(u_0)$, $f^2(u_0)$, . . . is called the orbit of the map whereas the iterates $f^n(u_0)$ are defined by $f^{n+1}(u_0) = f[f^n(u_0)]$ and $f^0(u_0) = u_0$. The following classification for the stability of the map $f(\bullet)$ is often used in chaos theory:

$$\begin{aligned}
|f'| > 1: &\quad \text{linearly unstable} \\
|f'| \leq 1: &\quad \text{linearly stable} \\
|f'| < 1: &\quad \text{strongly stable} \\
|f'| = 1: &\quad \text{marginally stable} \\
f' = 0: &\quad \text{superstable}
\end{aligned}$$

where f' is the slope of the map f at a fixed point with $|f'|$ denoting its absolute value. Note that the equation in discrete time form:

$$u_t/u_{t-1} = a(1 - u_{t-1})$$

has its critical parameter a acting as a bifurcation parameter in the sense that the qualitative behavior of u_t suddenly changes for different value of a. For example, the range $1 < a < 2$ defines monotonic growth of u_t converging to the steady state $u^0 = (1 - 1/a)$, but for $a > 3$ the steady state becomes unstable and a two-period cycle emerges. In fact the simulation studies by Lorenz (1963) showed that as a increases beyond $1 + \sqrt{6} = 3.45$, higher and higher even-order cycles emerge; beyond 3.57 he found that very higher odd-period cycles appear and so on. This type of chaotic behavior may sometimes be reduced or aggravated by the variance process in the stochastic process model.

3.2   DYNAMIC ADJUSTMENTS AND SECTORAL SPILLOVERS

The dynamic effects of openness in trade have been strongly emphasized in new growth theory. Export growth and the impact of the export-intensive sectors on the other sectors of the economy have played a very critical role in the rapid growth episodes of countries like the NICs in Southeast Asia. In new growth theory openness in trade has been viewed as a catalytic mechanism which alleviates the bottlenecks that impede the steady growth of the less developed countries (LDCs). Empirical studies of the growth of exports have revealed two broad trends for the successful NICs. Thus Bradford (1987) examined empirical data for more than a dozen countries over 1965–80 covering the link between structural change and economic growth, where the index of structural change was derived from 16 manufacturing sectors and concluded that high rates of growth and rapid structural change are closely associated with those countries which are the successful NICs. Moreover for some countries like South Korea the pace of rapid structural change was also associated with a change in export-mix in response to world competition. The shift from traditional to R&D intensive products in export growth has been remarkable for the four successful NICs in Asia as follows:

Table 3.1. Percentage Distribution of Exports to the US

		Traditional	Product group R&D intensive (general)	R&D intensive (sophisticated)
Hong Kong	(1966)	67.9	9.8	17.5
	(1986)	62.2	23.8	29.5
Korea	(1966)	56.5	2.0	3.9
	(1986)	52.7	19.2	29.6
Taiwan	(1966)	44.6	15.8	20.3
	(1986)	49.1	22.3	29.2
Singapore	(1966)	73.6	0.0	0.20
	(1986	13.9	58.2	78.1

This analysis by Kellman and Chow (1989) also showed another important characteristic, e.g., the traditional export items mainly from the primary sector were very dissimilar in pattern across the four countries above and also very insensitive to changes in relative prices but all the four countries were found to be very similar in the pattern of exports of certain sophisticated R&D intensive products such as electrical machinery, optical equipment and telecommunications and computer equipment and consumer electronics; also these R&D intensive products were found to be strongly responsive to international competition. In the more recent decade (1986–1996 this tendency has intensified due to two main reasons, e.g., (a) the impact of innovation in the semiconductor industry and its spillover effects on other sectors, and (b) the globalization of trade which has increased the competitive efficiency.

Several key channels have been identified in modern growth theory in order to explain the close association of the openness in trade via exports and the rapid overall growth. One channel is the 'trade–knowledge externality' which was originally emphasized by Alfred Marshall. The benefits of this trade–knowledge cannot be fully appropriated internally. As Caballero and Lyons (1992) have interpreted, the expression of 'trade–knowledge' includes according to Marshall not only R&D but also knowledge along the lines of process innovation and best practice technology in general. In Romer's (1990) endogenous growth theory, the capital input embodies this trade knowledge externality. The export sector's externality spills over to the other sectors and generates a feedback effect. A second channel of interaction why the export sector plays a leading role is that it is more productive and more intensive in modern technological inputs. Hence the export sector exerts a strong positive influence on the rest of the economy. A direct empirical test of this dominance effect of the export sector may be made by means of a two-sector model with outputs X and N for the export and the non-export sector subject to two production functions

$$N = F(K_N, L_N, X)$$
$$X = G(K_X, L_X, N) \tag{3.26}$$

where $K = K_N + K_X$ is total capital and $L = L_N + L_X$ is total labor. It follows therefore

$$\Delta N = F_K \, \Delta K_N + F_L \, \Delta L_N + F_X \, \Delta X$$
$$\Delta X = G_K \, \Delta K_X + G_L \, \Delta L_X + G_N \, \Delta N \tag{3.27}$$

where the subscripts on F and G denote the marginal productivity of the two inputs in the two sectors. A direct empirical estimate of the two sector model (3.27) from Korean national income statistics data produced the following results

	1964–83	1964–86	1969–86
F_X	1.92	1.00	0.99
G_N	0.28	0.31	0.31
F_X/G_N	6.90	3.20	3.11

It is clear that the dynamic interdependence effect from the export to the non-export sector is roughly between three and seven times larger than the reverse effect from the non-export to the export sector. The estimates for other successful NICs in Asia analyzed by Sengupta (1993) confirm this dominance hypothesis for the export sector. Finally, Lucas (1993) has emphasized the knowledge spillover effect as the most significant factor which explains the difference in capital productivity between an LDC and a developed economy. Thus the external benefits of human capital in his theory can be captured by specifying the production function for sector i (i=1,2) as

$$y_i = A_i x_i^\beta h_i^{\gamma_i}; \quad \Delta h_i = h_i (1 - u_i) \theta_i \tag{3.28a}$$

where the three variables y, x and h denote output, physical and human capital per effective worker. The term $h_i^{\gamma_i}$ is interpreted as an externality which multiplies the productivity of a worker at any skill level just as the shift factor A_i. For the export-intensive sector (i=1, e.g.) we have higher h_1 and higher γ_1 than the other sector. Also h_1 tends to grow faster over time, since the proportion $(1 - u_1)$ devoted to human capital accumulation and its productivity effect (θ_1) is likely to be higher for the export sector (i = 1).

There is an alternative way of modelling the knowledge spillover effect through human capital in the global economy. This follows the approach of Grossman and Helpman (1991) and more recently the learning models due to Jovanovic (1997), where endogenous quality increments follow the process of learning through research. Here there are invention costs but no adoption costs and the output of research is designs, which are sold by innovators to intermediate-goods producers. Specifically the use of the new intermediate good augments the productivity parameter A in (3.28a). This formulation allows the direct introduction of the Schumpeterian innovation process which is sufficiently important to affect the entire economy, as has been shown by Aghion and Howitt (1992).

In this aggregative model the economy is populated by identical infinitely lived households, who maximize their discounted objective functional:

$$U = \int_0^\infty dt \exp(-\rho t)[1 - \sigma)^{-1}\{c^{1-\sigma} - 1\}$$

(3.28b)

where c is per capita consumption, σ is the inverse of the intertemporal elasticity of substitution and $\rho = r - n$, r being the discount rate and n the growth rate of population. Each household has the budget constraint in per capita terms as

$$y = c + i_h + i_x - g$$

(3.28c)

where i_h and i_x are the gross investment flows of human and physical capitals and g is the net amount of lump-sum government transfers to households. Production function and the accumulation processes for the two types of capital are as follows:

$$y = A(n,g) F(x,h)$$
$$\dot{x} = i_x - (\delta_x + n)x$$
$$\dot{h} = B(n,\phi)i_h - (\delta_h + n)h \ .$$

(3.28d)

Here the scale parameter $B(n,\phi)$ captures the sequential effects of population growth affecting human capital accumulation and other learning effects in the public domain proxied by ϕ. When $\partial B/\partial n < 0$ this reflects the process of creative destruction in the Schumpeterian framework, where the prospect of more future research tends to discourage current research by threatening to destroy the rents from current research. However this congestion effect may be countered by the positive impact $\partial B/\partial \phi > 0$, when public sector capital and R&D process can create externalities for the private sector. Note that the depreciation rates δ_x, δ_h for the two types of capital reflect their variations in user costs. On using the Hamiltonian H

$$H = (1 - \sigma)^{-1}\{c^{1-\sigma} - 1\} + \lambda_1[A(n,g)F(x,h) + g - c$$
$$- i_x - (\delta_x + n)x] + \lambda_2[B(n,\phi)i_h - (\delta_h + n)h]$$

and the condition $\lambda_1 = \lambda_2$ for net marginal productivity equalization across factors, one can easily derive the result:

$$\frac{\delta_x - \delta_h}{A(n,g)} = f(w) - [B(n,\phi) + w]\frac{\partial f}{\partial w} = \psi(w,n,B) \qquad (3.28e)$$

where $w = n/x$ and $f(\bullet)$ is the neoclassical production function derived from $F(x,h)$ in per capita terms. Clearly if the Inada conditions hold for the production function $f(\bullet)$, then $\psi(o,n,B) = -\infty$, $\psi(\infty,n,B) = +\infty$ and under diminishing returns to each factor $\partial\psi/\partial w > 0$. Thus the equation (3.28e) yields a uniquely finite positive solution $w^* = w^*(\delta_h,\delta_x,A,B,n)$ which is constant over time in the steady state. The equilibrium value w^* of the ratio between the stock of human and physical capital stays constant at a finitely positive level. Also the optimality conditions for consumption and the resource constraint imply by equation (3.28e) that all per capita variables such as consumption, output, physical and human capital grow at the same positive rate. This agrees with the result of Romer (1990) that positive growth might be sustainable even under Inada conditions, if the accumulation of knowledge allows long run returns not to be diminishing.

3.3   SOURCES OF DYNAMIC INSTABILITY

Consider now the stochastic view of the bivariate interaction of the two sectors in the growth process model in the form (3.26). Assume a bivariate birth and death process satisfying the Chapman–Kolmogorov equations as before. Then the system of differential equations for the transition probability $p_{x,n}(t)$ at time t can be written as

$$dp_{x,n}(t) = -(\lambda_x + \mu_x + \lambda_n + \mu_n)p_{x,n}(t) + \lambda_{x-1}p_{x-1,n}(t)$$
$$+\mu_{x-1}p_{x+1,n}(t) + \lambda_{n-1}p_{x,n-1}(t) + \mu_{n+1}p_{x,n+1}(t)$$

$$(3.29)$$

for $x,n = 0,1,2...$ We now consider the application of the above system of differential equation to two special cases. The first case occurs when there is no death rate, i.e., $\mu_x = 0 = \mu_n$ and the deterministic system in $x(t)$ and $n(t)$ follows one way interdependence as follows

$$dx(t)/dt = \dot{x}(t) = b_1 vx(t)$$
$$dn(t)/dt = \dot{n}(t) = a_2 n(t) + b_2(1-v)x(t); \quad 0 < v < 1.$$

Here $n(t)$ depends on $x(t)$ for its growth, whereas $x(t)$ grows due to the high proportion of total output $x(t) + n(t)$ devoted to human capital, i.e., high level of v which implies a low level allocated for the growth of the $n(t)$ sector. The means (M_x, M_n) and variances (V_x, V_n) may then be calculated as

$$M_x(t) = \exp(b_1 vt)$$
$$V_x(t) = v(2 - v)^{-1} \exp(b_1 vt)[\exp(b_1 vt) - 1]$$

where the initial value $x(0)$ is set equal to one. However the non export sector output follows a different mean variance structure. The mean is

$$M_n(t) = b_2(1 - v)(b_1 v - a_2)^{-1} \exp(b_1 vt) + \exp(a_2 t)$$

but the variance is a more complicated function with a dominant term proportional to $\exp(2a_2 t)$. It is clear from these mean variance relationships that

$$\partial M_x(t) / \partial V_x(t) < 0 \text{ as } M_x(t) < 1/2$$

i.e., countries with a higher volatility of export output would tend to have a lower mean export level, otherwise $\partial M_x / \partial V_x > 0$ as $M_x(t) > 1/2$. Secondly, the allocation ratio v can be used directly by public policy favoring the export sector. The national government in NICs in Asia have always stressed these policy measures. For example the government planners in Japan and Korea have consistently allocated a growing share of domestic and foreign resources through credit rationing and other export subsidy measures to capital-intensive industries and also consumer electronics. Finally, as $t \rightarrow \infty$, the coefficient of variation (CV) measuring the relative level of fluctuations tends to settle down in both sectors,

$$CV_x \sim \left(\frac{v}{2 - v}\right)^{1/2}$$

This implies that the CV_x ratio increases as v rises.

A second case of the stochastic process model (3.28) occurs when the sectoral interdependence takes the following form

$$\lambda_x = \lambda_1 x, \mu_x = xf(x,n) = x(\mu_{11}x + \mu_{12}n)$$
$$\lambda_n = \lambda_2 n, \mu_n = nf(x,n) = n(\mu_{21}x + \mu_{22}n)$$

with $f(x,n) = \alpha_1 x + \alpha_2 n$ denoting the interaction term. This form allows various types of interaction effects through the functions $f(\cdot)$ and $g(\cdot)$. One could derive from this system differential equations involving the first two moments of the stochastic process as follows:

$$\dot{m}_{11}(t) = \lambda_1 m_{11}(t) - \mu_{11}m_{12}(t) - \mu_{12}\overline{m}_{11}(t)$$
$$\dot{m}_{21}(t) = \lambda_2 m_{21}(t) - \mu_{21}\overline{m}_{11}(t) - \mu_{22}m_{22}(t) \qquad (3.30)$$

Here $m_{11}(t) = E\{X(t)\}$, $m_{12}(t) = E\{X^2(t)\}$, $m_{21}(t) = E\{N(t)\}$, $m_{22}(t) = E\{N^2(t)\}$ and $\overline{m}_{11}(t) = E\{X(t)N(t)\}$ and the dot over a variable denotes its time derivative. Clearly if there is no interaction between the sectors, then the two sectoral outputs $m_{11}(t)$ and $m_{21}(t)$ grow at the exponential rates λ_1 and λ_2 respectively. But if $\mu_{12} = 0 = \mu_{21}$, and both μ_{11} and μ_{22} are negative, then both sectoral outputs tend to grow exponentially. The deterministic system corresponding to (3.30) may be specified as

$$\dot{X}(t) = \lambda_1 X(t) - \mu_1\alpha_1 X^2(t) - \mu_1\alpha_2 X(t)N(t)$$
$$\dot{N}(t) = \lambda_2 N(t) - \mu_2\alpha_1 X(t)N(t) - \mu_2\alpha_2 N^2(t)$$

Note that this system has a logistic time profile for the export sector output if $\mu_1\alpha_2$ is negligibly small, i.e.,

$$\dot{X}(t) = \lambda_1 X(t) - \mu_1\alpha_1 X^2(t)$$

with steady state values

$$X^* = \lambda_1 / (\mu_1\alpha_1), N^* = \frac{\lambda_2}{\alpha_2\mu_2} - \frac{\lambda_1}{\alpha_2\mu_1} .$$

The stability of these steady state values depends of course on the underlying characteristic roots. However the stability of the steady state values m_{11}^*, m_{21}^* of the stochastic system (3.30) depends on much more restrictive conditions. As May (1973) has shown that the probability of unstable steady states is much higher and there exist biological systems where this type of instability phenomenon is persistent. For example consider the second equation of the Lucas model (3.28) and assume a two-sector interacting framework as

$$\dot{h}_1 = h_1(t)f_1(h_1, h_2)$$
$$\dot{h}_2 = h_2(t)f_2(h_1, h_2) \tag{3.31}$$

where

$$f_1(\bullet) = k_1 - h_1(t) - ah_2(t)$$
$$f_2(\bullet) = k_2 - h_2(t) - ah_1(t) .$$

Here the coefficient a measures the symmetric competition between the two sectors for the common pool of human capital in the population and k_1, k_2 are the sector-specific parameters, which are constants in the deterministic case but random around a mean in a stochastic environment. In the steady state of the deterministic model the levels of h_1^* and h_2^* are found by putting the growth rates $\dot{h}_1 = \dot{h}_2$ to zero and then the linearized version around these steady states has the coefficient matrix

$$A = \begin{bmatrix} -h_1^* & -ah_2^* \\ -ah_1^* & -h_2^* \end{bmatrix}$$

Clearly both the eigenvalues of this matrix are negative if and only if the coefficient a < 1.0. This is the well known Gauss–Lotka–Volterra criterion for a stale bivariate population. Now let us consider a stochastic framework:

$$k_1 = k_0 + \gamma_1(t)$$
$$k_2 = k_0 + \gamma_2(t)$$

where the random parameters k_1, k_2 have a common mean value k_0 and $\gamma_1(t), \gamma_2(t)$ are two independent white noise random variables with zero mean and a common variance σ^2. Let R denote the root mean square measure of relative fluctuation as is used in (3.17) before. Then it holds approximately that

$$R^2 \sim \frac{\sigma^2}{k_0(1-a)} \ .$$

This result derived by May (1973) has two important implications. One is that the system is stable so long as a < 1.0 But as soon as the magnitude of a increases up to 1.0 the interaction dynamics provide a weaker and weaker stabilizing influence and in the limit R^2 tends to be explosive. Secondly, the common parameter k_0 is only assumed for simplicity, the result would hold even if it is different for the two sectors. Clearly as k_0 decreases to lower and lower values and satisfies the inequality $k_0(1-a) < \sigma^2$, then the fluctuations measured by R^2 in (3.32) would tend to be higher and higher. This implies a tendency favoring increased random fluctuations in the $h_i(t)$ process and hence in the output process $y_i(t)$ defined in the Lucas model (3.28).

3.4 STOCHASTIC LEARNING ALONG THE EFFICIENCY FRONTIER

Rapid growth episodes in the NICs in Asia have been closely associated with some key trends in these countries. One is the persistence of scale economies which tends to produce oligopolistic firms even if there are no formal barriers to entry under competitive world trade. In this framework the output of each firm is given by a Cournot–Nash equilibrium. Openness in world trade implying a larger market will tend to reduce the oligopolistic mark-up of price (p) over marginal cost (c). A second trend is the learning curve effect of cumulative experience of knowledge capital, which is undergoing an international spillover. For example Norsworthy and Jang (1992), have empirically shown this effect to be substantial in Japan and other Asian NICs in microelectronics and semiconductor industries in particular. in a dynamic limit pricing model discussed, e.g., by Sengupta and Fanchon (1997) the entry into the market by other oligopolistic firms depends on the mark-up of price over marginal cost, where the actual price lies somewhere between the short-run monopoly price and the competitive price, the exact positioning depending on the barriers to entry, risk aversion and the impact on cost reduction through cumulative experience and learning. The third trend in the rapidly growing NICs in Asia is to capture the cost savings over time due to building capacity ahead of demand and to adopt flexible manufacturing practices. In this set-up it is important to distinguish between current output ($\dot{y} = dy / dt$) and cumulative output $y(t)$ in the production function $F(y(t), x(t))$ where $x(t)$ denotes the variable inputs, e.g., the functional form

$$\dot{y}(t) = A \, y^{\delta} x(t)^{1/\gamma}$$

summarizes the dynamic process of producing the joint products of learning and output from resources and experiences. Assume now a duopolistic framework with two producers producing outputs $\dot{y}_1(t), \dot{y}_2(t)$ at prices $p_1(t)$, $p_2(t)$. The NICs may represent one producer and the rest of the world as the second producer. The dynamic optimization model for the first producer may then take the form

$$\text{Max } J_1 = \int_0^{\infty} e^{-rt}(p_1(t) - c_1(t)) \, \dot{y}_1 \, dt$$

subject to   (3.32)

$$\dot{y}_i(t) = F_i(y_1(t), y_2(t), p_1(t), p_2(t)); i = 1, 2$$

On using the current value Hamiltonian

$$H = e^{-rt}\{(p_1 - c_1 + \lambda_1)F_1 + (p_2 - c_2 + \lambda_2)F_2\}$$

and assuming the regularity conditions for the existence of an optimal trajectory the Pontryagin maximum principle specifies the following necessary conditions for optimality (for $i = 1, 2,$):

$$\dot{\lambda}_i = r\lambda_i - \frac{\partial H}{\partial y_i}$$

$$\dot{y}_i = F_i(y_1, y_2, p_1, p_2) \tag{3.33}$$
$$\partial H / \partial p_i = 0 \text{ for all } t$$

and $\lim e^{-rt}\lambda_i(t) = 0$ (transversality).

By using $\mu_{ii} = (\partial F_i / \partial p_i)(p_i / F_i)$ and $\mu_{ji} = (\partial F_j / \partial p_i)(p_i / F_j)$ when $i \neq j$ as the own price elasticity and cross elasticity of demand, the optimal price rule can be written as

$$p_1 = (1 + \mu_{11})^{-1}[\mu_{11}(c_1 - \lambda_1) - \lambda_2\mu_{21}] \tag{3.34}$$

with the optimal trajector for $\lambda_1(t)$ as

$$\dot{\lambda}_1 = r\lambda_1 + (c_1 - \lambda_1)F_{1y_1} - p_1 F_{1y_1} + c_{1y} F_1$$

i.e., $\qquad \lambda(t) = \int_t^\infty e^{-r(\tau-1)}\left[\left(\dfrac{p_1}{\mu_{11}} + \dfrac{\lambda_2\mu_{21}}{\mu_{11}}\right)F_{1y_1} + c_{1y_1}F\right]d\tau \qquad (3.35)$

where $\quad F_{1y_1} = \partial F_1 / \partial y_1$

$\qquad c_{1y_1} = \partial c_1 / \partial y_1 < 0$, i.e., future cost decline

$\qquad \mu_{11} < 0, \mu_{21} > 0.$

Clearly the optimal pricing rules involve the trajectory of both the current price $p_1(t)$ and the shadow prices $\lambda_1(t)$. The current pricing rule (3.34) shows the price to be much lower than the monopoly price $(1 + \mu_{11})^{-1}$ $\mu_{11}(c_1 - \lambda_1)$ since λ_2 is usually negative, since more competition hurts the market position of y_1 more. Secondly, the extent of future cost declines $(-c_1y_1 > 0)$ tends to reduce the dynamic shadow price $\lambda_1(t)$. Thirdly, if the demand function in (3.33) is a function of prices alone, i.e.,

$$\dot{y}_i = F(p_1, p_2)$$

then

$$\text{sign}(\dot{p}) = \text{sign}(-r\lambda_1 + c_{1t} - \lambda_2\mu_{21})$$

where $c_{1t} = \partial c_1 / \partial t$ is the decline of cost over time due to learning and experience since $c_{y_1} < 0$. This shows a strong pressure for price declines over time. This has happened exactly in the semiconductor and R&D intensive industries such as electronics, telecommunications and personal computers.

A simpler form of the decision model (3.32) results when we assume one average market price $p(t)$ for a homogeneous product and a dynamic

Cournot model with two outputs $\dot{y}_1$ and $\dot{y}_2$ as decision variables. In this case we reformulate the model as

$$\text{Max } J_1 = \int_0^\infty e^{-rt}(p(t) - c_1(t))\dot{y}_1 dt$$

$$\text{s.t.} \quad \dot{p}(t) = k(\tilde{p} - p), \; \tilde{p} = a - b(\dot{y}_1 + \dot{y}_2) \qquad (3.36)$$

where $\tilde{p} = \tilde{p}(t)$ is the demand price expected and p is the market price. Assuming quadratic cost functions, i.e., $c_1\dot{y}_1 = wu_1 + \frac{1}{2}u_1^2$ where $u_1 = \dot{y}_1$ and the parameter w declining over time due to learning and experience, the above is a linear quadratic control model and hence the optimal feedback strategies $u_i^*(t)$ can be easily calculated as

$$u_i^*(t) = [1 - bk\, h(t)]\, p(t) + bk\, m(t) - w \qquad (3.37)$$

with $\quad h(t) = (6k^2b^2)^{-1}[r + 4bk + 2k - \{(r + 4bk + 2k)^2 - 12k^2b^2\}^{1/2}]$

$\qquad m(t) = (r - 3b^2k^2h(t) + k + 2bk)^{-1}[w - ash(t) - 2bkwh(t)]$.

Here zero conjectural variation on the part of each player is assumed. Clearly this linear feedback form of the conjectural equilibrium output path in (3.36) yields a steady state price level p^* as

$$p^* = [2b(1 - bk\, h^* + 1]^{-1}\, [a + 2b(w - bk\, m^*)]$$

where h^*, m^* are the steady state values of $h(t)$ and $m(t)$ respectively.

Stochasticity in this framework may now be introduced in two simple ways. One is in the LQG (linear quadratic Gaussian) framework with the dynamic price equation rewritten as

$$dp(t) = k(\tilde{p} - p)dt + dv(t)$$

where $v(t)$ is a zero mean Gaussian process with stationary independent increments and a constant variance σ^2. The objective function now is to maximize the expected value of J_1 in (3.36). In this case the optimal $h(t)$ which is called the Kalman gain in filtering theory is directly influenced by the variances σ^2 of the error term and hence the steady state price level p^*

changes due to σ^2. Generally the price level p* gets higher with higher a. Secondly, the conjectural variation assumption that $\partial u_i / \partial u_j = 0$ for $i \neq j$ may not hold due to the presence of random noise in the market demand equation. In this case there may be stochastic instability in the convergence process and the steady state p*, u_i^* may not be stable. In such cases the duopolists may see implicit cooperation by 'subjective random devices' as proposed by Aumann (1974). As Ohyama and Fukushima (1995) have recently shown that in dualistic market structures of the NICs in Asia, the Asian producers adopt a two-tier policy. In the domestic front they act more like a monopoly and tend to exploit all scale economies due to learning and experience, whereas in the international market they attempt to build up implicit cooperation with the US producers, since they do not have a large base in R&D investment.

4. Recent Growth Episodes in NICs

The newly industrializing countries (NICs) of southeast Asia provide a fitting background for empirically testing some of the major tenets of endogenous growth theory developed over the last decade or so. Three major premises of new growth theory have generally been put forward in this connection. One is the role of openness in trade and export externality as a positive factor in promoting long run growth. Two mechanisms in the growth process appear to be important here. One is the dynamic productivity effect of the export sector's growth, which acts as a catalytic agent in the diffusion of modern technology. The second is the persistence of increasing returns to scale in the production of technology-intensive products which play an increasing role in the export trade of the NICs in Asia such as Japan, Korea (south), Singapore and Taiwan.

The second premise of new growth theory emphasizes the role of knowledge capital and the effects of learning by doing, where innovations are induced by market incentives and the expectation of future profits and the knowledge spillover occurs initially through foreign technology but spreads later through other sectors by the spread of information technology (IT). Like openness in trade the investment in knowledge capital takes place under conditions of increasing returns to scale (IRS) and this implies that the marginal product of capital need not decline over time to the level of discount rate and hence the incentive to accumulate this type of capital may persist indefinitely, thus sustaining a steady growth of national output.

Finally, the globalization of international trade and the emerging stock markets of the world have generated both positive and negative spillover effects of foreign investment in NICs. On the positive side competitiveness in open markets has helped increase the cost efficiency of export-intensive industries in general and knowledge capital intensive industries in particular. On the negative side the domestic economies of NICs are now more vulnerable to the international shocks originating in US and other countries and vice versa. The imbalance of imports and exports coupled with misalignment of domestic currencies in relation to US dollar may generate in this framework a balance of payments or foreign exchange crisis and the speculators' role in the international currency markets may accentuate this currency crisis as it happened in late 1997 for the NICs.

This chapter provides some empirical tests of the three premises of new growth theory described above, e.g., openness in trade and growth, scale economies in the technology-intensive sector and the impact of foreign exchange constraints on growth. Two countries e.g., Japan and Korea are selected among the successful NICs for our empirical applications, since they provide a fairly representative cross-section. Japan is a mature industrial economy, where the average share of exports in GDP is less than 15% in recent times, whereas for Korea and Taiwan it is more than 35%. The average GDP growth over the recent period 1984–90 is 4.62% in Japan as against 9.65% in Korea and 8.47% in Taiwan. But in terms of R&D expenditures as percent of GDP in 1988 Japan scores 2.8 as against 1.6 in Korea and 0.9 in Taiwan and 0.12 in Philippines. Our empirical tests are based on the modern theory of cointegration in time series models, which is used to test the persistence of long run growth and the growth contributions of labor, capital and export externality. The specification and estimation of the error correction models (ECM) which result from the cointegrated variables distinguish between the short and the long run and hence between the transitory and permanent shock to the growth process due to externality and other factors.

4.1 OPENNESS IN TRADE, PRODUCTIVITY AND GROWTH

Openness in trade and competition in world markets can be empirically measured in several ways. The protection measures and import tariff barriers have been used by Quah and Rauch (1990) for example to study the empirical relationship of openness and growth for over 81 developing countries over the period 1961–85. The relationship was found to be positive. The other measures of openness in trade that are frequently used in empirical growth studies are given by the ratio of exports to GDP and that of imports to GDP. Of these two the export ratio is a more convenient measure, since it can specify more directly the externality impact of the export sector over the other sectors. Using this measure the linkage between exports and economic growth in LDC has been traditionally analyzed by two groups of methods. One group of methods uses export growth to measure openness in trade and correlates it with per capita income. Thus Feder (1982), Chow (1967) and Edwards (1989) have used regression methods to explain income growth rates in terms of export growth for the developing countries. For a sample of 8 NICs, Chow (1967) carried out causality tests in the sense of Sims (1972) linking exports of manufactures and the manufacturing output and found a strong causal relationship from exports to income growth. The second group of methods attempted by Balassa (1983), Bradford (1987) and others looks at the composition of export products and uses its diversification to represent outward development or openness in world trade. Thus Bradford (1987) used empirical data for more than 12 countries either NICs, or next-tier NICs in the world over 1965–50 and found that high rates of income growth and rapid structural change are strongly positively correlated for those countries which are successful NICs. Here the index of structural change is derived from the share in GDP of the 16 manufacturing branches that are technology-intensive.

These empirical methods have however some basic limitations from an economic viewpoint. First of all, the correlation between exports and output growth may not have any structural long run significance, when the two variables are nonstationary over time. The modern theory of cointegration in dynamic economic modelling has emphasized this point very clearly. Thus consider a pair (y_t, x_t) of variables, where y_t is the dependent variable and it is assumed that both series are nonstationary. Let us assume that their first differences i.e., $\Delta y_t = y_t - y_{t-1}$, $\Delta x_t = x_t - x_{t-1}$ are stationary. Then the ordinary regression of y_t (e.g., output growth) on x_t (e.g., export growth) would frequently have high R^2 statistics typically displaying highly autocorrelated residuals (i.e., low Durban–Watson statistics), which produce a strong bias towards accepting the spurious relationships. As Phillips and Durlauf (1986) have shown that such regressions have the disturbing feature that the conventional t and F tests for the regression coefficients do not converge and there are no asymptotically correct critical values for the conventional significance tests.

Secondly, the researchers emphasizing a positive correlation between exports and output growth have usually employed a linear regression equation relating income growth Δy_t, openness x and other variables z:

$$E(\Delta y_t | x, z) = X\beta + Z\gamma \tag{4.1}$$

and they applied this formulation to the steady state version of these variables. Therefore they frequently use sample time averages of Δy_t, x and z in estimating the regression equation (4.1). However, due to nonstationarity, the time averaging process fails to reveal the dynamic relationships between growth and openness in cross-section samples. Thus

Levine and Renett (1990) found no robust relationship between the growth of the export–GDP ratio and the growth of GDP per capita. Recently Levine and Raut (1992) have shown that this lack of robustness may be due to neglecting significant nonlinearities in the relationship. Furthermore, if we let e_t as the additive error in the specification (4.1):

$$E(\Delta y_t | x, z) = f(X, Z) + e_t \qquad (4.2)$$

where $f(\bullet)$ may be a nonlinear function, one could test if the residuals e_t satisfy the condition of stationarity. For this purpose the modern theory of cointegration performs an augmented Dickey–Fuller (ADF) test by running an empirical regression of a generalized form:

$$\Delta e_t = \delta e_{t-1} + b_1 \Delta e_{t-1} + \cdots + b_p \Delta e_{t-p} \qquad (4.3)$$

and performing a t-test to determine if δ is significantly less than zero or not. Clearly if the output variable y_t is not stationary to the first order, the ADF test would reveal the inappropriateness of the regression model (4.2) as a long-run structural specification. It would also explain in part the lack of robustness obtained by the empirical studies of Levine and Renett (1990).

Recently, Edwards (1997) has used nine alternative indexes of openness in trade to empirically analyze the connection between trade policy and economic growth, where the latter is measured by the growth (Δy) of total factor productivity (TFP) or the Solow residual. Four of the nine indexes of trade orientation are most interesting e.g., World Bank index of outward orientation (x_1), average black market premium in the foreign exchange market (x_2), average import tariff on manufacturing (x_3) and the average ratio of trade taxes on imports and exports to the total revenue from trade (x_4). These indexes are easily updated on the basis of observed data and also easily available. The TFP growth regression estimated by the instrumental weighted least squares by Edwards (1997) appear in Table 4.1, with t-values in parentheses and the intercept term not reported. Here the decade long estimates of TFP growth (Δy) were constructed over the panel data for 1960–90 by using the estimated factor shares of physical capital and human capital and three sources of TFP growth are identified e.g., (1) the log of initial GDP per capita $G = \log(\text{GDP–65})$, (2) initial level of human capital ($H = $ Human capital–65) measured as the mean number of years of education in 1965 and (3) the index (x_i) of openness in trade measured in different

Table 4.1 TFP Growth Regression on the Trade Openness Variables

$$\Delta y = f(G, H, x_i)$$

Openness measure (x_i)	G (GDP–65)	H (Human Capital–65)	x_i	R^2	n (no. of countries)
x_1 (1973–82)	−0.011 (−2.04)	0.003 (2.35)	0.013 (3.36)	0.41	30
x_2 (1980s)	−0.008 (−2.32)	0.003 (2.23)	−0.019 (−1.95)	0.27	71
x_3 (1982)	−0.014 (−2.07)	0.003 (1.97)	−0.106 (−2.95)	0.10	64
x_4 (1980–85)	−0.040 (−2.42)	0.005 (2.28)	−1.67 (−2.15)	0.24	42

years due to nonavailability of data for each year. Note that if the time series y_t is nonstationary of order one, Δy is stationary and since the explanatory variables (G, H, x_i) are lagged in years, the regression estimates in Table 4.1 have some meaningful and possibly structural significance. Two results stand out very clearly. One is that the coefficient of human capital is consistently positive and statistically significant at conventional levels of t-test. Edwards (1997) notes that when alternative measures of human capital were used e.g., measures of the quality of education proxied by the teacher–student ratio etc. the thrust of the results was maintained. Secondly, there is a significant positive connection between openness in trade and productivity growth. When five indexes of openness in trade (the above three plus two other indexes of trade distortion) are combined into a grand composite index by the principal component method and the explanatory variable x_5 is used as the first principal component which accounts for more than 60% of the variation of the five indexes, the estimated results are as follows:

$$\Delta y = 0.08 - 0.013G + 0.005H - 0.07x_5$$
$$(2.0) \quad (-2.3) \quad (2.7)$$
$$n = 60; R^2 = 0.32$$

This reinforces the finding that other things being equal, more open countries tend to experience faster productivity growth than more protectionist countries with tariff barriers. Note that the coefficient of initial GDP per capita is negative though very small and statistically significant. This result seems to indicate that after controlling for the variables G and x_i, total factor productivity exhibits conditional convergence though at a slow rate. As it has been noted by Edwards (1997) when H and x_i are excluded from the regression equation, the coefficient of G becomes positive, thus providing evidence for rejecting the hypothesis of absolute TFP convergence.

One may also analyze the trend of TFP growth specifically for the individual NICs in East Asia, though comparable time series data are not easily available. One may refer here to two empirical studies. One is the study by Havrylyshyn (1990), who surveyed the existing research studies in this area and found capacity utilization and scale economies to be important factors behind the high share of TFP in GDP growth in these countries. Table 4.2 reports his empirical results from several sources, showing that the share of TFP in GDP growth is much higher for these Asian NICs than the average level of 30 to 35 percent observed for other countries. Note however that this share has fallen markedly in recent years since 1970 for Korea, Singapore and Taiwan.

The second empirical study is by Young (1995), who examined in great detail the diverse and heterogenous data structure of different NICs in Asia. Three major conclusions were reached by his empirical analysis. One is that the naive estimate of TFP growth over 1966–90 is reduced very significantly, when various adjustments are made due to weighting of labor input i.e., taking into account changes in age, sex and educational composition of the work force and also weighting of capital, i.e., placing a greater weight on the rapid growing stock of machinery.

1966–90	TFP Growth (% per annum)			
	Hong Kong	Singapore	Korea	Taiwan
Naive estimate	3.4	4.1	4.1	4.0
Final estimate after adjustment	2.3	0.2	1.7	2.1

Table 4. 2 Rates of Growth of Output and Shares of TFP (1952–80)

NIC	Source	Period	Average yearly rate of GDP growth (%)	Share of TFP in output growth (%)
Japan	Chen	1955–60	5.5	60.0
		1960–66	4.0	45.0
		1966–70	7.4	62.0
Korea	Chen	1955–60	2.0	47.4
		1960–66	4.1	59.3
		1966–70	5.1	50.1
Singapore	Chen	1955–60	3.7	69.0
		1966–70	5.1	44.0
	Tsao	1971–79	1.1	9.0
Taiwan	Chen	1955–60	3.1	60.0
		1960–66	6.0	55.0
		1966–70	1.8	23.0
	Kuo	1971–80	1.1	7.0

Young's second conclusion is that the TFP growth is declining in the recent period, particularly in the manufacturing sector which plays a prominent role in the export market. Thus according to his adjusted estimates TFP growth in Korea fell from 5.3% in 1970–75 to 0.8% in 1985–90, while for Singapore TFP growth was negative for both the decades 1970–80 (-0.9) and 1980–90 (-1.1). Since the labor participation rate has been significantly high in these countries, the labor share in TFP growth has been very high e.g., it rose from 47.7% during 1970–75 in Korea to 57.2% during 1985–90. Finally, the NICs of Asia excluding Japan have achieved rapid growth in large part through a spectacular mobilization of resources. Thus the rapid growth episodes in East Asia seems to be driven by extraordinary growth in inputs like labor and capital rather than by gains in efficiency.

Two points of caution must be made. The case of Japan is quite different from the so-called Asian 'tigers'. For Japan has grown both through high rates of input growth and high rates of efficiency (TFP) growth. Japan's historical performance gives an unmistakable record of technological catch-up with the US efficiency levels. But very recently Japan is experiencing a rapid productivity slow down and the rate of technological catching up faces a slump due to fluctuations in the foreign exchange market and volatility in stock markets. Secondly, the spillover of knowledge capital through foreign investment and the learning curve effects flowing from R&D investments have not yet had their full impact on the Asian NICs. Two important trends need be watched here. One is that a significant number of professionals of South Korean and Taiwanese origin have returned from the US to their countries of origin. Coupled with this trend, the government policies in these Asian NICs have stepped up their support of increased investment spending particularly for the technology-intensive export sector. Secondly, these economies stand out with some of the highest domestic saving rates in the world, coupled with substantial current account surpluses which indicate increased export of domestic savings. Table 4.3 shows the pattern of saving–investment behavior in the Asian NICs.

Table 4.3 Saving Investment Trend in the Asian Pacific Rim

	Savings average		Investment average	
	1971–80	1981–90	1971–80	1981–90
Hong Kong	28.4	30.7	27.8	27.9
Korea (South)	22.3	31.9	28.6	30.5
Singapore	30.0	42.5	41.2	42.0
Taiwan	32.2	32.9	30.5	22.6
Indonesia	21.6	32.0	19.3	30.4
Philippines	26.5	22.3	27.8	21.9
China	35.8	33.5	33.9	34.3

Source: Asian Development Outlook (1992)

In recent periods however the Asian NICs have experienced a slowing down of economic growth, thus reducing their domestic saving rates and current account surpluses. Now these countries face a currency market turmoil by the end of 1997 and IMF has to bail out countries like Korea, Malaysia and others to prevent massive fall in those currency values. But once the crisis is over and appropriate austerity measures adopted, these countries would revert to their goals of high investment rates supported by high domestic savings and improve their competitive position in the world markets. Like Japan these Asian NICs have to finally learn to adapt and improve the foreign technology imported from abroad and also step up the human capital investment in the form of R&D and skill development.

4.2   TIME-SERIES MODELS OF EXPORT EXTERNALITY

The contribution of the export sector to productivity growth through increased investment in human capital is difficult to assess empirically, because we do not have detailed reliable data on the composition of the export sector's output and the corresponding skill composition of human capital involved. Furthermore, the ordinary regression models do not have much of a structural significance if the variables are nonstationary. Hence there is a need to apply the modern theory of cointegration in this framework of export externalities.

Two types of specifications are attempted here to explore the link of exports and output growth for the three Asian NICs e.g., Japan, Korea and Taiwan which have proved most successful in world competition over the last two decades. These specifications involve export externality and the export elasticities. We apply here the theory of cointegration to develop tests for structural relationships between openness and growth. This theory essentially proposes two steps. In the first step we determine the order of integration of all the variables in a regression model which makes them stationary. In the second step suitable error correction models (ECM) are formulated by using the cointegrating vectors from the first stage.

A time series y_t is said to be integrated of order d, denoted I(d) if it must be differenced d times before it becomes stationary. Thus a time series y_t is I(0) if it is stationary, whereas if it is I(1), its first difference Δy_t is stationary. The concept of cointegration provides an important link between the interrelationships of integrated processes and the concept of steady state equilibrium. It was originally introduced by Granger (1969) and later extended by Engle and Granger (1987) and many others. Suppose a steady state relation holds as

$$y_t = \alpha' x_t = \sum_{i=1}^{m} \alpha_i x_{it}$$

or

$$z_t = y_t - \alpha' x_t = 0$$

where the time series z_t measures the extent to which the system is out of equilibrium and can therefore be termed the 'equilibrium error'. Hence if y_t and $\hat{x}_t = \alpha' x_t$ are both I(1), then the equilibrium error will be I(0) and z_t will rarely drift far from zero. In this case y_t and $\hat{x}_t$ must have long run components that virtually cancel out to produce equilibrium errors z_t. In such circumstances $\hat{x}_t$ and yt are said to be cointegrated and in this case only meaningful statistical inferences can be drawn by using the error correction models (ECM) to transform the original regression problem in nonstationary variables. Engle and Granger (1987) have shown that if y_t and x_t are both I(d), then there exists an error correction representation

$$A(L)(1 - L)^d y_t = -\gamma z_{t-1} + \theta(L)\varepsilon_t$$

where the error ε_t is white noise, $A(L)$, $\theta(L)$ are polynomial lag functions and $z_t = y_t - \alpha' x_t$ is the residual from the cointegrating regression. A special case of this representation occurs when $d = 1$ and $\theta(L) = 1$, i.e., the error term ε_t has no moving average part. The ECM then appears as:

$$\Delta y_t = b_0 + b' \Delta x_t - \gamma(y_{t-1} - \alpha' x_{t-1}) + \varepsilon_t$$

All terms here are I(0), hence no difficulties of statistical inference arise. In the steady state we have the long run equilibrium production behavior

$$y_t = \alpha' x_t + (b_0 / \gamma)$$

The tests of export externality and other specifications are primarily dependent on the order of integration of the variables used in the regression models. The order of integration of the variables was largely determined through the use of the DF statistic as mentioned in (4.3) before. For the export externality models the following variables were found to be integrated of order two at the 5% level of the DF test: GNPR (real gross national product), INV (gross investment), N (volume of employment) and X (total exports). Table 4.4 summarizes the ECM model. The order of integration of the other variables was as follows:

	Order of Integration Export Demand Variables		
	Japan (1962–87)	Korea (1967–87)	Taiwan (1962–87)
XGSR	2	3	2
PWR	2	3	2
YW	2	3	2

Here the variables are XGSR (real export of goods and services), PWR (domestic price level relative to the world price level) and YW (level of real world income). For the production function models discussed in the next section the variables selected are LGDPR (log of gross domestic product in real terms), LKR (log of real capital stock), LN (log of employment) and CRES (the cointegrating regression residuals). For each variable we add the term Di to indicate that it is integrated of order i = 1,2,3. The sources of data are Yearbook of Labor Statistics (ILO), International Financial Statistics Yearbook (IMF), IMF Supplement on World Trade Statistics, World Development Review (IBRD) and Taiwan Statistical Handbook. Since the capital stock series is not available from the data sources above we have used the Dadkhah–Zahedi (1986) formulation where gross capital stock K_t is defined as

$$K_t = \log 2 + 0.5 \log \sum_{i=0}^{t-1} (1-\delta)^i I_{t-i} + \frac{t}{2} \log(1-\delta) + \frac{1}{2} \log K_0$$

where K_0 is the capital stock for the initial year. This method has been widely adopted in the empirical development literature. The details of the statistical data are described elsewhere by Sengupta (1991, 1993).

Tables 4.4 and 4.5 provide the estimates of the error correction models for the impact of exports. These estimates show very clearly that the export variable (X) has a significant statistical impact on the real national income for all the three countries, though in absolute magnitude it is more important for Korea and Taiwan. One reason for this may be that the export share of GDP is on the average about 12.9 percent over the period 1968–86 for Japan whereas it is 30.6% for Korea and 56.7% for Taiwan. In terms of

Table 4.4 Error Corrections Models of Export Externality
Dependent Variable: GNPRD2

	A. Japan		B. Korea		C. Taiwan	
	Co-efficient	t-value	Co-efficient	t-value	Co-efficient	t-value
Intercept	−6.401	−1.61	−181.1	−1.95	6.541	1.24
INVD2	0.579	2.13	0.192	2.09	0.124	2.15
ND2	0.102	1.98	0.063	1.99	1.30	2.18
XD2	0.101	2.10	0.439	3.02	0.482	1.98
GNPRD2(-1)	0.102	1.64	0.194	0.71	0.145	1.89
XD2(-1)	0.092	1.98	0.101	0.62	0.211	1.08
XD2(-2)	−0.008	1.02	−0.054	1.02	0.013	0.78
INVD2(-1)	−0.031	1.89	-	-	-	-
Adj.R^2	0.702	-	0.692	-	0.714	-
DW Statistic	1.961	-	2.013	-	1.970	-
Sample Period	1967-86	-	1967-86	-	1967-86	
DF Statistic	−4.8; −7.14		−5.1; −7.2			

Source: Sengupta (1994)
Notes:
1. DW denotes the order of integration of the variables.
2. Adj. R^2 denotes R^2 adjusted for degrees of freedom
3. DF denotes the value of Dickey–Fuller statistics

Table 4.5 Error Corrections Models of Export Demand

A. Japan: Dependent Variable XGSRD2

	Coefficient	t-value
Intercept	−54.55	−0.19
PRWD2	−100.01	−1.83
YWD2	668.12	2.73
CRES(-1)	−1.25	−6.06
CRES(-2)	0.52	2.43
Adj. R^2	0.623	
DW Statistics	1.728	
Sample Period	1962–1987	
DF Statistic for residuals	−4.3; −6.1	

Table 4.5 (continued)

B. Korea: XGSRD3

	Coefficient	t-value
Intercept	3.81	0.01
PRWD3	−261.49	−2.96
YWD3	782.39	3.82
XGSRD3(-1)	0.92	2.17
PRWD3(-1)	−102.75	−1.34
YWD3(-1)	−1091.77	−3.00
CRES(-1)	−2.38	−4.81
CRES(-2)	3.92	3.84
CRES(-3)	−1.71	−2.74
Adj. R^2	0.752	
DW	1.900	
Sample:	1967–1987	
DF for residuals	−4.5; −7.4	

C. Taiwan: XGSDR2

	Coefficient	t-value
Intercept	4478.24	0.28
PRWD2	−3709.58	−1.86
YWD2	18464.47	1.32
CRES(-1)	−0.62	−2.70
CRES(-2)	0.41	2.03
Adj. R^2	0.259	
DW	2.175	
Sample	1962-1987	
DF Statistics	−5.3; −9.0	

Source: Sengupta (1994)

proportional growth rates of exports also, the figures are 8.7, 16.1 and 13.4% on the average for Japan, Korea and Taiwan respectively. One could interpret the significant impact of the export variable on income growth in three different ways. One is to drop exports (XD2) as a regressor and the value of adjusted R^2 declines by more than 0.25; also the signs of the other regressor (INVD2) become either negative or statistically insignificant. Secondly, if we decompose the income variable (Y) into a two-sector version with exports (X) and non-exports (M) as follows:

$$X = G(G_X, L_X, M)$$
$$M = F(K_M, L_M, X)$$
$$Y = X + M, K = K_M + K_X, L = L_M + L_X$$

with outputs X and M produced by the two sectors by using the two inputs capital (K) and labor (L), we could formulate a system of growth equations

$$\Delta M = F_K I_M + F_L \Delta L_M + F_X \Delta X$$
$$\Delta X = G_K I_X + G_L \Delta L_X + G_M \Delta M$$

where the subscripts on F and G denote the marginal productivities of the respective inputs in the two sectors. Note that if the two sectoral output X and M are integrated of order one, their first differences are integrated of order zero and the standard least squares regression are valid. However in our case the orders of integration turned out to be two for the two sectoral outputs for each of the three countries and the estimates of the coefficients F_X and G_M by the ECM models turned out to be as follows:

1967–87	Japan	Korea	Taiwan
F_X	0.29	0.99	0.182
G_M	0.16	0.32	0.20
F_X/G_M	1.8	3.1	9.1

If we use the ratio F_X/G_M of marginal productivities of the two sectors as a measure of export externality, clearly Korea and Taiwan have a far greater degree of export externality than Japan. Note that in an econometric sense this result has a structural and long run significance, which is absent in the ad hoc regression models of Feder (1982) and Bradford (1987). Finally, the estimates of ECM models of export demand in Table 4.5 show the long run impact of world income to be highly significant for both Japan and Korea, though not for Taiwan. Evaluated at their mean levels the income and price elasticities appear as follows:

	Price elasticity	Income elasticity
Japan	−0.67	1.63
Korea	−1.64	1.15
Taiwan	−1.86	1.34

Denoting the export demand time series by x_t, one could decompose it into its conditional mean and conditional variance as

$$x_t = E_{t-1}(x_t \mid z) + \varepsilon_t$$
$$\sigma_t^2 = E_{t-1}(\varepsilon_t^2)$$

where $E_{t-1}(x_t \mid z)$ is the conditional mean depending on information available up to the period t–1 and z is the set of regressors such as the relative price ratio (PRW) and world income (YW). Based on the estimated values of the residual ε_t one could test if the shocks to the export demand equation is persistent or not. Thus we set up the model known as the ARCH (autoregressive conditional heteroscedasticity)

$$\sigma_t^2 = \alpha_0 + \sum_{i=1}^{p} \alpha_i \varepsilon_{t-i}^2 + \sum_{i=1}^{p} \beta_i \sigma_{t-i}^2$$

for testing the time–varying nature of variance. For p = 1 one obtains the time–varying model for variance as

$$\sigma_t^2 = \alpha_0 + \alpha_1 \varepsilon_{t-1}^2 + \beta_1 \sigma_{t-1}^2$$

Clearly if the condition $\hat{\alpha}_1 + \hat{\beta}_1 = 1$ holds for the estimated parameters then the impact of exogenous shocks is persistent i.e., of a permanent nature. This implies that the hypothesis of cointegration cannot be rejected. When we performed such tests on the export demand function (Table 4.5) and the real output equation (Table 4.1) we could not reject the hypothesis of cointegration. These results seem to support two broad propositions. One is that the estimated parameters in the aggregate output and export demand equations do indeed reflect a long run equilibrium relationship between the variables involved. Secondly, the conditional variance tests imply that any exogenous shocks to the system due to technical innovation or world income changes would have persistent effects on output growth and export demand growth. These results are likely to be reinforced if we consider only manufacturing exports rather than total exports. Some detailed empirical tests of cointegration for manufacturing exports for Korea and Taiwan reported by Sengupta and Espana (1992) confirm this conjecture. This is also consistent with the recent findings by the trade economists such as Bhagwati (1988) that the export promotion strategies of the NICs help the growth of intra industry trade in manufactures among developing and developed countries to a significant extent.

One major source of export growth in the Asian NICs is the very high degree of capacity utilization and exploitation of increasing returns to scale.

Increasing returns to scale (IRS) has played a prominent role in the new growth theory. Two dimensions of scale economies are important for rapid economic growth. One is the presence of significant IRS in modern production, especially in the export sector which involves nonrival inputs to use a term due to Romer (1986). Nonrival input is one for which subsequent units have a significantly lower unit cost of production than the first. In the extreme case a nonrival input has a high cost of producing the first unit and a zero cost for subsequent units, e.g., a new design for a microprocessor which can be replicated at a negligible cost. The increasing use of such nonrival inputs has given a new dimension to commercial and non-basic R&D research thus intensifying the competitiveness in international trade. As Romer has pointed out that as a fraction of GDP Japan now spends considerably more on commercial nonbasic R&D than does the U.S.

The second dimension of IRS focuses on the knowledge spillover effects which improves labor productivity across the board. As Lucas (1988) pointed out this may be the most significant factor explaining the large difference in marginal productivity of capital between an LDC and a developed economy, when the concept of capital is broadened to include human capital. Thus the external benefits of human capital can be captured by specifying the production function as

$$y = Ax^{\beta}h^{\gamma} \qquad\qquad (4.4)$$

where the three variables y, x and h denote output, physical and human capital per effective worker respectively. The term h^{γ} is interpreted as an external effect, which multiplies the productivity of a worker at any skill level just as the intercept term A. It has also a spillover effect on other workers.

A direct empirical test of the existence of IRS can be obtained by estimating an aggregate production function with real GDP as the output variable (Y) and capital stock (K) and employment (L) as the two aggregate input variables. Two major difficulties of this approach are that the aggregate function may involve variables which are nonstationary. In this case the regression model may not have any structural significance.

Secondly, data on capital stock are not generally available in a reliable form from the official statistics. For this reason we restrict ourselves to the manufacturing sector alone, which is more relevant in the export performance and then we construct a series of capital stocks (K_t) based on investment streams (I_{t-i}) and depreciation rate (δ) by following the method due to Dadkhah–Zahedi (1986) as used before.

For the first difficulty we follow a method known as the variate difference method developed by Tintner (1969). This method decomposes a time series into two parts, one permanent and the other transitory and then builds a regression model based on the permanent components only. Thus let us write the permanent component hypothesis as

$$Y_t = Y_t^p + u_t; K_t = K_t^p + v_t; L_t = L_t^p + w_t$$
$$Y_t^p = F(K_t^p, L_t^p)$$

where the superscript p denotes the permanent component of each variable and u_t, v_t, w_t are the transitory components which are assumed to be statistically independent of the respective permanent components. An empirical test of the permanent component hypothesis consists in finding the functional form $F(\bullet)$ of the relation between the permanent output and the permanent components of capital and labor. To determine the permanent components of the time series we proceed as follows: Let x_t be the time series which is integrated of order d, then we know that the d–th difference of the series is enough to eliminate the trend in the variable x_t. Hence the permanent part x_t^p of x_t is given by the polynomial

$$x_t^p = a_0 + a_1 t + a_2 t^2 + \cdots + a_d t^d$$

The transitory component is given by the difference between x_t and x_t^p. Following this method and assuming a Cobb–Douglas form of the production function we obtain the following estimates in Table 4.6.

It is clear that the evidence of IRS is overwhelming. Moreover what is most striking is that the labor coefficient is about 3 to 4 times larger than the capital coefficient. This is definitely suggestive of the effect of 'learning by doing' or what has been called by Lucas (1990) the spillover effects of human capital. These effects multiply the productivity of a worker at any given skill level by a positive multiple depending on the technology used.

We may also mention the point that if each of the three variables output, capital and labor are detrended first and then the production functions reestimated, the persistence of IRS is upheld. This suggests that scale economies are structural and not transitory and the high values of adjusted R^2 are more indicative of the relative success of Cobb–Douglas production functions in capturing the process of overall output growth.

Table 4.6 Estimates of the Production Function Parameters in some Asian NICs

1961–87	Intercept	log K_t^p	log L_t^p	Adj R^2	DW
Japan	0.069	0.426** (2.89)	1.601** (2.69)	0.995	2.01
Korea	2.432**	0.359** (8.75)	1.462** (16.91)	0.989	1.95
Taiwan	5.271	0.625** (2.91)	1.725** (6.89)	0.991	1.89

Here the t-values are in parentheses and two asterisks denote significance at 1% level.

A direct estimate of the productivity of human capital in the form of externality effects as in the specification (4.4) is possible only when detailed data on the skill-intensity of the labor force in the exports and the manufacturing sector are available. Short of that the partial measures of the contribution of R&D and the intensity of new technical know-how may be used as proxy variables. Recently Enos and Park (1988) have studied the pattern of adoption and diffusion of imported technology in four major industries in Korea, e.g., petrochemical, synthetic fibers, machinery and iron and steel and compared this experience with Japan. On an overall basis they summarized the sources of growth of GNP due to labor, capital, economies of scale and technological advance (Table 4.7).

It is clear that Korea's growth has stemmed proportionally more from increases in labor supply and the associated augmentation of the skill factor and proportionally less from advances in technology. Furthermore if one analyzes the role of the major agents responsible for the adoption of foreign technologies, one basic difference emerges between Japan and Korea. In Korea at least until 1980, the government has been the primary agent; in

Japan it seems to have been since 1946 the large private firms. Also the number of foreign suppliers of technology scrutinized by the agents seems to have been greater in the case of Korea than in Japan. This explains the element of comparative advantage of the technology–intensive export sector in Korea.

Table 4.7 Sources of Output Growth

Sources of growth	USA 1948–69 (%)	Korea 1963–82 (%)	Japan 1953–72 (%)
Labor	22.0	35.8	17.1
Capital	19.8	21.4	23.8
Scale economies	10.5	18.0	22.0
Technological advance	29.8	11.8	22.4
Miscellaneous	17.7	13.0	14.7
Total	100.0	100.0	100.0

Source: Enos and Park (1988)

A comparison of Korea and Taiwan in terms of their growth performance discussed in some detail by Cho (1990) shows a broad pattern of similarity except in the degree of economic concentration. While Korea's economic growth has been based on an expansion of the size of firms yielding significant scale economies, Taiwan's growth has been largely in the form of an increase in the total number of manufacturing establishments rather than the average size. For example the average annual number of manufacturing establishments rose at an annual rate of 0.9 percent in Korea, whereas it rose at the rate of 9.6 percent in Taiwan during the period 1966–81. According to Cho (1990) the two countries, different approaches to financial policy may have played a significant role. For instance in Korea, 100 of the largest firms borrowed about 35% of total financial institutions' loans whereas the top 97 firms in Taiwan got only 11.6% of such loans. Also Korea's example is very close to Japan's where scale economies fostered by financial policies have played a big role in the growth of productivity. Furthermore in some countries like Korea the deliberate policy of promoting the HCI (Heavy and Chemical Industries Promotion Plan: 1973–79) yielded improved performance from 1986 onwards leading to rapid overall economic growth. As Lee (1991) has shown that the HCI sectors in Korea comprising such heavy industry projects as iron and steel, nonferrous metal, machinery, shipbuilding and capital were widely accepted as the leading sectors in self-sustained growth. The persistence of significant scale economies played a major role in this long run process.

Finally we conclude that the growth of human capital has played a much more important role than the physical capital for these three NICs. Not only has it made the scale economies more persistent in the manufacturing sector, it has also generated a dynamic resource reallocation process from the nonexports to the exports sector thereby augmenting the overall productivity of labor. Although the marginal productivity effect of the skill level and education could not be analyzed here due to lack of data, some recent estimates by Tallman and Wang (1990) for Taiwan suggest that the contribution of the skill factor may far outweigh that of labor. Thus using annual data over 1965–86 and an unrestricted Cobb–Douglas production function they found for Taiwan the following results:

	Constant	Employ-ment	Labor Skill	Capital	Adj. R^2
Coefficient	0.227	0.687	0.516	0.313	0.995
t-value	1.90	8.76	8.02	3.99	

4.3 ECONOMIC FLUCTUATIONS AND GROWTH IN JAPAN (1965–90)

In recent years two stylized aspects of new growth theory have attracted special attention. One is the question of convergence to the steady state level of income. New growth theory emphasizing endogenous growth predicts that countries need not converge, even if they have the same preferences and technology. A second aspect of new growth theory stresses the point that human capital in the form of knowledge diffusion and 'learning by doing' contributes to increasing returns in long run growth.

Our object in this section is to test the process of convergence to the steady state in terms of a model of input and output growth for Japan over the period 1965–90. The model of input and output growth which is developed here for Japan to test the time paths of convergence to the steady state has several novel features. First of all, the output growth path is modeled as a two-step optimization process decided by the representative producer. In the first step he derives the desired or target levels of input and output through a steady state cost minimization process. The second step minimizes a loss function based on the discounted stream of deviations of inputs from their desired or target levels determined in the first step. Whereas the first step is one of equilibrium at steady state, the second allows the dynamic adjustments in disequilibrium, which specify the transitional dynamics of the system. Convergence to the steady state equilibrium solution implies that the successive levels of disequilibria tend to disappear in the long run. Secondly, the 'learning by doing' effects on output through human capital are directly tested in our model through the relative speeds of adjustment of the two inputs, capital and labor as they converge to their steady states. Indirectly, the estimates of these adjustment equations for the inputs provide a measure of returns to scale, if it is increasing or not. Finally, the production frontier implied by the transitional dynamics in our model assumes that the inputs and output are all first difference stationary, i.e,. in the language of cointegration theory they are cointegrated of order one. This is significantly different from a static production function which assumes the inputs and output to be stationary or cointegrated of order zero.

To test the process of convergence to the steady state and the associated fluctuations, we propose here the approach of adjustment cost, which explicitly allows for the dynamic expansion path planned by the producer. In the first step the producer as the dynamic agent decides the optimal inputs by minimizing a steady state cost function, which gives rise to the long run equilibrium or target value. The second step then postulates an optimal adjustment rule towards the equilibrium or target level.

The first step optimization problem is

$$\text{Min}C_t = w'_t X_t \text{ subject to } Y_t = F(X_t) \tag{4.5}$$

where X_t and w_t are the column vectors of m inputs and their prices (prime denoting a transpose) and Y_t is the given level of output subject to the production function $F(\bullet)$, which may exhibit increasing returns to scale. Let X_t^* be the optimal solution and Y_t^* the associated output $Y_t^* = F(X_t^*)$, which specifies the allocative efficiency frontier.

The second step of the optimization model assumes a short run adjustment behavior for the producer, who finds that his current factor uses are inconsistent with the long run equilibrium path (X_t^*, Y_t^*) above as implied by the current relative factor prices and their expected changes in the future. Since the desired levels of inputs may change over time, the adjustment of producer's economic behavior frequently involves time lags in adjusting stocks to their desired levels. Thus all the expected future values of the target levels X_t^* of input demand, which implicitly depend on the expected levels of future prices become relevant to the current optimal decision. Assuming a quadratic adjustment cost the second optimization step requires the producer to minimize the expected present value of a quadratic loss function as follows:

$$\text{Min}_{x_t} E_t L \qquad\qquad (4.6)$$

where

$$L = \sum_{t=0}^{\infty} r^t [(x_t - x_t^*)' \Lambda (x_t - x_t^*) + (x_t - x_{t-1})' \Psi (x_t - x_{t-1})$$

where $E_t(\bullet)$ is expectation as of time t, $r = (1+\rho)^{-1}$ is the exogeneous rate of discount, $x_t = \ln X_t, x_t^* = \ln X_t^*$ and Λ, Ψ are the matrices of nonnegative weights. The first component of the loss function (4.6) is due to deviations from the steady state equilibrium i.e., disequilibrium cost and the second component characterizes the producer's aversion to fluctuations in input levels, i.e., the smoothness objective. The first is an inefficiency cost incurred due to deviations from the targeted level of optimal input usage. The second is purely an adjustment cost indicating the costs of successive movement toward the optimal input combinations. One can illustrate this optimal adjustment procedure by means of a single input case, as has been done by Kennan (1979) and Gregory, Pagan and Smith (1993).

For the case of Japan over the period (1965–90) we combine these two steps to derive and estimate a set of long run optimal input demand and the corresponding optimal output path. The empirical data are all obtained from the published official statistics and discussed in some detail by Sengupta and Okamura (1996). With L_t as total labor and K_t as capital and a Cobb–Douglas production function the desired levels of the two inputs L_t^* and K_t^* are determined by minimizing the static cost function now written as

$$\text{Min } w_t L_t + h_t K_t$$
$$\text{s.t.} \quad Q_t = B(A_t, V_t) K_t^a L_t^b$$

where Q_t is output and w_t, h_t are the respective prices of the two inputs:

labor (L_t) and capital services (K_t). The technical progress variable $B(\bullet)$ is assumed to be a function of exports (V_t) and an external shock variable A_t representing the international transmission of knowledge. In our empirical application the term $B(\bullet)$ has been assumed to be of the form $A_t V_t^\gamma$, where A_t is a time trend and V_t is the externality factor represented by the trend in real exports. Allowing for stochastic disturbances (ε_L and ε_K) the first order conditions of minimum cost are

$$\ln L_t^* = \ln(a/b)^{a(a+b)^{-1}} + (a+b)^{-1}$$
$$[\ln B_t - a \ln(w_t/h_t) + \ln Q_t] + \varepsilon_L$$

$$\ln K_t^* = \ln(a/b)^{a(a+b)^{-1}} + (a+b)^{-1}$$
$$[\ln B_t - b \ln(w_t/h_t) + \ln Q_t] + \varepsilon_K$$

Given these target levels of optimal inputs the producer minimizes the following loss function

$$\operatorname*{Min}_{X_t} E_t \sum_{t=0}^{\infty} r^t [(X_t - X_t^*) \Lambda (X_t - X_t^*)$$
$$+ (X_t - X_{t-1})' \Psi (X_t - X_{t-1})] \tag{4.7}$$

where r is the discount rate, $X_t = (\ln L_t; \ln K_t)$ is the vector of actual input levels and $K_t^* = (\ln L_t^*, \ln K_t^*)$ is the target levels determined in the first step above. Assuming diagonal weight matrices one obtains

$$\Lambda = \begin{pmatrix} \Lambda_L & 0 \\ 0 & \Lambda_K \end{pmatrix}, \quad \Psi = \begin{pmatrix} \Psi_L & 0 \\ 0 & \Psi_K \end{pmatrix}$$

The first order conditions for minimizing the intertemporal loss function (4.7) may then be written as:

$$\Lambda_L \left(\ln L_t - E_t(\ln L_t^*) \right) + \Psi_L \left(\ln L_t - \ln L_{t-1} \right)$$
$$- r \Psi_L (\ln L_{t+1} - \ln L_t) = 0$$

and

$$\Lambda_K \left(\ln L_t - E_t (\ln K_t^*) \right) + \Psi_K \left(\ln K_t - \ln K_{t-1} \right)$$
$$- r\Psi_K (\ln K_{t+1} - \ln K_t) = 0$$

Since these two equations are the same form, it is sufficient to analyze the labor demand equation only. By rearranging this equation yields

$$\theta_L E_t (\ln L_t^*) = (\theta_L + 2) \ln L_t - (1/r) \ln L_{t-1} - \ln L_{t+1}$$

where the ratio $\theta_L = \Lambda_L / \Psi_L$ measures the relative importance of the disequilibrium cost to the adjustment cost. On applying the lag operator Z and using the stable (i.e., nonexplosive root) μ_1 one could write as this

$$(1 - \mu_1 Z) \ln L_{t-1} = (1 - \mu_1) d_t^L$$

where

$$d_t^L = (1 - \mu_1) \sum_{s=0}^{\infty} \mu_1^s \ln L_{t+s}^*$$

This yields finally the optimal partial adjustment rule for labor demand:

$$\Delta \ln L_t = \phi_L (d_t^L - \ln L_{t-1}), \text{ where } \phi_L = 1 - \mu_1 \qquad (4.8)$$

Doing likewise for the capital input yields the optimal partial adjustment rule for capital:

$$\Delta \ln K_t - \phi_K (d_t^K \quad \ln K_{t-1})$$

Note also that one could derive here a relationship between the speed of adjustment parameter ϕ_i and the ratio θ_i of the weights on the two costs, i.e.,

$$\theta_i = -\phi_i r + \phi_i (1 - \phi_i)^{-1}, \quad i = L, K$$

Some general comments may now be added here about the specifications. First of all, we note that the estimate $\hat{\phi}_L$ of adjustment parameter for the labor demand equation is utilized here in three ways. One is to test the speed of convergence to the steady state level $\bar{d}_L$, which leads to the steady state level of output through the steady state production function. Secondly, the second step estimates of the adjusted demand functions provide an estimate of the scale economy of the aggregate production function. Thirdly, it provides an estimate of the ratio $\theta_L = \Lambda_L / \Psi_L$, which denotes the relative proportion of the two weights: Λ_L for deviations from the desired level of labor demand and Ψ_L for deviations from last year's level. Moreover one has to note that the desired levels of input demand d_t^L and d_t^K have to be estimated by the instrumental variables method by using all the exogenous variables such as past incomes, relative factor prices and past exports in the backward looking approach. For the forward looking approach the same exogenous variables in their future values have to be utilized. By comparing these two approaches one could test the existence of asymmetry in growth response from the past history versus future expectations.

Consider first the estimated results for the Cobb–Douglas production function reported in Table 4.8. Here the two inputs, labor and capital and also exports are taken in first difference terms. This is different from the conventional production function estimates in two ways. One is that the

Table 4.8 *Sources of Output Growth Measured by Loglinear Production Functions*

Dependent variable	$\Delta \ln Y$	Intercept	$\Delta \ln K$	$\Delta \ln L$	$\Delta \ln V$
1. GNP (real)	−0.005	0.597	0.071	0.067	0.496
(t-values)	(−0.258)	(2.714)	(1.692)	(1.235)	(2.08)
2. GDP (real)	0.0002	0.639	0.066	−0.033	0.501
(t-values)	(0.012)	(2.752)	(1.584)	(−0.620)	(2.14)

	ρ	R^2	DW	RTS
1. GNP (real)	0.496	0.719	2.03	0.734
2. GDP (real)	0.501	0.703	2.15	0.672

Notes: 1. ρ = first order autocorrelation coefficient, DW = Durban–Watson statistics, RTS = returns to scale.
2. Capital stock (K) and exports (V) are measured in real terms.

parameters are estimated here directly and not from the shares of national income accruing to labor and capital, as is done in Solow's growth accounting model. Secondly, the production function may be directly related to the incremental input demand functions formulated before. This can also be related to the error correction models used in cointegration theory.

The estimation results in Table 4.7 for the production frontier with two inputs have some interesting features. First of all, the role of capital is much more important than labor, both in magnitude of the respective coefficients and their t-values. Using data from the UN Comparison Project (1960–85) DeLong and Summers (1991) found a similar result on the dominant contribution of equipment investment to economic growth in Japan. They noted that the differences in equipment investment account for essentially all of the extraordinary growth performance of Japan relative to the sample of 25 countries over the period 1960–85. Secondly, the relative contributions of labor and exports are much smaller, implying that the phase of increasing returns is on the decline. Since exports is the only variable used as a proxy for eternality, it suggests a pattern different from the other NICs in Asia such as Korea and Taiwan for example. In 1986 the ratio of export to GDP was 17.2 per cent in Japan, whereas it was 48.1% in Korea and 84.0% in Taiwan. This ratio fell to less than 12% in Japan in 1993. As a mature industrial country the impact of openness in trade on the overall economic growth in Japan is much less than the other NICs in Asia. Another factor may be the existence of strong diminishing returns in the learning by doing process as has been established by Young (1991) in his empirical studies. Thus in the initial stage the development of new technologies leads to rapid learning by doing. After some time however the productive capability of these new technologies is exhausted and learning by doing slows down. Finally, the process of the externality factor measured by exports is not that important for the growth of the Japanese economy and its coefficient is not statistically significant at 5% level of t-test. This shows that the externality factor has been playing a declining role.

The estimates of the adjusted Solow residual reported in Table 4.9 clearly show its procyclical variations. For the U.S. economy and its major industrial sectors Hall (1990) found a similar pattern and attempted to explain it in terms of the market power and the trend in world oil prices. In our case the change in log GDP is found to be positively correlated with the adjusted Solow residual. However the oil shocks are negatively correlated. This finding is similar to that found by Hall for the U.S. economy.

The estimated results reported in Tables 4.10 and 4.11 are of major significance. This is due to several reasons. First of all, the optimal input demand equations for the two inputs show the speed of convergence to the steady state growth path. Of the two inputs which has faster convergence? The answer to this question holds the key to producer behavior in choosing the long run expansion paths. Secondly, the implied estimate of the total returns to scale (RTS) derived from the optimal adjusted equations provides a more dynamic estimate of scale than that provided by Table 4.7. This is for two reasons. One is that the implied estimates are derived from a two-step optimization model involving both short run and long run goals. A second reason is that the two different models for predicting long run targets can be employed here, e.g., the backward looking and forward looking formulation. Since these two formulations compare the roles of past history versus future expectations, this provides an indirect test of the stability of returns to scale. Finally, one could analyze the persistence of the growth paths of labor and capital in terms of the characteristic roots of the underlying dynamic system. If the root is very close to unity, this suggests a profile of persistence.

Table 4.9 Estimates of Solow Residuals ($\Delta \ln R$) Adjusted for Exports

	Year	$\Delta \ln R$	Year	$\Delta \ln R$
		Adjusted residual		
	1967	0.024	1979	−0.050
	1968	0.033	1980	0.011
	1969	−0.007	1981	0.001
	1970	0.004	1982	−0.007
A. Production	1971	−0.026	1983	−0.009
Function	1972	0.015	1984	0.016
Estimates	1973	−0.024	1985	−0.032
	1974	−0.042	1986	−0.009
	1975	−0.055	1987	−0.006
	1976	-0.005	1988	0.015
	1977	0.002	1989	0.031
	1978	0.078	1990	0.005

Average: 0.004, maximum: 0.0241, minimum: −0.0337

B. Correlation of	$\Delta \ln Y$	$\Delta \ln Z$
$\Delta \ln R$ with	0.461	−0.512

Notes: 1. Z denotes the index of world oil prices.
2. Y denotes GDP in real terms.

Table 4.10 Estimates of the Speed of Adjustment Parameters (ϕ_i) and the Weight Ratio $\theta_i = \Lambda_i/\Psi_i$ (i = K,L)

Output (ln Y_t)	Input (ln X_{it})		ϕ_i	θ_i	Characteristic Root $\mu_i = 1 - \phi_i$
	backward	K	0.0118*	0.016	0.882*
	looking	L	0.898*	7.873	0.102
I. GNP					
	forward	K	0.082*	0.007	0.918*
	looking	L	0.837**	4.281	0.163**
	backward	K	0.120	0.016	0.880
	looking	L	0.924*	11.231	0.076*
II. GDP					
	forward	K	0.086*	0.008	0.914*
	looking	L	0.569*	0.753	0.431*

Notes: 1. One and two asterisks denote significant t values at 5 and 1% levels.
2. The stable characteristic roots are derived from the optimal input demand equations as $\mu_i = 1 - \phi_i$

Consider first the estimates in Table 4.10. In terms of the speed of adjustment, labor adjusts much faster than capital. Thus the ratio ϕ_L/ϕ_K varies from 6.6 to 10.2. The implications of slow adjustment speed for capital are two-fold. First of all, the characteristic root for capital is very close to unity. Although its estimated value is less than one, it tends to equal or exceed unity, when the appropriate standard error is incorporated. Secondly, much of capital expansion is in the form of capital deepening and this reflects a stronger role of future expectations over past history. Thus the forward looking estimates of the characteristic root $\mu_K = 1 - \phi_K$ are higher than the backward looking ones. The producers tend to build capital ahead of current demand.

Table 4.11 Estimates of the Parameters of the Loglinear Production Frontier Implied by the Optimal Input Demands

Dependent Variable (ln Y)		Intercept	Capital (ln K_t)	Labor (ln L_t)	Exports (ln V_t)	R^2	RTS
	backward looking	4.43	−0.11	0.91*	0.64	0.65	1.44
I. GNP							
	forward looking	11.37	−0.14	0.81*	0.39**	0.59	1.06
II. GDP							
	backward looking	6.04	−0.20	1.26*	0.34*	0.64	1.40
	forward looking	6.80	0.02	0.41	0.43	0.27	0.86

Notes: 1. One and two asterisks denote significant t-values at 5 and 1% levels.
2. RTS denotes the degree of total returns to scale.

Finally, the estimate of θ_L which is the ratio of Λ_L to Ψ_L provides a strong contrast between the forward-looking and the backward-looking formulations for the labor demand equation. Since the labor input adjusts at a faster rate than capital, a value of θ_L greater than one suggests that the producers emphasize their long run targets much more than the short run fluctuations. This remains true even when we consider other dependent variables in the production function like exports. The details of these results are discussed in Sengupta and Okamura (1996).

Three important points emerge from the estimates of Table 4.11. First of all, the estimates of returns to scale (RTS) are uniformly lower for the forward looking model than the backward-looking model. The RTS is increasing for all cases except the GDP model in its forward looking version. This result is in striking contrast with the RTS estimates in Table 4.8, which displayed decreasing returns uniformly. Secondly, the export externality is found to be an important variable in the regression estimates. If one drops this variable in the estimating equation, then the RTS drops considerably resulting in diminishing returns to scale in most cases. Finally, the labor input which has the higher adjustment speed than capital appears to be the major factor contributing to growth. The role of learning by doing through labor as human capital comes through in our estimation most distinctly.

4.4 EXPORTS AND PRODUCTIVITY GROWTH IN KOREA AND OTHER NICs IN ASIA

The Korean growth episode provides in many ways a unique example of the successful NICs in Asia. This is so for several reasons. First of all, the endogenous policy change on the part of government has consistently emphasized on the liberalization and openness in trade along with other changes in macroeconomic policies. This is in sharp contrast to the experience of Latin American countries such as Mexico and Columbia. Renis (1990) has analyzed this contrast in terms of the following major policy components: (1) education, science and technology infrastructure including the patent laws, (2) significant land reforms, (3) the reform of the financial institutions in order to facilitate the privatization process thus permitting a shift of the public sector's role and finally (4) ensuring policy coordination in the public sector's role in maintaining balanced rates of real exchange rates, low tax rates as percent of GDP and low tariff rates on the external trade. The sequence in which these policy changes were introduced helped the trade liberalization process more strongly than Japan for example. To overcome the uncertainty of world competition the national policy markers shifted incentives to favor production for exports and assured exporters high initial profits. On top of substantial tariff exemptions exporters received exemptions from business taxes, 50 percent reductions in corporate and income taxes on export earnings and accelerated depreciation allowances for fixed capital used in export production. Secondly, the base for export-led growth drive in Korea in the 1960's was labor-intensive light manufacturing. Over the decade 1960–70 light manufacturing output grew from just 7.2 percent of GDP to 29.1 percent. Exports of light manufacturers increased from 24.2 percent of total exports to 60.3 percent, whereas the exports of primary products decreased from 63.5 percent of total exports to 11.3 percent. From this labor-intensive base of light manufacturing, Korea has shifted to heavy industries in the later decades. For example it has become the eighth largest steel producer in the world, the

95

second largest shipbuilder and the third largest producer of large capacity memory chips and a major supplier of cars and computers. Manufacturing now accounts for 30 percent of GDP, the same percentage as in Japan. Thus machinery, transport equipment and other manufactures jumped from 17 percent of total exports in 1974–76 to about 95 percent in 1985. Finally, the demand side factors have contributed to the Korean growth process very significantly over the last two decades. A World Bank country study (1987) reported that exports contributed 32.9 percent to output growth in manufacturing during the period 1980–83 and this is much larger than the contribution of investment which is about 19.8 percent. In the 1990's the export share of output growth in manufacturing has exceeded 38 percent.

Empirical growth episodes of the successful NICs in Asia suggest a close linkage of openness in trade and economic growth, when openness is measured by export growth and the overall economic growth by an index of structural change e.g., the average annual gain in percentage terms in the share of manufacturers in total exports and in total GDP (gross domestic product). Tables 4.12 and 4.13 show a very high degree of positive correlation between export growth and structural change in all the successful NICs in Asia, with Korea and Taiwan taking the lead. Japan, as a mature exporter, experienced less structural change in exports during this period, and it is conceivable that the role of exports in such a mature economy is less essential than it is in the export-oriented NICs.

Besides the increased concentration in the export of manufacturers, further specialization is taking place in the three more developed countries in the sample as the share of high-technology in total exports is constantly increasing. This process is especially pronounced in the case of Japan (see Table 12) and virtually nonexistent in the cases of Thailand and the Philippines. Again, the concentration of high-technology exports (HTX) seems to have been a correct strategical decision by Korea, given that the annual compounded growth rate of world demand for HTX of 13.3% has been higher than the growth rates of world demand for either manufactured or total exports of 12.3% and 7.9% respectively.

In Korea, growth of HTX was especially rapid, with a compounded annual growth rate, in terms of current value, of 45.5% for the period 1961–86. This may be seen in the background of a high degree of specialization in high-technology exports in different East Asian countries in Table 4.13.

Table 4.12 Structural Change and Economic Growth in East Asia

	(1) Growth Rate of Exports %	(2) X_{mfg}/X Initial %	(3) X_{mfg}/X Final %	(4) Total Gain (2)–(1)	(5) Degree of Structural Change	(6) Growth Rate of Output %
Korea	30.0	12.7	92.3	79.6	3.1	8.7
Taiwan	23.0	36.6	92.2	55.6	2.1	9.1
Thailand	14.1	1.4	52.3	50.9	1.9	6.8
Philippines	9.0	3.2	36.3	33.1	1.2	4.3
Japan	14.3	88.9	98.1	9.2	0.3	7.3

X_{mfg}/X = Share of Manufacturers in Total Exports, in percent. The periods covered are: Korea 1960–86; Taiwan 1961–87, Japan 1960–85, Thailand and the Philippines 1960–87. The growth rate of real output is computed using constant prices; the growth rate of exports is computed using current value of exports. Data sources are: (1) World Development Reports of World Bank, (2) Statistical Yearbooks of S. Korea, Taiwan, Thailand, Philippines and Japan.

It appears that export expansion in Korea was based on specialization in export areas experiencing higher than average growth rates, notably specialization in manufacturing exports. At the same time, further specialization was taking place as exports displayed an increasingly larger high technology component. The end result was a rapidly expanding exports sector increasingly specialized in the export of high technology goods, implying a rapid pace of structural change in the whole economy. Also we have to note that as a result of the increased production of manufacturers for exports, the share of manufacturing to GDP in Korea almost tripled during the period 1960–87 from 12.1 to 30.3. Other NICs also had similar experiences. Sengupta and Espana (1994) have discussed this export pattern in some detail.

Table 4.13   Specialization in High-Technology Exports (HTX) in East Asia

	(1) Initial and End Value of (HTX/X)			(2) Total Gain End–Initial Value of (1)	(3) Average Annual Gain in (HTX/X)
Korea	0.0	-	33.7	33.7	1.30
Taiwan	1.3	-	32.3	31.0	1.20
Thailand	0.0	-	11.9	11.9	0.44
Philippines	0.0	-	10.5	10.5	0.39
Japan	22.9	-	62.3	39.4	1.60

HTX = High-Technology Exports, represented by exports of machines and transport equipment, Section 7 of SITC.
(HTX/X) = Share of high-technology exports in total exports, both measured in current value terms.
Periods covered: Korea, Thailand, Philippines 1960–87; Taiwan 1961–87; Japan 1960–85.
Source of data: (1) World Bank Tables, (2) Statistical Yearbooks of Korea, Taiwan and Japan and (3) IMF World Economic Reports.

In our analysis of the Korean growth process we apply the cointegration theory and the ECM approach to two types of models. One is an aggregate model consisting of a production function that has been extended to include exports as an additional argument; the other is a two sector model comprising exports and non-exports. The aggregate model permits an estimation of the aggregate effects of exports on growth. It is applied to Korea and five other selected economies in order to compare the exports coefficient across different countries. The two-sector model is applied only to Korea. It is used to empirically determine in which sector primary factors are more productive, i.e., to determine the actual magnitudes of the marginal productivity coefficients. The two-sector model also allows for the determination of direction and magnitudes of externality effects across sectors.

Consider in the aggregate model, an extended production function with output (Y) depending on capital (K), labor (L) and exports (X):

$$Y = H(K,L,X) \tag{4.9}$$

Clearly if output and input variables are all nonstationary and integrated of order one, i.e., they are I(1), then their first differences are all I(0). Therefore by taking time derivatives of both sides of equation (4.9) one could derive:

$$\dot{Y} = H_K I + H_L \dot{L} + H_X \dot{X} \qquad (4.10)$$

where the dot over the variable denotes its time derivative and H_K, H_L, H_X are the marginal productivities of capital, labor and exports with $I = \dot{K}$ denoting investment. This equation (4.10) has two flexible features. One is that this dynamic specification does not suffer from the economic objection of spurious correlation or regression, since all the variables $\dot{Y}, I, \dot{L}$ and $\dot{X}$ are stationary and hence the standard OLS results with t-statistics retain their validity. Secondly, the dynamic model can be decomposed into a two-sector version, where the externality impact of the export sector on the non-export sector can be assessed both quantitatively and qualitatively. Thus we consider a simple two-sector model as

$$N = F(K_N, L_N, X)$$
$$X = G(G_X, L_X, N)$$
$$Y = N + X, \ K = K_N + K_X, \ L = L_N + L_X$$

with outputs X and N produced by the export sector and the rest of the economy (i.e., the non-export sector) by suing the two inputs K and L for the respective sectors. By taking time derivatives one can then easily derive the dynamic specification as:

$$\dot{N} = F_K I_N + F_L \dot{L}_N + F_X \dot{X} \qquad (4.11)$$
$$\dot{X} = G_K I_X + G_L \dot{L}_X + G_N \dot{N}$$

where the subscripts on F and G denote the marginal productivities of the respective inputs in the two sectors. Note that if all the sectoral variables are integrated of order one, their first differences are integrated of order zero and hence the standard OLS regressions are valid along with the t-statistics and R^2 values, i.e., the regression equations have a structural or equilibrium interpretation in the following sense: any deviations from the equilibrium relationship would tend to zero on the average and this would happen very frequently, since the regression variables are all stationary.

For the aggregate model (4.10) the OLS results for Korea are compared with those obtained when the export variables ($\dot{X}$) is left out. Thus we obtain

$$\dot{Y} = c + \hat{\alpha}I + \hat{\beta}\dot{L}$$

$$= -314.6 + 0.206I + 0.029\dot{L} \qquad\qquad R^2 = 0.568$$
$$(-0.529) \quad (4.553) \quad (2.245) \qquad DW = 2.033, \ \hat{\rho} = -0.037$$

$$\dot{Y} = c + \hat{\alpha}I + \hat{\beta}\dot{L} + \hat{\gamma}\dot{X}$$

$$= -2.08.9 + 0.151I + 0.024\dot{L} + 0.401\dot{X} \qquad R^2 = 0.641$$
$$(-0.372) \quad (2.875) \quad (1.921) \quad (1.805) \qquad DW = 1.965, \ \hat{\rho} = 0.016$$

Here the estimates are obtained from the time series data available from the World Bank Tables. The error corrected forms are not used here, since the first difference series are stationary. On the basis of these estimates the percentage contributions to output growth due to different inputs appear as follows: $I = 56$, $\dot{L} = 22$, $\dot{X} = 22$, with $\dot{Y} = 100$.

Clearly the impact of the export sector's role is very important, as much as the contribution of human capital in the form of $\dot{L}$. This suggests the existence of spillover effects of labor productivity due to export externality which has been strongly emphasized in the new growth theory in recent times. Note that if we assume the externality effect of exports is embodied as Harrod-neutral technical progress associated with labor productivity, then the aggregate production function (4.11) can be expressed as

$$Y = H(K,AL), \ A = A(X)$$

where AL is augmented labor with A depending on exports, which permit learning by doing effects of technical innovation.

To put the Korean estimation results in perspective the dynamic model

$$\dot{Y} = c + \alpha I + \beta\dot{L} + \gamma\dot{X}$$

of the externality effect of exports is also estimated for a group of selected developing and industrial countries in Table 4.14.

Here we have two export-oriented NICs in Asia, three mature industrial exporters and one LDC represented by the Philippines. Clearly the externality effect of exports is positive and statistically significant in all cases except Japan, where the export share of national output is much lower compared to the others. The Korean case is unique in this perspective in that both export growth and the export share of GDP are very high and exports grow at double the rate for output growth.

Next we consider the two-sector model (4.11) for estimating the intersectoral effects. Note that the externality impact of the export sector on the nonexport sector may be estimated by the marginal productivity parameter F_X/G_N may be used as a measure of dominance of the export vs. the nonexport sector if it is greater than one. The empirical estimates for Korea are as follows:

Parameter	1964–83	1964–86	1969–86
F_X	1.92	1.00	0.99
G_N	0.28	0.31	0.32
F_X/G_N	6.9	3.2	3.1

Table 4.14 Externality Effect of Exports on Growth 1967–86

	Korea	Taiwan	Japan	Belgium	Germany	Philippines
Intercept	−208.9	6.8*	−7.7*	−314.8*	−190.0*	−0.7*
I	0.151*	0.094*	0.615*	1.148	1.651	0.336*
I^2	-	-	0.384*	-0.001	-	0.003
$\dot{L}$	0.024*	0.050	0.119*	0.631*	0.028*	0.001
$\dot{X}$	0.401*	0.438*	0.116	0.333*	0.610*	0.389*
R^2	0.641	0.933	0.690	0.419	0.447	0.407
DW	1.96	1.56	1.98	1.95	2.44	1.52
X/Y	30.6	56.7	12.9	59.0	28.3	21.6
g_X	16.1	13.4	8.7	6.1	5.3	4.2
g_Y	8.0	8.1	5.4	3.0	2.7	3.6

Notes: 1. In case of the industrial countries in the sample an additional term I^2 is introduced to capture the nonlinearity effect.
2. X/Y = average share of exports in GDP; $g_X = \Delta X/X$ = rate of growth of exports in constant prices, $g_Y = \Delta Y/Y$ = rate of growth of total output in constant prices.

Clearly the externality effect of the export sector and its impact on the rest of the economy is most dominant, i.e., it is roughly 3 to 7 times larger than the reverse effect and furthermore the gap between the two externality effects is diminishing over time. This superiority in marginal productivity effects of the export sector has been empirically supported by other research workers in the field, e.g., Enos and Park (1988), Sengupta and Okamura (1996).

Now we perform cointegration tests on both the aggregate and two-sector models. Engle and Granger (1987) suggested seven possible cointegration tests, among them the Cointegrating Regression Durbin–Watson (CRDW) and the Dickey–Fuller (DF) tests. In the case of CRDW, after running the cointegrating regression, the Durbin–Watson statistic is tested to see if the residuals appear stationary. If they are non-stationary, the Durbin–Watson will approach zero and thus the test rejects non-cointegration (finds cointegration) if the DW is too big.

The DF tests the residuals of the cointegrating regression by running the following auxiliary regression,

$$\Delta\varepsilon_t = \delta\varepsilon_{t-1} + u_t, \ \Delta\varepsilon_t = \varepsilon_t - \varepsilon_{t-1} \tag{4.12}$$

Then the DF uses a test to determine whether or not δ is zero or negative. The t statistic for δ is then the DF statistic. If δ is found statistically to be equal to zero or negative, then the null hypothesis of non–cointegration is rejected. The augmented DF test runs the empirical regression of a more generalized form

$$\Delta\varepsilon_t = \delta\varepsilon_{t-1} + b_1\Delta\varepsilon_{t-1} + \cdots + b_p\Delta\varepsilon_{t-p} + u_t$$

and performs a t-test to test whether or not δ is significantly less than zero.

An alternative method of modelling a nonstationary time series with changing mean and variance is to use integrated variables to define an ARCH (autoregressive conditional heteroscedastic) model that has been widely applied in dynamic modelling of nonstationary series.

Here the conditional variance $\sigma_t^2 = E_{t-1}(\varepsilon_t^2)$ may be modelled as

$$\sigma_t^2 = a_0 + \alpha_1\varepsilon_{t-1}^2 + \beta_1\sigma_{t-1}^2 \tag{4.13}$$

where the errors ε_t are estimated by the deviations $\dot{X}$ and $\dot{N}$ from their mean levels. Clearly if the condition $\hat{\alpha}_1 + \hat{\beta}_1 = 1$ holds for the estimated parameters $\hat{\alpha}_1, \hat{\beta}_1$ then the volatility due to shocks is of a permanent nature, i.e., the null hypothesis of cointegration cannot be rejected then.

The empirical results of the different cointegration tests for Korea over the period 1964–86 may now be discussed for both the aggregate and sectoral models. In case of the estimated aggregate model

$$\dot{Y}_t = c + \hat{\alpha}\dot{I}_t + \hat{\beta}\dot{L}_t + \hat{\gamma}\dot{X}_t + \varepsilon_t; R^2 = 0.641, DW = 2.033, \hat{\rho} = 0.037$$

the results are as follows:

Test	DW	DW	t	t	Test of H_0
CRDW	2.033	0.455**	-	-	Reject
DF	-	-	−4.591	−4.07**	Reject

Notes: 1. Two asterisks denote the critical value of the test statistic for α = 1%. In the case of the CRDW, this is the critical value for q = 3, i.e., three independent variables.

2. The null hypothesis for both tests is non-cointegration. Thus, our results seem to reject H_0 in favor of cointegration.

For the two-sector model (4.11) the results of the cointegration test appear in Table 4.15.

Table 4.15 Estimates of Cointegration Test Statistics

Test	DW	Nonexports sector ($\dot{N}$) DW	t	t	Test of H_0
CRDW	1.916	0.511**	-	-	Reject
Eq. (4.13)			−0.847	−1.717**	Accept $(\alpha_1 + \beta_1 = 1)$
CRDW	2.452	Exports sector ($\dot{X}$) 0.511	-	-	Reject
Eq. (4.13)	-	-	−0.924	−1.717	Accept $(\alpha_1 + \beta_1 = 1)$

Notes: 1. One asterisk denotes the critical value of the DW statistic with 5% level of significance. The null hypothesis here is non–cointegration.

2. Two asterisks denote the critical value of t at 1% level and Eq. (4.13) tests whether or not $(\alpha_1 + \beta_1 = 1)$. Thus the null hypothesis of a constant variance and by implication the cointegration of the variables seem to be accepted here.

Clearly the statistical results from the cointegration tests above seem to support two broad propositions. One is that the estimated parameters in the aggregate and sectoral models do indeed reflect a long run equilibrium relationship between the variables involved. Secondly, the growth model based on first differences seems to exhibit persistence in variance, which implies that any exogenous shocks to the system due to technological innovation would have permanent effects on output growth. We have to note in concluding this section that we applied two other tests of cointegration mentioned by Engle and Granger (1987), e.g., the portmanteau statistic based on the autocorrelation coefficients of residuals and the Box–Pierce statistic but since the results are not different they are not discussed here.

4.4.1 Test of Demand Dominance

Now we turn to the question: which of the two forces, demand or supply play a more dominant role in the dynamic growth process of the Korean economy? Empirical modeling of this issue involves disequilibrium analysis, since demand does not necessarily equal supply in such a framework. Two types of econometric tests can be applied here. One is by estimating the disequilibrium model

$$D = D(p, z_1); \quad S = S(p, z_2)$$
$$Q = \min(D, S) \tag{4.14}$$

where we consider for example a commodity market where demand (supply) is influenced by price and an exogenous variable z_1 (z_2 for supply) but both D and S are unobserved. What is observed is Q which is the minimum of D and S. For macroeconomic situations such a disequilibrium formulation in terms of labor and goods markets has been analyzed by Benassy (1982). A second method is to consider which of the two constraints, the savings–investment gap and the foreign exchange constraint has been binding on the rapid economic growth in Korea. Since foreign exchange is the most important element of demand growth and inadequate domestic savings the most important limitation on capacity expansion of output, the disequilibrium denoted by $Q = \min(D, S)$ is replaced in this approach by

$$g = \min(g_d, g_x) \tag{4.15}$$

where g is the observed growth rate of per capita income or output, g_d and g_s are respectively the foreign-exchange constrained growth rate and savings-constrained growth rate of per capita output. Bacha (1984) used this framework and distinguished between a programming view and a structuralist view of export growth and its impact on national income growth. In the programming view the net export ratio is viewed as a government instrument in a standard Keynesian open-economy multiplier model and its optimal value is chosen by policymakers by maximizing national growth rate subject to the capacity constraints. In the structuralist view the maximum export ratio is lower than the desired level and the foreign exchange constraint is binding so that there is less than full capacity utilization. On applying Bacha's steady-state growth equation the following estimates are obtained for Korea:

	1967–76	1972–81	1977–86	1967–86
g_s	12.07	10.86	8.75	10.69
g_d	9.31	8.52	8.15	9.32

Clearly the foreign exchange constraint has been binding (i.e., $g_d \leq g_x$). This view is also confirmed by other independent estimates. For example Kwon (1986) estimated an index of capacity utilization rate of the Korean manufacturing sector over the period 1961–80 and found that it rose from 0.46 during 1961–64 to about 0.75 in the 1970's and almost to full capacity in the late 1980's. Although this capacity utilization index is defined as the ratio of actual consumption of electricity to the maximum possible consumption, it is suggestive of the general pattern. As Lee (1990) noted that the Korean government exercises complete control over the allocation of foreign loans between industries and sectors and because of this the actual rate of growth of national income during the first three five-year plans in Korea (1961–76) consistently exceeded the target rates set by the planners and did so during the second five-year plan (1967–71). Thus the fundamental philosophy underlying the planning process in Korea has been that the planners have always been prepared to borrow abroad to achieve a target rate of growth, i.e., to pursue an expansionary demand policy in order to maintain a high rate of growth.

In applying the test for the disequilibrium model (4.14) we convert it to a macrodynamic framework and specify the demand supply functions in a growth rate form

$$\Delta D = F(I, \Delta G)$$
$$\Delta S = H(I, \Delta L)$$
$$\Delta Q = \min(\Delta D, \Delta S)$$

Here the demand equation ΔD represents the typical Keynesian variables represented by investment demand (I) and autonomous government expenditure (ΔG), where investment demand includes both domestic and foreign demand. The supply equation is the production function with capital and labor inputs. Estimating these two equations by linear regression for Korea over the period 1967–86 we obtain the estimated series of $d = \Delta D$ and $s = \Delta S$. Then to test whether $d > s$ or $s > d$ we obtain the following regression

$$d = a + bs$$

of estimated demand and supply. For Korea the following result is obtained

$$d = 225.1 + 0.850 * s, \quad R^2 = 0.86, \quad DW = 2.2$$
$$\quad (1.6) \qquad (1.3)$$

Clearly $d < s$, hence $q = \Delta Q = d$. A similar set of calculations for the other countries in our sample produced the following results:

	$q = \min(d,s)$	$g_X = \Delta X/X$	$g_Y = \Delta Y/Y$
Korea	d	16.1	8.0
Taiwan	d	13.4	8.1
Japan	d	8.7	5.4
Belgium	s	6.1	3.0
Philippines	s	4.2	3.6
Germany	d	5.3	2.7

Clearly the demand factor was more binding in the dynamic growth process of the successful NICs in Asia. Since this implied that the demand–induced growth was more persistent, i.e., less volatile and the planners in Korea targeted it as a long run objective, the response of supply was in the typical Keynesian fashion, i.e., increased capacity utilization in the short run and building capacity ahead of demand in the long run. The latter was greatly helped in Korea and Taiwan by a policy of low real interest rates and significant economies of scale in the manufacturing sector over the last two decades.

4.4.2 Trends in Productivity in Manufacturing

Substantial gains in productivity in the Korean manufacturing sector have been frequently stressed in the literature as the basis of Korean growth miracle over the last two decades. Hence it is of great importance to study the productivity trend in this sector, which has contributed so significantly to the spectacular export growth in Korea. The basic data used by our study is from Kwon (1986), who analyzed the growth of total factor productivity in Korean manufacturing over the period 1961–80 and found that it has grown at 3% per annum, of which technical change contributed 45%, scale economies 38% and the change in capacity utilization rate about 17%. These estimates were derived from a translog cost function fitted over the input quantities and their prices for this period. The empirical data consist of annual time series for Korean manufacturing (1961–80), which is updated till 1986. The time series consists of aggregate output and the quantities and prices of labor, capital, energy and materials. The index of manufacturing production is used as a measure of aggregate output while the quantity of labor input is measured by the total manhours worked. Total costs are defined as the sum of four components: expenditures on labor, energy, material and the value of flow services of capital. The quantity as well as the price indices of net capital stock are obtained from Kwon (1986) and Lee (1990). Two limitations of the data set have to be mentioned. One is that there is no direct measure of technical change in the form of labor augmenting or capital augmenting technical progress. Kwon (1986) uses time itself as a proxy variable for this purpose, which of course is not always satisfactory. Secondly, there is no direct measure of capital usage in the sense of capacity utilization. Here also Kwon (1986) used a proxy utilization rate defined by the ratio of actual consumption of electricity to the maximum possible consumption. However, this proxy variable is not very suitable in our case, since other parameter estimates are very sensitive to it.

Kwon's OLS estimate of the aggregate cost function for Korean manufacturing assumed a translog specification which ignored the problem of nonstationarity in the input output data and the high value of $R^2 = 0.978$ appears to be misleading, since it is associated with a very low DW statistic. Moreover some of the critical parameters such as the coefficient of log output is negative implying that in some domains of output the marginal cost may be negative. Also the standard t-tests applied here may be of doubtful validity, since all the inputs and outputs are observed to be nonstationary.

In our approach we attempt to estimate the error correction model as follows. First, we start with a loglinear production function

$$y_t = \sum_{i=0}^{4} \alpha_i x_{it} + e_t \tag{4.16}$$

where in logarithmic terms y is output and x_1 through x_4 denote the four inputs: capital, labor, energy and materials and x_0 is one for all t. Following Granger (1969) we perform a simple test to identify error-correction by running a regression of (4.16) using least squares and then asking if $\hat{e}_t = y_t - \hat{\alpha}'x_t$ is integrated of order zero or not. The standard time series method for doing this is to look at the correlogram of $\hat{e}_t$ and then decide, by eye, if it is declining fast enough for I(0) to be appropriate. The same method presumably has to be applied to decide that y_t and x_t are both I(1). This procedure however is not very efficient and hence we apply the Dickey–Fuller (DF) and the augmented Dickey–Fuller (ADF) tests proposed by Engle and Granger (1987). The DF test first runs a regression of the change $(\Delta \hat{e}_t)$ in estimated residuals

$$\Delta \hat{e}_t = \delta \hat{e}_{t-1} + u_t$$

where $\Delta \hat{e}_t = y_t - \hat{\alpha}'x_t$. In the next step the DF performs a t–test to test if the estimated coefficient δ is negative and significantly different from zero. The t-statistic for the coefficient δ is the DF statistic. But the ADF test runs the linear regression

$$\Delta \hat{e}_t = \delta \hat{e}_{t-1} + b_1 \Delta \hat{e}_{t-1} + \cdots + b_k \Delta \hat{e}_{t-k} + u_t \tag{4.17}$$

and then performs a t-test to see whether or not δ is significantly less than zero. The t-statistic for δ is the ADF statistic. Based on the estimates of the Cobb–Douglas (CD) production function in Table 4.16, we compute the estimates of the cointegration regression equation (4.17) as follows:

δ	b_1	b_2	b_3
−0.901**	−0.061	−0.0001	−0.0004

where two asterisks denote significance at 1% level of the t-test. Thus the ADF test rejects the null hypothesis of no cointegration among the variables. The DF test also rejects the null hypothesis at 1% level.

As a further test we ran a least squares regression Δy_t on $\Delta x_{1t},...,\Delta x_{4t}$ and tested the residual if it is white noise. The tests did not reject the null hypothesis of a white noise process for the residual error. As a second step we combine the white noise test for e_t in (4.16) by building a more general model as

$$y_t = \alpha' x_t + \sum_{k=1}^{p} \alpha_j(y_{t-k} - y_{t-k-1})$$
$$+ \sum_{k=0}^{q} \beta_j(x_{t-k} - x_{t-k-1}) + \varepsilon_t$$

where ε_t should be white noise if p and q are chosen large enough to pick up any temporal structure in the I(0) variable e_t in (4.16). Grainger (1969) has shown that this model permits an efficient estimate of the production function model. It is clear that a similar procedure can be followed for estimating a dynamic cost function, where costs depend on output and its changes over time. Thus if c_t denotes cost in logarithmic units we have the dynamic cost function

$$\Delta c_t = \gamma_0 + \gamma_1 \Delta y_t - \theta(c_{t-1} - \alpha_0 - \alpha_1 y_{t-1}) + \varepsilon_t \qquad (4.18)$$

where ε_t is white noise and the effect of incremental output on costs is captured by Δy_t. Note that the steady state cost function is specified by $c = \alpha_0 + \alpha_1 y$. These cost estimates are in Table 4.17.

Finally, the output growth process is characterized by changes in labor productivity $z = f(z_1, z_2)$ where in logarithmic terms z is output–labor ratio in year t, z_1 is capital–labor ratio in year t and z_2 is the output–labor ratio in year t–1. Here z_2 is used as a proxy for technical process as is frequently done in econometric modeling for development. The production function estimates then take the loglinear form.

$$\Delta z_t = a_0 + a_1 \Delta z_{1t} + a_2 \Delta z_{2t}$$
$$-\gamma(z_{t-1} - \alpha_0 - \alpha_1 z_{1t-1} - \alpha_2 z_{2t-1}) + \varepsilon_t$$

and in steady state

$$z_t = \alpha_0 + \alpha_1 z_{1t} + \alpha_2 z_{2t} + \eta_t$$

Note that we have reported in Tables 4.16 and 4.17 alternative estimates based on the criterion of the least sum of absolute values of errors (LAV), which yields the linear programming (LP) method of estimation. To apply this LAV method in our case consider the production frontier specification above, where the error terms ε_t are nonpositive. This yields

$$-\varepsilon_t = \beta' Z_t - \Delta y_t \geq 0; \quad t = 1, 2, \dots, \tau$$

Table 4.16 Regression and LP Estimates of the Dynamic Production Function (1961–86) in Korean Manufacturing

Variables	CD	LP	Mixed
Constant	−0.212	0.412	0.324
x_1, t−1	−0.091	0.023	0.029
x_2, t−1	0.424*	0.245*	0.304*
x_3, t−1	−0.141	0.041*	0.039
x_4, t−1	0.592*	0.592*	0.512*
Δx_2	0.414*	0.512*	0.493*
Δx_4	−0.012	0.013*	0.009*
b_0	−1.213	0.014	0.005
R^2	0.640	-	0.894
Ave slack	-	0.065	-

Notes: 1. One asterisk denotes for regression models significant t-values at 5% level, and for LP models similar t-values are indicated by assuming the asymptotic standard error formula based on truncated normal with range zero to infinity.
2. 'Ave slack' denotes the average value of error in the LP estimates.
3. CD regressions and LP estimates are based on equations (4.12) and (4.18) respectively.
4. Data sources are Kwon (1986) and the Statistical Yearbook of Korea.

Table 4.17 Regression and LP Estimates of the Dynamic Cost Function
(1961–86) in Korean Manufacturing

Variable	Regression (CD)	LP	Mixed
Constant	0.021	0.223	0.135
y_{t-1}	0.752*	0.612*	0.652*
Δy_t	−0.121	0.109	0.094
γ_0	0.103*	0.941*	0.853*
R^2	0.912	-	0.946
Ave slack	-	0.031	-

Notes: 1. The footnotes of Table 4.16 are applicable here for asterisks.
2. Regression and LP estimates are based on models in (4.19).
3. Data sources are as in Table 4.14.

Table 4.18 Changes in Labor Productivity over Two Subperiods

Variables	Period I (1961–73)		Period II (1974–86)	
	CD	LP	CD	LP
Constant	0.491	0.214	−0.159	0.154
$z_{1,t-1}$	−0.279*	0.141	0.142	0.245
$z_{2,t-2}$	0.598*	0.768*	1.004*	0.981
Δz_1	−0.021	0.007	−0.014	0.021
Δz_2	0.768*	0.798*	0.894*	0.779*
a_0	−1.201	0.978	0.123	0.479
R^2	0.894	-	0.912	-
Ave slack	-	0.051	-	0.047

Notes: 1. Asterisks have the same meaning as in Table 4.5.
2. CD and LP estimates are based on Tables 4.16 and 4.17.

where Z_t' is the row vector comprising $(1, \Delta x_t, z_{t-1})$ where $z_{t-1} = y_{t-1} - \alpha' x_{t-1}$ and β is the corresponding vector of parameters. Minimizing the sum $\sum\limits_{t=1}^{\tau} |-\varepsilon_t| = \Sigma(-\varepsilon_t)$ over t points belonging to the convex hull we obtain the final form of the LP model used to estimate the dynamic production frontier as follows:

$$\text{Min} \sum_{i=1}^{k} \beta_i \bar{Z}_i$$

subject to

$$\sum_{i=1}^{k} \beta_i Z_{it} \geq \Delta y_t; \quad t = 1,2,...,\tau$$

$$\beta_i \geq 0; \quad i=1,2,...,k$$

where k is the total number of parameters and $\bar{Z}_i = (1/\tau) \sum\limits_{t=1}^{\tau} Z_{it}$ is the mean level of the regressor variable Z_i. Note that for the case of the dynamic cost function (4.18) we would have to minimize the sum $\sum\limits_{t=1}^{\tau} \varepsilon_t$, when $\varepsilon_t \geq 0$.

The econometric estimates in Tables 4.15 through 4.17 may now be interpreted. First of all, the role of error correction models is clearly brought out in both the regression and the LP estimates. Whereas OLS regressions yield negative coefficients for capital and energy inputs, the LP estimates generate positive values. The estimates of the dynamic production function based on first differences and the dynamic production frontier based on LP computations are more meaningful and statistically more acceptable, since the residual errors are tested to be stationary and white noise. Furthermore the LP estimates clearly show the dominant impact of capital. Note that the mixed estimates show the capital coefficient to be highly significant at 5% level of t-test. Bur the extent of scale economies appears to be much less when we apply the LP model. This may be due to two reasons. One is due to the prevalence of allocative or price efficiency, since the factor markets in Korean manufacturing have been highly competitive and flexible as noted by Kwon (1986). Secondly, the data on capital stock is highly heterogenous particularly due to the new technology.

Secondly, the cost function estimates in Table 4.16 clearly show significant economies of scale both in the CD regression and the LP formulation but since the output coefficient (0.612) is lower in case of the LP model, it implies higher economies of scale. Furthermore the impact of the incremental output is to augment the scale economies by a greater amount. This result is in agreement with the empirical finding of Kwon (1986) and Feder (1982) that the rapid growth in Korean manufacturing output over the last two decades has been achieved by the successful utilization of scale economies and capacity expansion. Finally, the estimates of labor productivity changes in Table 4.17 show that in recent years (period II: 1974–86) the scale economies have been reduced. For the Korean economy the first period (1961–73) was a period of self-sustaining growth, whereas the second period was the period of transition toward the heavy and chemical intensive manufacturing. In both periods however the role of technical progress measured by the proxy variable z_2 has been very dominant. This shows the importance of the dynamic forces in the production and cost function studies.

4.4.3 Educational Achievement and Human Capital in Economic Growth

The role of human capital in the overall growth process can be analyzed in principle in two different ways. One is to look at investment for education in different levels and trace the impact of improved educational achievements on the labor quality and skill levels. The second is to assess the growth in R&D spending in both public and private sectors and also evaluate the extent of foreign technology transfer that contributes to domestic learning and growth.

The role of educational achievements in improving labor quality has a more persistent and self–sustained impact on growth, since the R&D expenditures are still very small in proportion in Korea and other NICs in Asia. Thus Singapore and Taiwan spend about 1 percent of GNP on R&D, while Korea spends about 2.5 percent, which is almost the same as in OECD countries. Two significant aspects about Korea's R&D effort are how fast it was built up and also the inversion of the relative roles of public and private sectors in funding R&D research. In the mid-1970s Korea was spending about 0.5% of GNP on R&D and about 80% of it was financed by the public sector. By 1990 there was a five-fold increase in R&D and 80% of it was undertaken in the private sector. Two main reasons may be cited.

One is that in augmenting technology-intensive exports firms found it increasingly necessary to be able to understand, improve and integrate the relevant technologies. Secondly, new institutions like the Korean Productivity Center with its Flexible Automation demonstration centers deliberately promoted the diffusion of extensive training in the use of new technologies. This helped the learning process of firms which began to undertake their own technological efforts such as the development of some electronic components and products. As Kim (1995) has reported that spurred by various incentive programs the number of corporate R&D laboratories increased from one in 1970 to 1201 in 1990, which reflects the intensity with which the Korean firms are investing in 'learning by R&D'. Although small and medium–sized firms account for about 50 percent of the total number of corporate R&D centers, the large monopoly conglomerates known as *chaebol* dominate the R&D activities. This latter dominance makes it possible to exploit the scale economies and large-scale diffusion of the knowledge capital.

The role of education in enhancing the skill levels of the labor force engaged in the manufacturing and the export sector can be directly quantified through the optimal demand equations such as (4.8) applied for the case of Japan. We consider the annual data for Korea over the period 1971–94 and define the following variables $y_t = \ln Y_t$, $n_t = \ln L_t$, $k_t = \ln K_t$ and $h_t = \ln H_t$, where Y_t is the real GDP, L_t the aggregate labor force, K_t is real capital formation and H_t is human capital proxied by the sum of education levels in high school, junior college, technical colleges and universities. the estimated partial adjustment equations corrected by the Cochrane–Orcutt procedure for autocorrelation appear as follows:

$$n_t = -1.371 + \underset{(t=3.242)}{0.416}\ n_{t-1} + \underset{(2.526)}{0.364}\ \hat{n}_{t+1} + \underset{(0.225)}{0.434}\ y_t - 0.025t$$

$$\overline{R}^2 = \text{Adjusted } R^2 = 0.986; \quad \rho = -0.208$$

$$k_t = -0.380 + \underset{(3.554)}{0.566}\ k_{t-1} + \underset{(3.665)}{0.496}\ \hat{k}_{t+1} - \underset{(-0.243)}{0.029}\ y_t - \underset{(-0.196)}{0.006}\ t$$

$$\overline{R}^2 = 0.997; \quad \rho = -0.014$$

$$h_t = 2.015 + \underset{(8.160)}{0.498} h_{t-1} + \underset{(12.516)}{0.513} \hat{h}_{t+1} - \underset{(-2.223)}{0.211} y_t + \underset{(1.378)}{0.019} t$$

$$\overline{R}^2 = 0.998; \quad \rho = -0.381$$

Here the future values of n_{t+1}, k_{t+1} and h_{t+1} are replaced by their estimated values in order to reduce the bias. Two features are clearly brought out in these estimates. One is that the future expected demand for human capital (represented by h_{t+1}) plays a stronger role than the past (represented by h_{t-1}). Also the time trend of human capital is rising. A more direct estimate of the growth rate of human capital produces the following result

$$\Delta h_t / h_{t-1} = \underset{(1.845)}{0.374} - \underset{(-1.692)}{1.212} h_{t-1}; \quad \overline{R}^2 = 0.094$$

which shows a relative decline in the growth rate as the level of h_{t-1} rises.

Recently Tallman and Wang (1993) have used educational achievement data for Taiwan over the period 1965–89 to incorporate a labor quality index into the labor input in an aggregate Cobb–Douglas production function with physical capital, raw labor input and a human capital index proxied by a measure of education level. Their result shows considerable improvement in the performance of the Solow-type growth model and a significant coefficient for the human capital index suggesting self-sustained growth due to the sum of the three coefficients exceeding unity.

5. Growth Stabilization and Exchange Rate Instability

Economic growth and trade policies are closely interrelated. Openness in trade and the spillover of information technology have intensified this process of globalization of trade. Over the last two decades 1976–96 the newly industrializing countries (NICs) of the Asian Pacific rim have experienced a very high rate of economic growth on the average due primarily to the large expansion of their export sectors and the heavy inflow of foreign capital and technology. For example South Korea's growth rate of 22.9% accompanied the average annual growth rate of per capita real income of 6.4% over the 1965–87 period. Experiences of the other successful NICs in Asia are very similar. This record of export growth is now facing a serious challenge from the fluctuations in the foreign exchange markets. By the end of 1997 the NICs in Asia started facing a crisis in the foreign exchange market due to a balance of payments imbalance. Some of the major sources of the exchange market volatility are: (1) the speculative attack on the international reserves of the central banks of these countries, (2) imbalance between a country's external liabilities and the lagging productive capacity and (3) the international transmission of shocks across the stock markets of the world.

One major impact of the speculator's role in the foreign exchange market has been that the national governments of developing countries have felt constraints on their monetary policies and they have to continually intervene in such markets through deliberate trading in order to maintain an orderly market. The second source of volatility arises as follows. The flow of international capital in a developing country tends to mobilize local resources and thereby over expands beyond the existing productive capacity of the country. In that case a country's external liabilities go up but its productive capacity fails to keep up. This imbalance can manifest itself in a currency crisis. Finally, the investors today are increasingly participating in international portfolios and hence the volatility in one stock market may be transmitted to other markets. This is more easily possible now a days due to currency hedging i.e., investment today are increasingly made under conditions of currency hedging, thus requiring little or no cross-border transfer of capital. In such a situation an increase in the external liabilities of a country in the wake of foreign investment may not be followed by an inflow of foreign savings. On the other hand foreign capital investment may reduce the volume of domestic savings by crowding out or a boom in the asset market. Thus the external imbalance may induce an imbalance between domestic savings and investment. This is a potential source of foreign exchange market crisis. Recent trends in volatility in foreign exchange markets have undergone and are still undergoing rapid and significant change. Dramatic decline in the role of fundamentals such as interest rate differentials and inflation rates, significant pulls of speculative expectations and stochastic bubbles in the form of chaotic instability are some of the new distinguishing features in these markets. Over the last two or three decades four types of stylized facts have dominated the exchange market scenario, which requires detailed analysis and interpretation. The first is the apparent collapse of the purchasing power parity (PPP) paradigm in explaining the exchange rate movements in terms of such fundamental factors as interest rate differentials. Thus the detailed empirical study by Frankel (1991) for the pound–dollar and franc–mark showed that the PPP held up very well in the 1921–25 period but not at all in the period 1973–79. For more recent periods the slope coefficients relating exchange rate movements to inflation and interest rate differentials are often insignificant or even wrong-signed. Secondly, the regime of fixed exchange rates for the period 1960–73 has changed to that of floating rates since 1974 and this is evident in the time series of monthly changes in exchange rates, which has been analyzed by Krugman (1991) in some detail. His estimates for the 1960–86 period show that the variance of monthly changes in the real exchange rate between US and Germany was 15 times as large in the second half of the sample period (1974–86) as in the first (1960–73). This trend in higher conditional variances is continuing still. Krugman argues that in a world of highly volatile exchange rates, firms have an incentive to adopt a 'wait and see' attitude toward both trading and pricing decisions. The result has been a significant delinking of prices of identical commodities in different countries. Thirdly, the foreign exchange market today is by far the largest financial market with a daily turnover exceeding 1.3 trillion dollars in 1996. By contrast the total international trade of goods and services constitutes less than 2 percent of annual foreign exchange transactions. Two aspects of this global finance are most important. One is that the bulk of these currency transactions is presumed to be speculative in nature. Private speculators are program traders with vast sums of assets who seek to make profits on exchange rate fluctuations. Their activities tend to distort the price signals in foreign exchange markets for long run investment and trade. Tobin (1994) has strongly emphasized this aspect of volatility in global finance and proposed a tax so as to curb the speculative component of currency transactions, which is presumed to generate stochastic bubbles and instability. The second aspect of global finance is a shift from bond to bank loans and then to equity markets as a method of financing capital flows from industrial to developing countries. In the 1920s the US bond market carried the bulk of financing international capital flows, then the bank loans took over in the 1970s. Since 1984 however the equity market has provided the bulk of global finance. This has made the exchange market transactions to be more sensitive to volatility. US investors and program traders have increasingly invested in global stocks and thereby the volatility of the New York stock market has been carried over to foreign exchange markets all over the world. Recently the empirical study by Sengupta and Sfeir (1997a,b) has found some evidence of chaotic dynamics and instability in the global financial markets. Finally, the central banks today continue to intervene in the foreign exchange markets in order to maintain an 'orderly market' through open market trading. This sometimes leads to the so-called problem of time inconsistency due to heterogeneous stabilization goals pursued by different countries and also due to the so-called overshooting phenomena. Short of a full-fledged global currency union with powers of coordinating the diverse and heterogeneous exchange rate policies the outcome is likely to be market volatility. For example, one could discern three distinct types of stabilization policy in the world today. One is the device of a high reserve ratio against foreign funds adopted by the Latin American countries such as Chile and Colombia with the objective of holding the real exchange rate within a target zone. The second policy is by the East Asian countries, e.g., South Korea, Malaysia, who adopted a policy of sterilization to confront the real appreciation of their domestic currencies. The third is the open market policy of the developed industrial countries, e.g., US and Germany which has the implicit objective of holding the exchange rate within a target zone by pursuing a loose policy of mutual coordination among countries. Note that the inconsistency problems due to lack of coordination of exchange rate policies contribute to instability due to unexpected fluctuations in foreign currency purchases and sales. Recently Hall and Henry (1988) formulated a macrodynamic model involving governments' and central banks' policy aspirations and showed how the inconsistency of mutual policies due to lack of coordination may lead to volatility in exchange markets.

Our objectives in this chapter are threefold. One is to empirically test the influence of fundamental factors on the exchange rate volatility and the second is to model the speculative agents' demand for foreign currency and its fluctuations over time. By relating the fluctuations in speculative demand to the volatility of the exchange market, one could empirically estimate the effects of so called fads in the exchange market. Thus indirectly it provides a test of the monetary hypothesis recently advanced by Frankel (1991) that the exchange rates are nothing but asset prices and as such they are very strongly dependent on heterogeneous expectations about the future and their asymmetry. The third objective is to empirically test the nonlinear dynamics in the foreign exchange markets of US, Europe, Asia and Latin America.

5.1   STOCHASTIC MODELS OF VOLATILITY

To model the fundamental factors affecting the exchange rate we use an optimizing model of the trading behavior of exporting firms, whereas the speculative side of the foreign exchange market is formulated in terms of a decision model for the representative speculator who has to decide on the optimal amount of forward purchases of foreign currency.

It is assumed that the representative producer faces competitive prices for his output and inputs, where he produces exportable output X_t subject to a quadratic cost function. To lessen the impact of uncertainty of a nominal bilateral exchange rate at a future rate he decides to enter into a forward contract. His profit in period $t+1$ can then be written as

$$\pi_{t+1} = b_1 s_{t+1} X_t + b_2 X_t + (s_{t+1} - f) \tag{5.1}$$
$$K_t - (1/2)X_t^2 - (1/2)\alpha(X_t - X_{t-1})^2$$

where s_{t+1} = spot rate at time $t+1$ quoted in terms of domestic currency per unit of foreign currency

f = one period forward rate at time t for delivery at time $t+1$
K_t = firm's net purchases of foreign currency for delivery at a future date
b_1 = unit net receipts from foreign trade denominated in foreign currency
b_2 = unit net receipts from the foreign trade in the firm's domestic currency
α = weight on export fluctuations measured by $(X_t - X_{t-1})^2$, $0 < \alpha < 1$.

The exporting firm adopts a mean–variance strategy for choosing the optimal levels of X_t and K_t, where his risk adjusted profit function takes the form

$$\text{Max}\phi = \sum_{t=1}^{\infty} \rho^t \left[\overline{\pi}_{t+1} - \frac{a}{2} \text{var } \pi_{t+1} \right]$$

where

$$\overline{\pi}_{t+1} = bX_t + rK_t - \frac{1}{2}X_t^2 - \frac{1}{2}\alpha(X_t - X_{t-1})^2$$
$$\text{var } \pi_{t+1} = (b_1X_t + K_t)^2\sigma^2; b = b_1\overline{s} + b_2$$

$\overline{s}, \sigma^2$ = the conditional mean and variance of s_{t+1}

ρ = constant rate of discount

$r = \overline{s} - f$ = risk premium.

The optimal solutions are

$$K_t = r(a\sigma^2)^{-1} - b_1X_t \tag{5.2}$$
$$(1 + \alpha + \alpha\rho)X_t - \alpha\rho X_{t+1} - \alpha X_{t-1} = b - b_1r$$

At the steady state

$$K = r(a\sigma^2)^{-1} - b_1X$$
$$X = (1 + 2\alpha)^{-1}[b - b_1r] \tag{5.3}$$
$$= b - b_1(\overline{s} - f), \text{ if } \alpha = 0$$

Two points emerge from these optimal decision rules. One is that trade varies inversely with risk premium; likewise the firm's demand for foreign currency is lower if the spot rate fluctuates more. Hence it follows that it is optimal for the exporter to enter into a forward contract to his trade transactions of amount b_1X with a positive b_1. Secondly, the oscillations in X_t are determined by the characteristic equation of (5.2), which has its two roots real and therefore nonoscillatory.

The model for the representative speculators assumes that they have unlimited arbitrage funds and their actions insure that the covered interest parity holds. The speculator has to decide on the optimal amount of forward purchases H_t. Again assuming the mean variance approach he maximizes the risk adjustment objective function

$$\underset{H_t}{\text{Max}\,\varphi} = \sum_{t=1}^{\infty} \rho^t \left[\overline{V}_{t+1} - \frac{a}{2}\,\text{var}(V_{t+1}) - \frac{\alpha}{2}(H_2 - H_{t-1})^2 \right]$$

subject to $\qquad V_{t+1} = iV_t(s_{t+1} - f)H_t$

where

V_t = speculator's initial wealth with its mean $\overline{V}_{t+1}$

i-1 = domestic rate of interest

H_t = forward purchases of foreign currency

$r = \overline{s} - f, (\overline{s}, \sigma^2)$ = mean and variance of s_{t+1}.

The optimal decision rule is then of the form

$$(a\sigma^2 + \alpha\rho + \alpha)\,H_t - \alpha\rho H_{t+1} - \alpha H_{t-1} = r \qquad (5.4)$$

At the steady state

$$H = (a\sigma^2)^{-1} r, \quad r = \overline{s} - f \qquad (5.5)$$

It is clear from the steady state equation (5.5) that the speculators require a nonzero forward rate bias to engage in the purchase or sale of foreign currency. Also H rises with r but a larger variance or a greater risk average reduces the amount of speculative transactions. The characteristic equation underlying (5.5) also suggests that there are zones of instability due to complex roots and also explosive roots.

On combining the two optimization models (5.2) and (5.4) for the exporters and the speculators, i.e., $X_t = F(r, K_t)$, $H_t = g(H_{t-1}, r)$ and expressing real exchange rate $RX_t = h(X_t, H_t, r)$ as a function of X_t, H_t and the risk premium r we can derive an estimating equation for testing the role of fundamentals versus fads. The fundamentals here refer to interest rate differentials and price differentials which are proxy variables for risk premiums. The fads on the other hand refers to unexpected monetary shocks and the low risk aversion of the speculative agents under a regime of target zones for the exchange rate. Also when the target zones attempted by different national governments are not mutually consistent, then this raises the policy inconsistency problems and also heteroscedasticity of the conditional variance of exchange rates. Hence the fads can be modeled through second order variance process models which are closely related to the Arch models in econometrics.

5.1.1 Empirical Estimates and Their Implications

Assuming exchange rates to be passively adjusting to the disequilibria due to interest rate differentials and trade imbalances, one could test this hypothesis by specifying the following relationship

$$RX_t = f[RI - RIUS)_t, (EX - IM)_t]$$ (5.6)

where RI = real rate of interest in the foreign country, RIUS = real interest rate in the US, and $(EX-IM)_t$ is export minus imports at month t. A more generalized specification would have to include the rate of inflation as another explanatory variable, where the rate of inflation is measured by the monthly change in wholesale price indices (WPI). Two aspects of the specification (5.6) are to be noted. One is that the usual least squares method (OLS) may not be appropriate in case the real exchange rate series is nonstationary. If the series RX_t is a random walk, then the first difference series $\Delta RX_t = RX_{t-1}$ is stationary and hence least squares method is appropriate for the dependent variable ΔRX_t. Secondly, future expectations play an equally important role as the past trends in exchange rates. Hence RX_{t+1} may provide an additional explanatory variable. This is also in line with the target zone models first introduced by Krugman (1991), where the formation of market expectations is consistent with the existence of a band constraining the possible future paths of exchange rates. Krugman's model implies a deterministic nonlinear relationship between the exchange rate's deviation from its central parity on the one hand and also the interest rate differentials and 'fundamentals' on the other.

The following two forms of specifications are finally selected as the exchange rate equation

$$\ln RX_t = \alpha + \beta_1 \ln RX_{t-1} + \beta_2 \ln RX_{t+1} + \beta_3 (RI - RIUS)_t$$
$$+ \beta_4 (RI - RIUS)_{t-1} + \beta_5 \ln[(EX_t / IM_t) / (EX_{t-1} / IM_{t-1})]$$
$$+ \beta_6 \ln(EX_t / IM_t)$$ (5.7)

and

$$\ln RX_t - \ln RX_{t-1} = \alpha + \beta_1 RI_{t-1} + \beta_2(WPI_t - WPI_{t-1})$$
$$+ \beta_3(RI_{t+1} - RI_t) \tag{5.8}$$

Our empirical applications seek to test which of the several fundamental forces, i.e., past history, future expectations, interest rate differentials and trade balances play a dominant role in the evolution of the real exchange rate process for the four industrial countries: France (FR), Japan (JP), United Kingdom (UK) and Germany (GR) over three sample periods based on monthly data as follows: Sample I (February 1985 through January 1988), Sample II (February 1988 through January 1991) and Sample III (February 1991 through August 1995).

The real exchange rate (RX) is calculated here as SP*/P, where S is the nominal exchange rate expressed in the domestic currency per unit of the foreign country. The monthly data on the nominal exchange rate are obtained from IMF *International Financial Statistics*, while the consumer price indices are from DRI data bank. With US as the foreign country the following four industrial countries: France (FR), Japan (JP), United Kingdom (UK) and West Germany (GR) are used here with three sample periods: Sample I: February 1985 to January 1988, Sample II: February 1988 to January 1991 and Sample III: February 1991 to August 1995. These sample periods are selected from the pattern of the graphic plots.

Following the standard unit root models we calculated the estimated residuals e_t from the fitted equation:

$$RX_t = \alpha + \beta_1 RX_{t-1} + \beta_2 RX_{t-2} + \beta_3 RX_{t-3} + \varepsilon_t \tag{5.9}$$

and then used a six-month moving average estimate of conditional variance $\hat{\sigma}_t^2 = E_{t-1}(e_t^2)$, where e_t is the estimated residual $\hat{\varepsilon}_t$.

The temporal dynamics of the real exchange rate series was first tested for random walk by running the regression equation (5.4) in the form $\Delta RX_t = (\beta_1 - 1)RX_{t-1} + \beta_2 \Delta RX_{t-2}$ and testing if the estimated coefficient $(\hat{\beta}_1 - 1)$ is significantly different from zero. The ADF (augmented Dickey–Fuller) test statistic was used with a sample size n=33 and in each of the four cases FR, JP, UK and GR the test statistic showed that the our series are not stationary, i.e., the unit root exists thus implying a random walk with a temporal variation over time.

Tables 5.1 and 5.2 provide ordinary least squares estimates of the exchange rate equations (5.7) and (5.8) respectively. A number of conclusions emerge from these monthly estimates. First of all, the impact of past trend $(\hat{\beta}_1)$ and the future expectations (coefficient $\hat{\beta}_2$) are both statistically significant, suggesting both to be equally important as driving forces in all the cases for three sample periods. For the recent period (i.e., sample III) the case $\hat{\beta}_2 > \hat{\beta}_1$ holds for both France and Germany, suggesting a more dominant role of future expectations than past history. Secondly, all the other slope coefficients $\hat{\beta}_3$ through $\hat{\beta}_6$ are statistically insignificant, implying that the interest rate differential and the export–import ratio have no explanatory value at all. Hence dropping these variables does not alter the estimates of β_1 and β_2 at all. Thus the recent time series behavior of exchange rates supports the hypothesis advanced by Frankel (1991) that the fundamentals such as interest rate differentials are often insignificant or wrong-signed. Thirdly, the estimates of Table 5.2 show some influence of the inflation rate measured by the increase in wholesale price indices, although the coefficients are not always significant in a statistical sense. Also in such cases interest rates fail to play any significant explanatory role. Also one notes that R^2 values adjusted for degrees of freedom are very poor in Table 5.2 compared to Table 5.1. Thus we may broadly conclude that the fundamentals are much less important today in explaining the volatility of the real exchange rate process.

An important stylized fact in the current periods of floating exchange rates is that the variance of monthly changes in exchange rates has increased enormously. This has been due to three major forces. One is the wait and see attitude of exporting firms and the incentive to hedge. The second is the role of the speculative traders who tend to be driven more often by fads than fundamentals. The third is the interaction of heterogeneous expectations of different governments who have uncoordinated stabilization goals.

One econometric way of modelled exchange rate volatility is to postulate a model of time-varying variances of exchange rates. The random shocks to the mean exchange rates, which may cause volatility are represented here by what is known as the Arch (autoregressive conditional heteroscedastic) model and its various generalizations in the modern financial literature. The simplest version of the Arch model uses the following specification for the conditional variance

$$y_t = E_{t-1}(y_t) + e_t; \quad \sigma_t^2 = E_{t-1}(e_t^2)$$
$$\sigma_t^2 = w + \alpha e_{t-1}^2 + \beta \sigma_{t-1}^2 \tag{5.10}$$

Table 5.1 Impact of Fundamentals on Real Exchange Rates

	Sample I			
	FR	JP	UK	GR
$\hat{\alpha}$	−0.549	0.002	−0.019	0.07
	(−1.87)	(0.01)	(−0.74)	(0.46)
$\hat{\beta}_1$	0.938**	0.516**	0.458**	0.53**
	(4.13)	(4.38)	(4.67)	(3.87)
$\hat{\beta}_2$	0.374*	0.484**	0.509**	0.426
	(2.39)	(4.17)	(4.74)	(2.86)
$\hat{\beta}_3$	−0.01	−0.003	0.005	−0.002
	(−1.01)	(−0.35)	(0.66)	(−0.24)
$\hat{\beta}_4$	0.005	0.005	-0.004	0.004
	(0.64)	(0.54)	(−0.54)	(0.44)
$\hat{\beta}_5$	0.185	0.028	−0.013	0.148
	(1.35)	(0.43)	(−0.23)	(0.66)
$\hat{\beta}_6$	−0.175	−0.014	0.002	−0.16
	(−0.86)	(−0.16)	(0.03)	(−0.48)
$\overline{R}^2$	0.86	0.98	0.93	0.97
n	17	34	34	34

	Sample II			
	FR	JP	UK	GR
$\hat{\alpha}$	−0.06	−0.072	−0.035	−0.006
	(−0.58)	(−0.16)	(−0.46)	(−0.12)
$\hat{\beta}_1$	0.507**	0.536**	0.455**	0.519**
	(4.83)	(5.21)	(3.46)	(4.94)
$\hat{\beta}_2$	0.519**	0.479**	0.494**	0.481**
	(5.15)	(4.31)	(4.74)	(3.52)
$\hat{\beta}_3$	−0.001	−0.012	0.007	−0.001
	(0.11)	(−1.13)	(0.97)	(−0.13)
$\hat{\beta}_4$	0.003	0.012	−0.006	0.002
	(0.28)	(0.94)	(−0.85)	(0.17)
$\hat{\beta}_5$	0.148	−0.014	0.032	0.007
	(0.93)	(−0.25)	(0.53)	(0.69)
$\hat{\beta}_6$	−0.458	−0.009	−0.01	0.025
	(−1.84)	(−0.14)	(−0.12)	(0.21)
$\overline{R}^2$	0.91	0.91	0.88	0.89
n	34	34	34	34

Table 5.1 (continued)

Sample III

	FR	JP	UK	GR
$\hat{\alpha}$	0.005	−0.169	−0.013	0.008
	(0.04)	(−1.16)	(0.45)	(0.17)
$\hat{\beta}_1$	0.442**	0.558**	0.474**	0.44**
	(5.44)	(9.57)	(7.58)	(5.57)
$\hat{\beta}_2$	0.559**	0.476**	0.496**	0.566**
	(6.98)	(8.85)	(7.14)	(8.32)
$\hat{\beta}_3$	4.2E-5	0.003	−0.009	0.006
	(0.01)	(0.41)	(−1.26)	(0.76)
$\hat{\beta}_4$	−0.014	−0.005	0.005	−0.01
	(−0.23)	(−0.77)	(0.79)	(1.22)
$\hat{\beta}_5$	0.032	−0.007	0.015	−0.011
	(0.36)	(−0.23)	(0.33)	(−0.11)
$\hat{\beta}_6$	−0.036	−0.003	0.016	−0.13
	(−0.39)	(−0.06)	(0.25)	(-0.77)
$\bar{R}^2$	0.83	0.98	0.93	0.92
n	53	53	53	53

Note: Here t-values are in parenthesis and one and two asterisks denote significant values at 5% and 1% levels respectively.

where y_t is the real exchange rate and $E_{t-1}(y_t)$ is its conditional mean as of time t−1. The variance term σ_t^2 is conditional on information up to time point t−1, i.e., $E_{t-1}(e_t^2)$ is the conditional expectation of the error term e_t^2. Note that the random shock to mean exchange rate is e_t and the shock to variance is $[E_t(e_t^2) - E_{t-1}(e_t^2)] = \xi_t$, where ξ_t is a random term. However since the estimate of the coefficient a in (5.10) frequently turns out to be statistically insignificant, one could run a second order variance process model as

$$\sigma_t^2 = w + \beta_1\sigma_{t-1}^2 + \beta_2\sigma_{t-2}^2 + \text{error} \tag{5.11}$$

which yields the characteristic equation

$$\lambda^2 - \beta_1\lambda - \beta_2 = 0$$

Table 5.2 Impact of Interest Rate and Inflation

	$\hat{\alpha}$	$\hat{\beta}_1$	$\hat{\beta}_2$	$\hat{\beta}_3$	$\bar{R}^2$	n
Sample I						
JP	−0.0089	−0.0007	0.0163	−0.0044	−0.002	34
	(−0.21)	(−0.1)	(1.58)	(−0.36)		
UK	−0.0343	0.0044	0.0306	0.0332**	0.28	34
	(−1.02)	(0.77)	(−1.29)	(3.07)		
GR	-0.059	0.0132	0.0211	0.0448*	0.14	34
	(−2.03)	(1.48)	(1.07)	(2.55)		
Sample II						
JP	0.0172	−0.0049	0.0312*	0.0224	0.15	34
	(0.58)	(−0.69)	(2.13)	(1.39)		
UK	0.0076	−0.0043	0.0271	0.0205*	0.09	34
	(0.26)	(−0.79)	(1.27)	(2.12)		
GR	0.0115	−0.0061	0.0452	0.0246	0.16	34
	(0.65)	(−1.59)	(1.79)	(1.58)		
Sample III						
JP	−0.0001	0.0013	0.0493**	0.0111	0.18	53
	(−0.01)	(0.39)	(3.75)	(1.21)		
UK	0.0035	−0.0004	0.0047	−0.0234*	0.03	53
	(0.18)	(−0.09)	(0.29)	(−2.04)		
GR	−0.0138	0.0047	−0.0421*	−0.0058	0.05	53
	(−1.1)	(1.27)	(−2.08)	(−0.45)		

Notes: 1. t-statistics in parentheses
2. *: significant at the 5% level
3. **: significant at the 1% level
4. Due to insufficient data France is excluded.

with two roots. The character of the two roots determine the stability or oscillatory property of temporal variance σ_t^2. This model can be used to test the exchange market volatility due to fads and the speculators' unanticipated expectations about the future. Table 5.3 provides the empirical estimates, which show that the two characteristic roots calculated from these estimates are complex for each case of samples II and III except for Japan in the third sample. For example the two roots for UK are: 0.601 $\pm$ 0.612i (Sample II) and 1.444 $\pm$ 0.771i (Sample III) with amplitudes R = 0.857 and 0.669 respectively. Even for Japan, which is a special case due to its persistent trade surplus with US for a long time, a complex root of 0.631 $\pm$ 0.149i is exhibited by the estimates of the second order variance process equation. Thus the variance process exhibits a persistent feature of oscillations. Also it is clear from the regression coefficient estimate of β_1 in Table 5.3 that it is not statistically different from unity, thus implying an explosive pattern for the variance process.

Two other developments seem to be important in this context. One is the international comovement of speculative exchange rates, which has been analyzed by Arch and generalized Arch models by recent researchers. Secondly, the volume of transactions in the exchange market has increased substantially over the last decade due mainly to the speculative transactions and the national governments' active trading. This has aggravated the vola-

Table 5.3 *Estimates of the Linear Second-Order Variance Process*

$$\sigma_t^2 = w + \beta_1 \sigma_{t-1}^2 + \beta_2 \sigma_{t-2}^2$$

	Sample	w	β_1	β_2	$\overline{R}^2$	n
FR	I	0.008	0.903**	−0.041	0.72	29
	II	0.016*	1.036**	−0.489**	0.66	29
	III	0.012**	0.991**	−0.329**	0.63	48
JP	I	16.72	1.263**	−0.421*	0.81	29
	II	18.0*	1.265**	−0.717**	0.75	29
	III	6.962**	1.219**	−0.51**	0.74	48
UK	I	1.49E-4	0.809**	−0.083	0.64	29
	II	0.0002**	1.202**	−0.676**	0.72	29
	III	0.0001*	1.444**	−0.670**	0.86	48
GR	I	0.002	0.974**	−0.143	0.72	29
	II	0.002**	1.054**	−0.470**	0.69	29
	III	0.002**	0.992**	−0.321**	0.63	48

Note: One and two asterisks denote significance at 5% and 1% of t statistics

tility pattern due to 'good news', 'bad news' effects and so on.

5.2 NONLINEAR DYNAMICS IN EXCHANGE RATE FLUCTUATIONS

Foreign exchange markets have been most volatile over the last several years and the researchers have paid increased attention to understanding the sources of this volatility and their international transmission from Asia, Latin America, to Europe and to the US. Recently applied econometricians have attempted to model this volatility in terms of nonlinear dynamic models. These models can be broadly divided into four broad categories, e.g., (a) nonlinear dynamics in the real exchange rate process; the major question here is whether hysteresis exists in the time series of real exchange rate movement, (b) nonstationarity in the conditional variance process for exchange rates; the major question here is the implication of explosive roots and chaotic dynamics, (c) nonlinearity in the trading behavior of speculative and other agents involving currency exchange and portfolio returns from currency trends; the major issue here is the variety of interactions among heterogeneous traders, some offering positive feedback and some negative, and (d) the remaining group where the interplay of central banks and monetary authorities pursuing heterogeneous policies tend to generate endogenous fluctuations.

Our object in this section is to analyze the recent empirical data of selected countries of the world in order to test the realism and relevance of the recent nonlinear dynamic models which are either in current use or newly developed by us. The selected countries are divided into three groups as follows:

A. Industrial developed countries, e.g., US, UK, France (FR), Germany (GR) and Japan (JP).
B. Developing countries in Asia, e.g., Indonesia, South Korea (KO), Malaysia (MA), Singapore (SI), Thailand (TH).
C. Developing countries in Latin America, e.g., Brazil (BR), Chile (CH), Colombia (CO), Mexico (ME).

The two main objectives of our empirical analysis are to quantify the persistence of volatility if any in the real exchange rate processes over time and then to discuss their possible policy implications for the global investment markets in the future.

5.2.1 Nonlinear dynamics in volatility

Two types of nonlinear models have been very frequently applied in econometric studies to model volatility in the exchange markets. One is the conditional variance model, which is frequently known as the ARCH (autoregressive conditional heteroscedastic) model and its generalized variants known as GARCH models. The simplest version of the ARCH model uses the following specification for conditional variance

$$y_t = E_{t-1} + e_t; \quad \sigma_t^2 = E^{t-1}(e_t^2)$$
$$\sigma_t^2 = \theta(B)\sigma_t^2 + \psi(B)e_t^2 + w_t \qquad (5.12)$$

where $\theta(B)$ and $\psi(B)$ are lag polynomials in B, the backshift operator, e_t is the random shock to the mean exchange rate and the shock to variance is $\xi_t = \{E_t(e_t^2) - E_{t-1}(e_t^2)\}$. For the first order lag this model reduces to

$$\sigma_t^2 = \alpha e_{t-1}^2 + \beta \sigma_{t-1}^2 + w_t \qquad (5.13)$$

Clearly this conditional variance model can be estimated by the maximum likelihood method (or by least squares if ξ_t is approximately or exactly normally distributed), since an estimated series $\{\hat{\sigma}_t^2\}$ can be constructed from the estimated residuals $\hat{e}_t$ obtained from (5.12). If the sum $(\alpha + \beta)$ of the coefficients in (5.13) equals or exceeds one is a statistically significant sense, then the variance shocks are persistent or permanent and the expected variance process $E(\hat{\sigma}_t^2)$ will tend to be unbounded.

An alternative version of the variance process model (51.3) is the second order process

$$\sigma_t^2 = \beta_1 \sigma_{t-1}^2 + \beta_2 \sigma_{t-2}^2 + \text{error} \qquad (5.14)$$

where we replace $E(e_{t-1}^2)$ by the term σ_{t-2}^2 yielding the characteristic equation

$$\lambda^2 - \beta_1 \lambda - \beta_2 = 0$$

with two roots, whose characteristics determine the oscillatory and stability properties of the temporal variance process. Both these specifications in (5.13) and (5.14) share two important limitations. One is that the expectations here are all *non anticipative*, so that the future state of the foreign exchange market is not allowed to have any impact. Secondly, the role of asymmetry which is only captured by the higher moments (e.g., good news, bad news effects are markedly different) is not recognized at all. To offer partial remedies to these limitations one may propose two modifications. One is to introduce a feed forward effect along with a feedback effect in the variance process as:

$$\sigma_t^2 = \alpha + \beta_1 \sigma_{t-1}^2 + \beta_2 \sigma_{t+1}^2 + u_t \tag{5.15}$$

and test if β_2 is negligible in comparison with β_1 or not. If it is negligible or statistically insignificant, then the feedforward effect is of little consequence to the temporal dynamics of the variance process. The relative bias in the estimate of β_2 is reduced by replacing the observed levels of σ_{t+1}^2 by an estimated series $\hat{\sigma}_{t+1}^2$ where $E(\hat{\sigma}_{t+1}^2) = \sigma_{t+1}^2$. A second modification is to introduce a logistic model for the variance process:

$$\sigma_t^2 / \sigma_{t-1}^2 = \alpha + \beta(1 - \sigma_{t-1}^2) + error \tag{5.16}$$

which yields the canonical form of the Lorenz model of chaos

$$\sigma_t^2 / \sigma_{t-1}^2 = \beta(1 - \sigma_{t-1}^2) + e_t \tag{5.17}$$

A second type of nonlinear model which has been frequently applied in econometric studies of the exchange rate dynamics involves tests of stationarity of the time series of real exchange rates. If y_t denotes the real exchange rate in logarithms, then the $\{y_t\}$ series is tested for the random walk hypothesis by running the regression equation

$$\Delta y_t = a - b\, y_{t-1} + \sum_{i=2}^{3} c_i \Delta y_{t-i} + u_t$$
$$b,\ c_i > 0 \tag{5.18}$$

and testing if the estimated coefficient b is significantly different from zero.

Sengupta and Sfeir (1997a,b) have applied this test for Group A countries over monthly time series data for two sample periods: Feb. 1988 to Jan. 1991 and Feb. 1991 to Aug. 1995. With US as the base country and using respective consumer price indexes the real exchange rate series for France (FR), Germany (GR), UK and Japan (JP) all exhibited nonstationarity, i.e., the existence of unit roots thus implying a random walk. Since the existence of unit roots or nonstationarity implies the absence of any mean reversion, it follows that nominal exchange rates and prices would then diverge from their equilibrium and this divergence may remain persistent in the long run as $t \to \infty$. Two types of nonlinearities may be introduced here so as to allow the rate of mean reversion to vary. One results from the interaction of two types of traders in the exchange market as formalized by Frankel and Froot (1986). The first group of traders comprises the fundamentalists who bet on a return to the perceived long run equilibrium (i.e., they are pro mean reversion and hence favor convergence). The second group is composed of the chartists who emphasize positive serial correlation in exchange rate movements with very little concern about the fundamentals (i.e., they are pro divergence and hence anti mean reversion). The interplay of these twin forces yields a nonlinear model

$$\Delta y_t = a - b(y_{t-1} - x_t)^3 + \sum_i c_i \Delta y_{t-i} + u_t \qquad (5.19)$$

where x_t is the equilibrium level in the short run which may be proxied by the last three months' moving average and the cubic regressor reflects asymmetry in the rate of mean reversion. This implies that if the influence of the fundamentalist traders is small close to equilibrium, then there may be local divergence due to the chartist traders but at greater distances from the equilibrium value, hysteresis is weaker and the mean reverting behavior dominates.

A second way to introduce nonlinearity is through the interaction of three types of currency traders in the foreign exchange market. Let us denote by $r_t = \Delta y_t$ as the change in exchange rates or return from holding the currency. To formulate an equation for the change of r_t we introduce three types of stylized market participants, e.g., the fundamentalists, the chartists, and the market specialist. As before the fundamentalist traders are 'information traders', the chartists are 'noise traders' and the market specialists mediate market transactions in order to maintain an orderly market. The equation for the rate of change of $r_t = \Delta y_t = y_t - y_{t-1}$ which captures the effects of the interplay of the three types of traders may take this form:

$$\Delta r_t = b_0 + b_1 r_{t-1} + b_2 (r_{t-1} - \bar{r}_{t-1})^3 + b_3 y_{t-1} + \varepsilon_t \qquad (5.20)$$

where $\bar{r}_t$ is the moving average of last three months. Here b_1 and b_3 are the negative feedback coefficients of the fundamentalists and the market specialists, whereas b_2 is the positive feedback of the chartist traders. Whereas negative feedbacks contribute to mean reversion of the market return the positive feedback moves the return process away from equilibrium. It is well known that positive feedbacks offer some of the major sources of chaotic dynamics in economic systems and Brock (1990) has discussed their empirical relevance in stock market dynamics.

5.2.2   Tests of nonlinear volatility

Statistical tests of volatility are difficult to devise for the empirical models due to two main reasons. One is the presence of nonlinearity of parameters where the method of nonlinear maximum likelihood cannot be applied in most cases in exact form. The method of scoring or modified gradient algorithms which are usually applied here must satisfy appropriate conditions of convergence and also detect the situation when the maximum achieved is local and not global. Secondly, the empirical data on exchange rates are in general low dimensional and hence chaotic dynamics which are present in high dimensional (say of dimension ten or more) chaos cannot be detected. High dimensional deterministic chaos is not distinguishable from randomness in practice. Here the very concept of randomness or stochastic variability is in question with the time-series data of real exchange rates. The Lorenz model of logistic curve for the conditional variance in equation (5.17) is not appropriate here for deterministic chaos, since the estimated series $\{\sigma_t^2\}$ is already mixed with noise. In this framework only calibration and Monte Carlo methods are permissible as tools for testing chaotic instability.

The nonlinear elements have been introduced in the ARCH formulation (5.13) by relaxing the restrictive assumption of a quadratic mapping between σ_t^2 and the past history of e_t. Thus Nelson (1991) assumes σ_t^2 to be an asymmetric function of the past data as follows:

$$\ln \sigma_t^2 = w + \sum_{j=1}^{p} \beta_j \ln \sigma_{t-j}^2$$

$$+ \sum_{k=1}^{q} \alpha_k \left[\theta \psi_{t-k} + \eta \left(| \psi_{t-1} | - (2/\pi)^{0.5} \right) \right] \qquad (5.21)$$

where $\psi_t = e_t / \sigma_t$ and this specification is called the exponential GARCH (p,q) model. In empirical estimation η may be set equal to unity. For stock market return data there is some weak evidence that σ_t^2 may indeed by an asymmetric function for past data and since the exchange rates generate returns for the currency traders, it is expected that this type of EGARCH (1,2) model may be more appropriate, see e.g. Kearns and Pagan (1990). We have already noted in (5.19) this asymmetric impact in our specification of the near-random walk model.

An alternative way to test the asymmetry hypothesis is to set up a conditional skewness model, just like the conditional variance model. If s_t is the conditional skewness, then the test of persistence of skewness is

$$s_t = a_0 + b_1 s_{t-1} + b_2 s_{t-2} \qquad (5.22)$$

The so-called phenomenon of skewness preference by the investors in a bullish market tends to disturb the normal mean variance relationships of exchange market returns. This phenomenon says that if the average global investor is optimistic about the future in the sense that tomorrow's returns are likely to be higher than today's, then this 'good news' effect tends to depress the conditional variance estimated from the past data in a backward looking sense. Thus the mean variance relationship is negatively correlated in a bullish market and vice versa in a bearish market.

The existence of chaotic dynamics has drawn considerable attention in current economic literature, e.g., sunspot equilibria, volatility in stock markets and long run temporal instability in several monetary indicators. Recently Brock (1990), Day and Chen (1993) and Wen (1996) have explored the theoretical and empirical basis of chaotic dynamics in economic theory and financial economics. Empirically Wen (1996) found strong empirical evidence of continuous-time chaos from the loglinear detrended Standard and Poor 500 series of 1952–83. He also found by calibration that the interplay of the three types of traders, the fundamentalists, the chartists and the market specialists may generate a similar series of a chaotic attractor.

Tests for some 'hidden structure' in the time series of $\{y_t\}$ of real exchange rates have recently attracted considerable attention in economic literature. How can one know if there is some function $f(\bullet)$ such that the difference equation

$$y_{t+1} = f(y_t, y_{t-1}, \ldots, y_{t-s})$$

generates the observed data set $\{y_t\}$? Chaos theory seeks to determine some notion of 'dimension' of $\{y_t\}$ and testing if it is small, e.g., s=2. One notion of dimension used with experimental data in chaos theory is the correlation dimension of Grassberger and Procaccia (1983), which uses the correlation function defined by

$$C(m, \varepsilon, t) = \#\{(t,s): \|y_{t,m} - y_{s,j}\| < \varepsilon\} / T^2$$

where $y_{t,m} = (y_t, \ldots, y_{t-m+1})$, $y_{s,m} = (y_s, \ldots, y_{s-m+1})$, and $\|y\|$ is the norm max $\{|y_i|, i=1,2,\ldots,m\}$ for any m dimensional vector y and $\#\{\bullet\}$ denotes the number of elements. The idea behind this test is quite simple. Given a data record of T observations, $\{y_t, t=1,2,\ldots,T\}$ we form all possible 'm-futures', $y_{t,m}$ and $y_{s,m}$ and then count the number of pairs of date (t,s) where they differ by less than ε. The measure C is the fraction of pairs of m-futures that differ in distance by less than ε. Brock, Dechert and Scheinkman (1986) have shown that if $\{y_t\}$ is purely random, then the expression

$$B(m, \varepsilon, T) = T^{0.5} \; [C(m, \varepsilon, T) - C(1, \varepsilon, T)^m]$$

converges to a normal distribution N(0,V) with mean zero and variance V = V(m,ε,T) as $T \to \infty$. It follows that the statistic

$$W(m, \varepsilon, T) = B(m, \varepsilon, T) / V^{0.5} \qquad (5.23)$$

converges to a unit normal N(0,1) distribution. This provides the basis of the so-called BDS statistic that is not difficult to use. Thus for the real exchange rates series $\{y_t\}$ we calculate the W-statistics (5.23) as above and if W is large in absolute value, we reject the hypothesis of randomness at the significance level read off from a standardized normal table. This test has been widely applied to financial time series data, where the test identified many models of deterministic chaos of low dimension as nonrandom. Following this procedure one could use the estimated residuals form an autoregressive equation AR(5) of order 5 or more of the real exchange rate process and compute the conditional variances $\hat{\sigma}_t^2$ used in the logistic map (5.17). However this method has two difficulties. One is that the data set required should be quite large and secondly, the structure of volatility may change from one phase to another.

5.2.3   International aspects of volatility

Under the current trend of liberalization of world trade and globalization of financial market, two aspects of the international transmission of volatility appear to be important in a policy framework. One is the difference in patterns of volatility between the industrial and developing countries. For countries growing at a faster rate from a low level, the relative prices of tradables may change substantially thus inducing nonstationarity in real exchange rate dynamics. Thus the developing countries are expected to have a higher unit-root rejection rate than industrial countries. Secondly, the Lorenz-type chaotic dynamics in exchange rate fluctuations may be more prevalent in the industrial countries due to two reasons, e.g., more openness of their economies and the stronger role of future expectations than the past trends in the investors' behavior. By comparing the behavior pattern of the three groups of countries, the industrial and the developing economies of Asia and Latin America one could thus test if volatility clustering is dependent on country-specific growth and price differentials.

Empirical patterns of real exchange rate fluctuations at an international level are presented in Tables 5.4 through 5.13. The countries and sample periods are selected by considerations of data availability and structural changes in policy regimes.   The empirical monthly data are from International Financial Statistics published by IMF and the US dollar is used as the base country in terms of which the other currencies re expressed. The real exchange rate (RX_t) is calculated as SP*/P, where S is the exchange rate of the domestic country per unit of foreign currency, P* is the consumer price index of the foreign country and P is the consumer price index of the domestic country. For example the real exchange rate of Japan = Yens per dollar times the ratio of US price index to the price index in Japan.

One may note several broad results from the cross-country Tables 5.4 through 5.13. First of all, stationarity in the real exchange rate process is rejected uniformly and with more intensity for Asia and Latin America. The conditional variance series analyzed by the ARCH and GARCH models also exhibits nonstationarity. This implies that the variance series has a finite probability of an explosive behavior. The estimates of the characteristic roots from the second order variance equation show in many cases the existence of oscillatory behavior. These two results tend to support earlier studies of the Asian Pacific region by Verbiest (1989) and Cheung and Lai (1977), who found in their cross-country results that the developing countries tend to have a higher rather than lower unit root rejection rate than industrial countries. Thirdly, the role of speculative traders is clearly evidenced in the impact of future expected variance (σ^2_{t+1}) on the current variance (σ^2_t) as reported in Tables 5.5 and 5.10. For the industrial economies the results are very similar, e.g.,

	Intercept	$\hat{\sigma}^2_{t-1}$	$\hat{\sigma}^2_{t+1}$	$\overline{R}^2$
		Sample V (Jan. 1980 to Dec. 1985)		
FR	−0.004	0.503**	0.554**	0.91
JP	0.409	0.307**	0.651**	0.78
UK	−0.0002	0.588*	0.595**	0.83
GR	0.0	0.505**	0.538**	0.91

For some countries like Japan and UK the impact of future variance has been markedly higher than the past. Thus future expectations and variances rather than past trends and the so-called asymmetry effects (e.g., good news, bad news effects) are likely to play a dominant role in the exchange markets in the future. This suggests very strongly that the nonlinear aspects of exchange rate dynamics require a more thorough analysis. Finally, the Lorenz models of volatility estimated in Tables 5.8, 5.12 and 5.13 exhibit two characteristics very clearly. The critical parameter β which generates a chaotic behavior when it exceeds 3.46 is well above 4.5 for two Asian countries (MA and SI and also TH for Sample II) and these are statistically significant at 5% level. For Latin American countries the chaotic instability is almost nonexistent. For Mexico the parameter β is in the chaotic range but statistically insignificant. Secondly, the industrial countries exhibit far more strongly the prevalence of chaotic instability, e.g., the cases of France, UK and GR. Indirectly this may reflect the stronger role of speculative investors in these markets, when the tendencies for global finance and more liberal monetary policies are becoming more persistent. Short of a currency union at an international level there appears to be a clear need for reducing the scope of Lorenz type chaos in the exchange markets of the industrial world today. There is clearly some justification for a Tobin-type tax in this framework. However, this type of tax measure to be really effective has to counteract the impact of expected future variance by following the sliding mode technique of variable structure control laws as discussed recently by Yu (1996). The transformed Lorenz model would then appear as

$$\sigma_t^2 / \sigma_{t-1}^2 = \alpha + \beta(u)[1 - \sigma_{t-1}^2]$$

where $\quad u = \begin{cases} u^+, \text{for } s > 0 \\ u^-, \text{for } s < 0 \end{cases}$

is the control law and s specifies the sliding mode.

Table 5.4 Impact of Interest Rate Inflation

	$\hat{\alpha}$	$\hat{\beta}_1$	$\hat{\beta}_2$	$\hat{\beta}_3$	$\overline{R}^2$	n
Sample I						
JP	−0.0089	−0.0007	0.0163	−0.0044	−0.002	34
	(−0.21)	(−0.1)	(1.58)	(−0.36)		
UK	−0.0343	0.0044	0.0306	0.0332**	0.28	34
	(−1.02)	(0.77)	(−1.29)	(3.07)		
GR	−0.059	0.0132	0.0211	0.0448*	0.14	34
	(−2.03)	(1.48)	(1.07)	(2.55)		
Sample II						
JP	0.0172	−0.0049	0.0312*	0.0224	0.15	34
	(0.58)	(−0.69)	(2.13)	(1.39)		
UK	0.0076	−0.0043	0.0271	0.0205*	0.09	34
	(0.26)	(−0.79)	(1.27)	(2.12)		
GR	0.0115	−0.0061	0.0452	0.0246	0.16	34
	(0.65)	(−1.59)	(1.79)	(1.58)		
Sample III						
JP	−0.0001	0.0013	0.0493**	0.0111	0.18	53
	(−0.01)	(0.39)	(3.75)	(1.21)		
UK	0.0035	−0.0004	0.0047	−0.0234*	0.03	53
	(0.18)	(−0.09)	(0.29)	(−2.04)		
GR	−0.0138	0.0047	−0.0421*	−0.0058	0.05	53
	(−1.1)	(1.27)	(−2.08)	(−0.45)		

Notes: 1. t-statistics in parentheses
2. *: significant at the 5% level
3. **: significant at the 1% level
4. Due to insufficient data France is excluded

Table 5.5 Real Exchange Rate Fluctuations in Asia

$$RX_t = \alpha + \beta_1 RX_{t-1} + \beta_2 RX_{t-2} + \beta_3 RX_{t-3}$$

	$\hat{\alpha}$	$\hat{\beta}_1$	$\hat{\beta}_2$	$\hat{\beta}_3$	$\overline{R}^2$	n
Sample I (Jan. 1980–Dec. 1985)						
IN	25.77	1.006**	−0.04	0.02	0.95	69
	(0.68)	(8.31)	(−0.26)	(0.21)		
KO	−11.42	1.098**	−0.22	0.142	0.94	
	(−0.92)	(9.08)	(−1.26)	(1.19)		
MA	0.14	1.124**	−0.24	0.06	0.92	69
	(1.55)	(9.31)	(−1.31)	(0.53)		
SI	0.15	0.906**	0.20	−0.17	0.90	69
	(1.64)	(7.58)	(1.26)	(−1.43)		
TH	0.57	0.980**	0.09	−0.08	0.94	69
	(0.62)	(8.03)	(0.51)	(−0.65)		
Sample II (Feb. 1991–Aug. 1995)						
IN	46.35	1.240**	−0.32	0.06	0.96	55
	(0.72)	(8.86)	(−1.45)	(0.40)		
KO	31.23	1.339**	−0.25	−0.12	0.95	55
	(0.96)	(9.26)	(−1.04)	(−0.80)		
MA	0.17	1.074**	0.04	−0.17	0.92	55
	(1.33)	(7.73)	(0.20)	(−1.19)		
SI	0.02	1.036**	−0.14	0.10	0.96	55
	(0.25)	(7.19)	(−0.71)	(0.67)		
TH	0.17	1.246**	−0.49*	0.24	0.94	55
	(0.14)	(0.07)	(−2.33)	(1.67)		

Notes: 1. t-statistics in parentheses
2. *: significant at the 5% level
3. **: significant at the 1% level
4. $\overline{R}^2$ is multiple correlation squared adjusted or degrees of freedom

Table 5.6 Variance Process Model for Asia

$$\sigma_t^2 = \alpha + \beta_1 \sigma_{t-1}^2 + \beta_2 \sigma_{t+1}^2$$

	$\hat{\alpha}$	$\hat{\beta}_1$	$\hat{\beta}_2$	$\overline{R}^2$	n
Sample I (Jan. 1980–Dec. 1985)					
IN	−338.3	0.548**	0.548**	0.93	65
	(−0.88)	(14.26)	(14.26)		
KO	−25.8*	0.552**	0.566**	0.93	65
	(−2.54)	(14.12)	(14.51)		
MA	0.0	0.539**	0.544**	0.89	65
	(−1.44)	(11.36)	(11.51)		
SI	0.0	0.547**	0.542**	0.89	65
	(−1.41)	(11.07)	(11.20)		
TH	−0.01	0.548**	0.548**	0.93	65
	(−0.99)	(13.59)	(13.59)		
Sample II (Feb. 1991–Aug. 1995)					
IN	−45.2	0.562**	0.577**	0.94	48
	(−1.60)	(13.99)	(14.33)		
KO	−8.78**	0.633**	0.513**	0.96	48
	(−2.36)	(18.76)	(15.73)		
MA	0.0	0.545**	0.546**	0.92	48
	(−1.37)	(11.00)	(10.90)		
SI	0.0	0.542**	0.536**	0.90	48
	(−1.24)	(9.89)	(9.78)		
TH	−0.01	0.576*	0.558*	0.78	48
	(−1.18)	(8.06)	(7.66)		

Table 5.7 Arch Model for Variance in Asia

$$\hat{\sigma}_t^2 = \alpha + \beta_1\hat{\sigma}_{t-1}^2 + \beta_2\hat{e}_{t-1}^2$$

e_t : residual from $RX_t = \alpha + \beta_2 RX_{t-1} + \beta_2 RX_{t-2} + \beta_3 RX_{t-3} + \varepsilon_t$

$\hat{\sigma}_t^2$: 6 months' moving average variance of e_t

	$\hat{\alpha}$	$\hat{\beta}_1$	$\hat{\beta}_2$	$\overline{R}^2$	n
Sample I					
IN	−27.1	0.833**	0.180**	0.85	62
	(−0.06)	(17.23)	(0.02)		
KO	−1.85	0.791**	0.218**	0.80	62
	(−0.29)	(13.91)	(8.02)		
MA	0.0	0.776**	0.111*	0.67	62
		(11.36)	(2.88)		
SI	0.0	0.865**	0.164**	0.86	62
		(17.85)	(6.93)		
TH	0.0	0.831**	0.168**	0.83	62
		(16.18)	(8.40)		
Sample II					
IN	−8.7	0.805**	0.235**	0.91	48
	(−0.75)	(19.86)	(8.40)		
KO	−2.6	0.996*	0.132**	0.92	48
	(−1.41)	(22.19)	(11.34)		
MA	0.0	0.793**	0.221**	0.87	48
		(14.87)	(8.08)		
SI	0.0	0.583**	0.113	0.54	48
		(7.32)	(1.41)		
TH	0.0	0.660**	0.216**	0.66	48
		(8.19)	(5.58)		

Table 5.8 Logistic Model for Variance in Asia

$$\sigma_t^2 / \sigma_{t-1}^2 = \alpha + \beta(1 - \sigma_{t-1}^2)$$

	$\hat{\alpha}$	$\hat{\beta}$	$\overline{R}^2$	n
Sample I				
IN	2.43*	0.0	0.0	66
	(2.18)	(0.38)		
KO	1.34**	0.001*	0.06	66
	(10.59)	(2.13)		
MA	−136.7*	138.21*	0.05	66
	(−2.07)	(2.09)		
SI	−123.5*	124.90*	0.07	66
	(−2.36)	(2.39)		
TH	2.94	0.37	0.0	66
	(1.93)	(0.51)		
Sample II				
IN	1.32**	.0.0	0.01	49
	(9.47)	(1.18)		
KO	1.49**	0.002	0.015	49
	(6.66)	(1.32)		
MA	−151.6	153.91	0.02	49
	(−1.44)	(1.46)		
SI	−282.9*	284.27*	0.07	49
	(−2.16)	(2.16)		
TH	−3.01	4.651*	0.09	49
	(−1.73)	(2.43)		

Table 5.9 Real Exchange Rate Fluctuations in Latin America

$$RX_t = \alpha + \beta_1 RX_{t-1} + \beta_2 RX_{t-2} + \beta_3 RX_{t-3}$$

	$\hat{\alpha}$	$\hat{\beta}_1$	$\hat{\beta}_2$	$\hat{\beta}_3$	$\overline{R}^2$	n
Sample I (Jan. 1980–Dec 1985)						
BR	0.71	1.127**	−0.254	0.12	0.98	69
	(0.67)	(9.08)	(−1.38)	(0.95)		
CH	−0.04	0.767**	0.262	−0.01	0.97	69
	(−0.005)	(6.21)	(−0.11)	(−0.11)		
CO	−16.10**	1.493**	0.658**	0.21	0.99	69
	(−3.77)	(12.30)	(−3.19)	(1.67)		
ME	0.36	0.738**	0.168	0.0	0.76	69
	(1.58)	(5.94)	(1.10)			
Sample II (Feb. 1991–Aug. 1995)						
BR	0.0	0.670**	0.244	0.036	0.81	52
		(4.65)	(1.43)	(0.25)		
CH	0.31	1.133**	-0.316	0.178	0.93	52
	(0.02)	(8.18)	(−1.55)	(1.22)		
CO	7.08	1.229**	−0.126	−0.118	0.98	52
	(0.51)	(8.08)	(−0.53)	(−0.75)		
ME	0.38	0.848**	0.119	−0.080	0.75	52
	(1.50)	(5.88)	(0.63)	(−0.54)		

Table 5.10 Variance Process Model for Latin America

$$\hat{\sigma}_t^2 = \alpha + \beta_1 \hat{\sigma}_{t-1}^2 + \beta_2 \hat{\sigma}_{t+1}^2$$

	$\hat{\alpha}$	$\hat{\beta}_1$	$\hat{\beta}_2$	$\overline{R}^2$	n
Sample I					
BR	−0.47	0.544**	0.545**	0.92	65
	(−0.96)	(12.86)	(12.83)		
CH	−18.19	0.543**	0.532**	0.91	65
	(−0.88)	(12.06)	(11.80)		
CO	−4.18*	0.679**	0.424**	0.99	65
	(−2.34)	(26.39)	(21.06)		
ME	−0.01	0.542**	0.540**	0.92	65
	(−0.95)	(12.36)	(12.30)		
Sample II					
BR	0.0	0.513**	0.531**	0.92	48
		(9.03)	(8.52)		
CH	−9.34	0.621**	0.558**	0.87	48
	(−1.94)	(10.55)	(10.17)		
CO	−33.71	0.551**	0.551**	0.94	48
	(−1.22)	(13.09)	(13.07)		
ME	−0.01	0.537**	0.536**	0.94	48
	(−0.71)	(11.37)	(11.40)		

Table 5.11 Arch Model for Variance in Latin America

$$\hat{\sigma}_t^2 = \alpha + \beta_1 \hat{\sigma}_{t-1}^2 + \beta_2 \hat{e}_{t-1}^2$$

		Sample I			
	$\hat{\alpha}$	$\hat{\beta}_1$	$\hat{\beta}_2$	$\overline{R}^2$	n
BR	−0.03	0.847**	0.166**	0.85	62
	(−0.06)	(17.31)	(8.28)		
CH	5.97	0.851**	0.140**	0.87	62
	(0.36)	(18.45)	(7.22)		
CO	0.21	0.758**	0.205**	0.84	62
	(0.32)	(15.03)	(8.73)		
ME	0.0	0.841**	0.203**	0.86	62
		(17.47)	(9.79)		
		Sample II			
BR	0.0	0.765**	0.230**	0.93	45
		(21.24)	(4.32)		
CH	−0.63	0.827**	0.194**	0.83	45
	(−0.17)	(13.28)	(6.80)		
CO	1.97	0.844**	0.154**	0.83	45
	(0.09)	(13.47)	(5.82)		
ME	0.0	0.823**	0.197**	0.90	45
		(17.24)	(8.93)		

Table 5.12 Logistic Model for Variance in Latin America

$$\sigma_t^2 / \sigma_{t-1}^2 = \alpha + \beta(1 - \sigma_{t-1}^2)$$

	$\hat{\alpha}$	$\hat{\beta}_1$	$\overline{R}^2$	n
	Sample I			
BR	1.76**	0.023	−0.005	66
	(4.79)	(0.82)		
CH	1.99**	0.001	−0.007	66
	(2.88)	(0.74)		
CO	1.28**	0.0	−0.007	66
	(11.57)			
ME	−5.01	12.893	−0.006	66
	(−0.33)	(0.78)		
	Sample II			
BR	3.89	−2.100	−0.02	49
	(0.88)	(−0.42)		
CH	1.83**	0.007	0.02	49
	(4.60)	(1.46)		
CO	2.29**	0.0	−0.01	49
	(2.79)			
ME	-61.33	191.94	−0.02	49
	(−0.13)	(0.38)		

Table 5.13 Lorenz Logistic Model for Variance for Industrial Countries

$$\sigma_t^2 / \sigma_{t-1}^2 = \alpha + \beta(1 - \sigma_{t-1}^2)$$

	Sample	$\hat{\alpha}$	$\hat{\beta}_1$	$\overline{R}^2$	n
FR	I	−1.74	3.30	0.04	30
		(−0.84)	(1.44)		
	II	−20.1	22.4	0.07	30
		(−1.69)	(1.81)		
	III	−5.96	7.36*	0.12	49
		(−2.16)	(2.56)		
JP	I	1.303**	0.002	0.02	30
		(7.21)	(1.21)		
	II	1.46**	0.01	0.11	30
		(8.04)	(2.11)		
	III	1.69**	0.017	0.14	48
		(5.42)	(1.51)		
UK	I	−261.6	262.9	0.07	30
		(−1.77)	(1.77)		
	II	−383.5	384.7	0.01	20
		(−1.13)	(1.13)		
	III	−164.7	166.0	-0.01	49
		(−0.76)	(0.77)		
GR	I	−27.1	28.7	0.07	30
		(−1.71)	(1.79)		
	II	−205.3	207.8	0.05	30
		(−1.58)	(1.59)		
	III	−63.3**	64.8**	0.08	48
		(−2.79)	(2.84)		

Sample I: Feb. 1985 through Jan. 1988
Sample II: Feb. 1988 through Jan. 1991
Sample III: Feb. 1991 through Aug. 1995

5.3 TESTS OF NONLINEARITY IN EXCHANGE MARKETS

Two types of specific forms of nonlinearity are empirically analyzed in this section. One is a test of the near-random walk hypothesis. The other is a test for the existence of positive feedback loops in the returns from investment in currency stocks. The linear random walk model, which implies mean reversion assumes that the rate of reversion of the real exchange rate to its mean level is constant. This is specified by the parameter b in the augmented Dickey–Fuller regression equation (5.18). Since b is assumed to e constant by assumption, the rate of mean reversion is the same irrespective of how far the real exchange rate has deviated from the mean level. By contrast the near random–walk model assumes that rate of mean reversion to vary, e.g., in the stable case it is assumed to increase as the real exchange rate gets further away from the mean. This yields the cubic model (5.19) discussed before in terms of the chartists' behavior. This model predicts near-random walk behavior when y_t is close to x_t in (5.19), with increasing mean reversion as one moves away from the equilibrium level x_t. Increasing adjustment cost may provide another argument for this asymmetric behavior. Table 5.14 presents the test results for near random walk hypothesis for one common period (January 1980 through December 1985) for Asia, Latin America and Europe. It is clear that the cubic regressor is highly significant at 1% level of t-test in all the cases; even the first order autocorrelation coefficient $\hat{\beta}_1$ turns out to be either negligible or insignificant in most cases. The very high value of the $|\hat{\beta}_2|$ coefficient with $\hat{\beta}_2 < 0$ suggests a strong degree of mean reversion, also a high degree of asymmetry. Thus when $y_{t-1} > \bar{y}_t$ for a subperiod, y_t tends to revert to its mean; whereas for $y_{t-1} < \bar{y}_t$ it tends to increase to its mean level. Thus there occurs greater hysteresis near the equilibrium level. Thus the influence of the fundamentalist traders is very small when the exchange rate is close to equilibrium but at greater distance from the equilibrium, hysteresis is weaker and the mean reverting behavior dominates. It is quite remarkable here that in presence of the cubic regressor the first order autocorrelation coefficient $\hat{\beta}_1$ turns out to be rather negligible and insignificant, although in Table 5.5 and 5.9 it is close to one or higher in many cases and highly significant in a statistical sense. Although not presented here this hypothesis of near-random walk behavior holds uniformly for the other periods for the countries considered here.

The second aspect of nonlinearity involves the existence of positive feedback loops in the return process model (5.14) mentioned before. Wen

(1996) calibrated this model in the continuous time domain and found the persistence of chaotic behavior. Even in linear forms this specification yields on estimation unstable feedback loops for the countries in Latin America (Table 5.14).

Table 5.14 Test of Near-Random Walk by a Cubic Regressor

$$\Delta y_t = \alpha + \beta_1 y_{t-1} + \beta_2 (y_{t-1} - \bar{y}_t)^3$$
$$y_t = \ln RX_t$$

Asia: Sample I (Jan. 80–Dec. 85)

	$\hat{\alpha}$	$\hat{\beta}_1$	$\hat{\beta}_2$	$\bar{R}^2$
IN	−0.045	0.007	−145.53**	0.41
KO	0.165	−0.023	−378.08**	0.47
MA	0.025	−0.023	−4306.33**	0.19
SI	0.021	−0.022	−2511.09**	0.33
TH	−0.035	0.011	−5.18.95**	0.38

Latin America: Sample I (Jan. 80–Dec. 85)

	$\hat{\alpha}$	$\hat{\beta}_1$	$\hat{\beta}_2$	$\bar{R}^2$
BR	−0.097	−0.015	−22.75**	0.30
CH	0.006	−0.002	−3066.71**	0.22
CO	−0.032	0.004	−659.38**	0.14
ME	−0.040	0.037	−-00.05**	0.54

Europe and Japan: Sample V (Jan. 80–Dec. 85)

	$\hat{\alpha}$	$\hat{\beta}_1$	$\hat{\beta}_2$	$\bar{R}^2$
FR	0.092*	−0.038*	−1005.27**	0.36
JP	0.082	−0.015	−1482.18**	0.32
UK	0.005	−0.014	−852.49**	0.37
GR	0.066**	−0.056**	−725.85**	0.31

* Significant at 5% level of t-test
**Significant at 1% level of t-test

Table 5.15 Estimates of Feedback Loops

Latin America
Sample I (Jan. 1980–Dec. 1985)

	$\hat{b}_0$	$\hat{b}_1$	$\hat{b}_2$	$\bar{R}^2$	n
BR	0.073	0.0954**	−0.020	0.45	70
CH	0.180	1.1201**	−0.034	0.56	70
CO	0.213	0.6554**	−0.037**	0.33	70
ME	0.126	1.1742**	−0.106	0.62	70

Sample II (Feb. 1991–Aug. 1995

BR	−0.513	1.2102**	−0.094	0.63	53
CH	0.434*	0.8433**	−0.073*	0.46	53
CO	0.229	0.8134**	−0.035	0.46	53
ME	0.143	1.0148**	−0.124	0.55	53

With the cubic regressor the results are made stronger. Thus there exist periods in the international cross-section data when the chaotic force persists and this has a finite probability of transmission across national borders.

The policy implications of the presence of these nonlinearities are several. First of all, in the chaos theory it is well known that forecasting in the long run is of very little value, since the steady state may not exist. Secondly, the cycles generated by chaotic dynamics are not very easy to test by the existing methods of parametric statistical estimation. Finally, there is some merit in the recent proposals by Tobin (1994) and others to institute a global tax in order to curb the so called speculative motive which may be prevalent in the chartist traders' behavior. Problems of course arise as to the actual implementation of this tax mechanism. Short of the existence of a global customs union, there may arise serious problems of coordination due to heterogeneous expectations about the future developments in the international monetary affairs.

International finance and global trade have reached a new phase in recent times, where the fundamental forces such as price and interest rate differentials are playing much less important roles in the dynamic behavior of the international foreign exchange markets. The speculative forces, the chartist traders and global investors involved with large capital inflows and outflows are playing more dominant roles. Lack of coordination of national monetary policies and divergent future expectations of the evolution of the world economy are also contributing to the instability of the international foreign exchange markets today.

5.4   EXCHANGE RATE IMBALANCE AND GROWTH

The recent increase in fluctuations in the foreign exchange market has raised great concern in the developing countries all over the world and in particular the NICs in Asia. Three major implications of these fluctuations are of great importance in this framework. One is the so-called 'emerging stock markets' in the developing countries which have provided the major attraction of foreign capital inflows in these countries. This has sometimes induced a boom in asset prices and domestic consumption thereby reducing the volume of domestic savings and creating the saving investment imbalance. Such imbalances may tend to affect growth rate adversely. Secondly, the speculative movement of interantional capital tend to foster the extent of volatility in the currency market, pushing up the marginal cost of hot money and thus discouraging real investment for growth. Finally, the imbalance in balance of payments tends to have an adverse effect on the growth of real output. Recently Edwards (1997) performed an international cross-section regression study based on 1980 averages, where the productivity growth measured by TFP growth (Δy) was regressed on the following three variables x_1 = GDP 1965, x_2 = human capital 1965 and x_3 = the average value of the black market premium in the foreign exchange market during the 1980s. The results are as follows:

$$\Delta y = a_0 - \underset{(-2.32)}{0.008} \; x_1 + \underset{(2.23)}{0.003} x_2 - \underset{(-1.95)}{0.019} \; x_3$$
$$n=71, \; R^2 = 0.27$$

$$\Delta y = a_0 - \underset{(-2.07)}{0.014} \; x_1 + \underset{(1.97)}{0.003} x_2 - \underset{(-2.95)}{0.106} \; x_4$$
$$n=64; \; R^2 = 0.10$$

where x_4 represents an average import tariff and n is the number of countries included in the sample. Clearly the higher the imbalance in the foreign exchange market as represented by variables x_3 and x_4, the lower the productivity growth of the economy. The t-values in parentheses also confirm the finding that other things being given, more open countries will tend to experience faster productivity growth than more protectionist countries which set up import tariffs and trade barriers.

6. Growth and Development Policy

From a policy maker's standpoint economic growth may be viewed in two perspectives, a short to medium term perspective of about 5 to 8 years and the long run perspective of one to two decades or so. The latter is usually called structural and the empirical studies of total factor productivity (TFP) growth or the Solow residual usually treat technological progress as the prime mover of long run growth. Unlike Solow's model the new growth theory treats technological progress as endogenous rather than exogenous. This transformation has implications for deliberate policymaking, which are striking and catalytic. For one thing, the technological advance and the associated process of research and learning may be deliberately pursued as a growth objective and if openness in trade helps this process the policy makers may attempt to pursue a policy of outward oriented exports in the technology-intensive products. Secondly, the human capital element of technological innovation may be accumulated by investment in the educational sectors such as schools, colleges and technical institutions and the public sector may play a catalytic role along with the private sector in raising the educational standards and skill levels of the working population currently and in the future. With an aggregate production function

$$Y_t = A_t K_t^{\alpha}(H_t L_t)^{\beta}, \text{ where } H_t = E_t^{\delta} \qquad (6.1)$$

with real output (Y) and two traditional input measures, physical capital (K) and labor (L) we obtain by adding H_t as the level of human capital proxied by E_t as a measure of the education level:

$$\dot{Y}_t / Y_t = \alpha(\dot{K}_t / K_t) + \beta\left[(\dot{L}_t / L_t) + \delta\frac{\dot{E}_t}{E_t}\right] + \dot{A}_t / A_t \qquad (6.2)$$

where dot denotes the time derivative. Clearly this model can generate sustained and perpetual growth of output even when there is constant returns to scale in both physical and human capital stocks, i.e., $\alpha + \beta = 1$, since the positive impact (δ) of the growth of educational standards generates overall increasing returns to scale. Finally, if we do not distinguish

153

between human capital and technological know-how, then the spillover of knowledge from abroad can enter into the production function (6.1) above and generate increasing returns and hence unbounded growth. Thus one can replace the term H_t above in (6.1) by s_t which stands for workers' knowledge capital in a country, which evolves in relation to the world knowledge capital S_t as follows

$$\dot{s}_t = \delta (S_t / s_t)^\alpha u$$

where u is the fraction of time spent in learning foreign technology. Parente and Prescott (1994) used this type of formulation to highlight the importance of knowledge spillover across countries as an important component of external economies through international trade. Eaton and Kortum (1995) have provided some estimates of knowledge spillover, where the interdependence is very significant. For example their estimates show that the fraction of productivity growth in Japan due to research performed in US is about 9 percent, whereas Japan's research activity contributes 19 percent of the productivity growth in US. To a large extent this has been fostered by US–Japan technological alliances in such industries as semiconductors and telecommunications.

The short and medium term growth problems are essentially problems of adjustment and disequilibrium. In a policy framework these may be viewed in two different ways. One is to assume that the short run adjustment behavior of the producers seeks to minimize the expected loss due to the deviations of actual output form the optimal trajectory in the long run. Assuming a quadratic adjustment cost function in an intertemporal framework, this yields an optimal decision rule in a linear form, which can be estimated and updated over time. This framework of planned adjustment of various input and output demands to their long term equilibrium or optimal values facilitates the application of simple decision rules over time. The second approach is to view the divergence between the short and the long run paths as a disequilibrium behavior and then analyze the role of various policy interventions and their impact on the disequilibrium behavior. Thus the analysis of the multi market models of disequilibrium may involve various types of buffer fund and/or price support programs. The savings investment imbalance and the balance of payments disequilibrium may involve various types of monetary and fiscal policies and also exchange rate policies. In a multi-sector framework this leads to the general model structure known as CGE (computable general equilibrium) models, which combine a generalized form of Leontief-type input–output model with econometrically estimated demand functions in order to simulate the impact of alternative policy measures. Various World Bank studies have adopted this framework for quantitative policymaking in developing economies.

The object of this chapter is to discuss this policy framework in its short and long run contexts. Clearly the long run framework is closely related to the endogenous growth theory, though the short run framework has important repercussions on the long run trajectory.

6.1   DYNAMICS OF ADJUSTMENT POLICIES

One practical way to study the dynamics of the adjustment process due to macroeconomic policymaking is to compare the experiences of the successful countries with those not so successful. For example the East Asian high performers like Korea, Singapore and Taiwan provide a contrast to Brazil and Mexico, the two large Latin American economies where the growth performance in the last two decades has not been so rapid. Recently Dahlman and Nelson (1995) have done a comparative study of fourteen countries and their national innovation systems and found some common characteristics of the technological leaders who experienced fairly rapid growth episodes. They identified four key areas as critical elements for a successful technology policy which is conducive to world competition. These are: (a) acquiring foreign technology efficiently, (b) diffusing modern technology across the domestic sectors in an efficient manner, (c) improving, developing and integrating the acquired technology and (d) developing an adequate base of human and knowledge capital.

The following Table 6.1 reproduced form their estimates provides an interesting framework for comparison.

Several features stand out in these comparative measures of economic performance. First of all, the openness in trade measured by the export–GDP ratio and the import of capital goods ratio to gross domestic investment is strikingly higher for the successful NICs compared to the less successful ones like Brazil, Mexico and India which focussed on inwardly oriented policy regimes. Secondly, the successful NICs had much lower inflation rates than the less successful ones. Thus the impact of macroeconomic instability on the growth performance is very significant. Since this instability can also be generated by the imbalance in the external trade, it is useful to look at the empirical perspective of the influence of other macroeconomic factors on the overall growth performance. Recently

155

Table 6.1   Indicators of Economic Performance of Selected Developing Countries

	SI	KO	HK	TI	BR	ME	IN
1. GDP per capital (average growth rate 1965–88)							
	7.2	6.8	6.3	6.5	3.6	2.3	1.8
2. Average inflation rate (1965–88)							
	4.0	12.0	7.1	6.6	99.8	34.7	8.2
3. Exports as % of GDP (1970–88)							
	158.0	31.0	94.9	44.5	8.5	11.2	5.8
4. Potential scientists and engineers as % of total population							
	1.58	0.24	2.62	-	1.12	-	0.3
5. Secondary level education enrollment ratio (1988)							
	71	88	74	90	39	53	39
6. Ratio of R&D to GNP							
	0.9	2.12	-	1.16	0.4	0.6	0.9
	(1987)	(1989)		(1987)	(1985)	(1984)	(1986)
7. Ratio of private to public R&D							
	61/39	80/20	-	48/50	33/67	-	12/88
8. Import of capital goods as % of GDI							
	86.9	27.9	47.0	37.0	9.0	13.4	5.3
9. Average annual population growth							
1965–80	1.6	2.0	2.0	2.3	2.4	3.1	2.3
1980–88	1.1	1.2	1.5	1.4	2.2	2.2	2.2

Source: Dahlman and Nelson (1995)

Fischer (1993) computed the regression of growth rate of real GDP (Δy) on several macroeconomic variables such as inflation rate (x_1), ratio of budget surplus to GDP (x_2), change in terms of trade (x_3) and the black market exchange rate premium (x_4) for 22 countries over two sets of data. One is the cross-sectional data where the average growth rate for the period 1961–88 is considered for each country, whereas the second data set is used for panel regression, where both the time series variation within each country and the cross-sectional variations are utilized. The estimates are as follows with t-statistics in parenthesis

	x_1	x_2	x_3	x_4	no. of observations
cross-section	−0.026	0.277	−0.040	−0.041	22
data	(−1.34)	(3.36)	(−0.20)	(−3.32)	
panel data	−0.039	0.228	0.043	−0.017	351
	(−4.65)	(4.49)	(2.71)	(−2.76)	

These results support the conclusion that high inflation, large budget deficits and exchange market distortions tend to be associated with a lower growth rate on the average. Although these correlations between inflation and exchange market distortions with the growth rate do not imply any causality, they provide significant suggestive evidence that very high inflation rates and large distortions in the foreign exchange market are not consistent with long term sustained growth of real GDP. This provides a rationale for pursuing optimal monetary and exchange rate policies for countries interested in pursuing goals of sustained economic growth.

Finally, the comparative analysis of recent technological developments of 14 developing countries by Dahlman and Nelson (1995) also found a strong positive correlation of the level of educational attainment and the intensity of R&D expenditures with the national growth rates. Two aspects of the trend in R&D expenditure are important for the Asian NICs with a highly successful growth rates over the last two decades. One is the increasing tendency of the private sector to undertake R&D investment. The second is the learning process through which the firms keep up with the advances in technology made in US and other countries. The first tendency works through the profit incentives so as to emphasize the commercial applicability of the R&D expenditures. Hence the economies of scale and economies of scope due to appropriate changes in output-mix are viewed by private entrepreneurs as long term factors which may contribute to a high rate of sustained growth. The second tendency facilitates the process of technology transfer, where modern technology borrowed from the US are learned, developed, improved and then diffused by countries such as Japan and Korea. Thus the inward-oriented policies in India and Brazil have generated the highest shares of R&D expenditures by government, whereas the private sector industries play a dominant role in Japan and Korea. Recently Duysters (1996) has studied the empirical database until 1989 of three industrial sectors such as computers, telecommunications and semiconductor industry, all engaged in the information technology developments. His object is to study the scope of strategic alliances by multinational companies and the extent of internationalization. The following table (Table 6.2) clearly shows a strong tendency of internationalization in technological alliances in the computer and semiconductor industries.

Table 6.2 Distribution of Strategic Technology Alliances Between and Within Economic Blocs (Percentages)

	Total		Computers		Semiconductor		Telecom	
	78–85	86–93	78–85	86–93	78–85	86–93	78–85	86–93
US–EU	21.2	18.0	24.2	16.1	20.7	16.4	20.5	22.6
US–JP	21.5	13.5	21.9	19.7	32.9	30.5	14.6	5.2
JP–EU	3.5	3.2	7.0	4.0	3.2	6.1	2.6	3.0
EU–EU	21.0	14.9	14.8	7.2	13.1	13.8	26.5	22.6
US–US	27.3	42.4	25.8	45.8	25.7	19.3	28.5	35.1
JP–JP	5.5	7.9	6.3	7.2	4.5	13.8	7.3	11.7
Total	100	100	100	100	100	100	100	100

Source: Duysters (1996).

However the intensity of such technological alliances across the international frontier may tend to increase in recent years in the R&D areas also, since strategic R&D partnering policies may help reduce substantial transaction costs. Also by integrating previously separate activities, the cooperative alliances and partnering may augment the total values of demand and thereby significant scale economies can be obtained. Indirectly this suggests a tendency for conditional technological convergence in some industries dealing with modern information technology.

6.2   LEARNING AND GROWTH

The neoclassical growth model assumes a competitive framework of general equilibrium, where the profit maximization goal of the producer determines the path of optimal demand for the various inputs and hence the optimal output. However this process of achieving the optimal levels of input demand may be far from instantaneous due to several reasons such as uncertainty of future prices, relative fixity in some inputs and the externalities of international trade. Hence one has to analyze the dynamics of the disequilibrium behavior of the adjustment process in the short to medium term horizon. Learning from past experience and adopting a rational policy for the expected future market form the cornerstone of this dynamic adjustment process. We consider here an empirical application of a dynamic adjustment model with learning by doing for analyzing the pattern of input and output demand in Japan over the period 1965–90. The details of statistical data and the econometric method are discussed by Sengupta and Okamura (1996).

The disequilibrium model of adjustment cost involves a two-step decision process for the producer. In the first step he decides the optimal inputs by minimizing a steady state cost function, which gives rise to the long run equilibrium or target value. The second step then postulates an optimal adjustment rule towards the equilibrium or the target level. The first stage problem is thus:

$$\text{Min } c_t = w_t' X_t \text{ subject to } Y_t = F(X_t)$$

where X_t and w_t are the column vectors of m inputs and their expected prices (prime denoting a transpose) and Y_t is the output level given by the production function $F(X_t)$ which may exhibit increasing returns to scale due to the human capital input or knowledge spillover. Let X_t^* be the optimal input levels and Y_t^* be the associated output on the efficiency frontier.

The second step of the optimization model assumes a short run adjustment behavior for the producer, who finds that his current factor uses are inconsistent with the long run equilibrium path (X_t^*, Y_t^*) above as implied by the current relative factor prices and their expected changes in the future. Since the desired levels of inputs may change over time, the adjustment of producer's economic behavior frequently involves time lags in adjusting stocks to their desired levels. Thus all the expected future values of the target levels X_t^* of input demand, which implicitly depend on the expected levels of future prices become relevant to the current optimal decision. Assuming a quadratic adjustment cost the second optimization step requires the producer to minimize the expected present value of a quadratic loss function as follows:

$$\underset{x_t}{\text{Min}} E_t L$$

where   (6.3)

$$L = \sum_{t=0}^{\infty} r^t [(x_t - x_t^*)'G(x_t - x_t^*) + (x_t - x_{t-1})'H(x_t - x_{t-1})]$$

where $E_t(\bullet)$ is expectation as of time t, is the exogenous rate of discount, $x_t = \ln X_t, x_t^* = \ln X_t^*$ and G, H are the matrices of nonnegative weights. The first component of the loss function is due to deviations from the steady state equilibrium, i.e., disequilibrium cost and the second component characterizes the producer's aversion to fluctuations in input levels, i.e., the smoothness objective. For simplicity and convenience it is assumed that the weighting matrices G and H are diagonal with positive diagonal elements and the production function is Cobb–Douglas in form, i.e., $y_t = f(x_t)$ where $y_t = \ln Y_t$ and $f(\bullet)$ is log linear in form. On applying the first order condition for the minimization problem in (6.2) one obtains the optimal linear decision rule (LDR) as follows:

$$[-(1/r)(P + (1+r)I_m)Z + (1/r)Z^2 + I_m]x_{t+1} = -(1/r)PE_t x_t^* \quad (6.4)$$

where $P = H^{-1} G$, I_m = identity matrix of order m and Z is a backward lag operator. It is well known that the characteristic equation of this linear difference equation system (6.4) will have half of its roots stable and half unstable. Let μ be the square matrix of stable roots of the system. Then one could define a long run target input demand vector as d_t:

$$d_t = (I_m - r\mu) \sum_{s=0}^{\infty} r^s \mu^s x_{t+s}^*$$

On using this in the optimal LDR equation (6.4) we derive the linear adjustment rule (LAR) of the transitional dynamics as follows:

$$\Delta x_t = \phi(d_t - x_{t-1}) \tag{6.5}$$

where $\phi = I_j - \mu$, d_t is derived above and it is assumed that the rational expectations hypothesis holds, i.e., $E_t(x_{t+1}) = x_{t+1}$. This assumption implies that the future expectations $E_t(\bullet)$ are realized in terms of the observed variables x_{t+1}. Under conditions of perfect foresight and the possibility of no arbitrage such an assumption appears reasonable and it has been frequently applied in recent intertemporal macroeconomic literature.

The equations for the disequilibrium transition dynamics (6.5) can be estimated in principle by two different ways. One is the forward-looking approach, where the future value of $x_{t+1}^* = hW_t + \eta_t$ with W_t as the instrument variables and η_t as the error process are utilized in the estimation of the d_t series. The second is the backward looking approach where the past values (x_{t-s}^*) are used to estimate the d_t process, before the disequilibrium dynamics (6.5) is estimated. If the underlying time series variables are stationary, these two approaches may generate estimates which are very similar but since the condition of stationarity fails for the observed data set these need not produce similar results.

The adjustment model is estimated in two steps in order to obtain consistent estimates for the OLS parameters, since the desired input levels X_t^* are approximated in their error parts by AR(3) processes of all exogenous variables. Kennan's method of approximation by AR(1) process fails here in case of heterogeneous labor. The first step specification of the partial adjustment rules yields:

$$\Delta \ln X_{it} = c_i - \phi_i \ln X_{i,t-1} + \phi_i d_{it}$$

where i denotes the three inputs (K_t, F_t, L_t), c_i is the constant intercept and ϕ_i is the speed of adjustment parameter. The three inputs are: F_t is total hours of female labor, L_t is male labor with skills up to secondary education level and K_t includes both physical and human capital, where the latter is skilled labor with higher than secondary level of education. The estimates of these parameters ϕ_i and their associated characteristic roots are reported in Table 6.3. Only those roots which are stable are included here, since we are interested in the convergent paths to the steady state.

The estimates of the speed of adjustment parameter ϕ_i are utilized in a two-step method to handle the cross equation restrictions imposed by the steady state cost minimization problem (6.4). We follow Kennan's (1979) procedure here to obtain consistent estimates for the two-step method. For example in the two-input case the linear labor demand equations appear as follows:

Step 1 $\quad \Delta \ln L_t = f(\ln L_{t-1}, \ln Y_{t-1}, \ln RW_{t-1})$

Step 2 $\quad Z_t = f(\ln Y_{t-1}, \ln RW_{t-1})$ $\hspace{2cm}$ (6.6)

where

$$Z_t = \hat{\theta}_L \left[\alpha_L + (\alpha_K + \alpha_L)^{-1} \alpha_L \ln\left(\frac{W_L}{W_k} \right)_{t-1} \right.$$

$$\left. + (\alpha_k + \alpha_L)^{-1} \ln Y_{t-1} \right]$$

$$\hat{\theta}_L = -\hat{\phi}_L + (1 - \hat{\phi}_L)^{-1} \hat{\phi}_L$$

Here RW_t is the relative factor prices of labor to capital W_L/W_k and α_L, α_K are the coefficients of the Cobb–Douglas production function denoting the elasticities of aggregate labor and capital. Note that the estimate $\hat{\phi}_L$ of the adjustment parameter for the labor demand equation (6.5) is utilized here in three ways. One is to test the speed of convergence to the steady-state level $\bar{d}_L$, which leads to the steady state level of output through the steady-state production function. Secondly, the second step estimates of the adjusted demand function in (6.6) provide an estimate of the scale economy of the aggregate production function. Thirdly, it provides an estimate of the ratio a $= g_2/h_2$, which denotes the relative proportion of the two weights: g_2 for deviations from the desired level of labor demand and h_2 for deviations from last year's level. If the desired levels of input demand follow independent AR(3) processes, then the OLS method followed in the above two steps has been shown to be statistically consistent by Kennan (1979) and others. These estimates are presented in Table 6.4 and the details of statistical data and their sources are given in Sengupta and Okamura (1996). Finally, we estimate also the contribution of three types of labor (i.e., F_t for female labor hours, L_t for manhours with skill level of up to secondary education

Table 6.3 Estimates of the Speed of Adjustment Parameters (ϕ_i), the Stable Characteristic Roots (ζ_i) and θ_i

Output (ln Y_t)	Input (ln X_{it})	ϕ_i	ζ_i	θ_i
GNP	K	0.702*	0.298	1.659
(without exports)	F	0.335**	0.665	0.169
	L	1.071*	−0.070	−16.42
	S	0.418*	0.582	0.299
GNP	K	0.328*	0.672	0.162
(with exports)	F	0.689*	0.311	1.524
	L	1.027*	−0.027	−39.61
	S	0.826*	0.174	3.921

Notes: 1. One and two asterisks denote significant values at 5% and 10% levels of t-test respectively.

2. Labor is shown here separately for skilled (S) and less skilled (L) manhours and female (F) labor.

level and S_t for skilled labor with education levels higher than the secondary) along with physical capital. But since S_t is a good proxy for skill and learning curve effects, it is lumped with the capital input K_t. Thus we specify the dynamic production equation as

$$\Delta y_t = \beta_0 + \sum_{i=1}^{5} \beta_i \Delta x_i$$

where y_t = GNP in real terms, $x_1 = \ln F_t, x_2 = \ln L_t, x_3 = \ln K_t$ (augmented), $x_4 = \ln U_t, x_t = \ln V_t$ where the Hicks-neutral technical progress function is related to the openness in trade measured by the ratio V_t of exports to GNP and the learning curve effect U_t. The estimates are as follows:

$$\Delta y_t = 0.012 + \underset{(t=0.991)}{0.302} \ \Delta x_1 - \underset{(-0.141)}{0.030} \ \Delta x_2 + \underset{(3.204)}{0.790} \ \Delta x_3$$

$$- \underset{(-1.293)}{0.028} \ \Delta x_4 + \underset{(0.133)}{0.014} \ \Delta x_5$$

$$R^2 = 0.49; \ DW = 1.92, \ RTS = 1.076$$

Here the sum of elasticity coefficients tends to exceed one and the externality factor though not statistically significant has positive impact on the growth of real GNP. Also the role of capital is much more important than labor in this dynamic setup. This result is upheld even when the skilled manhours are not included in the definition of augmented capital stock. On using data from the UN Comparison Project (1960–85) DeLong and Summers (1991) found a similar result on the dominant contribution of equipment investment to economic growth in Japan. The noted that the differences in equipment investment account for essentially all of the extraordinary growth performance of Japan relative to the sample of 25 countries over the period 1960–85. Secondly, the relative contributions of labor and exports are much smaller, although the overall returns to scale is increasing. Since exports is the only variable used as a proxy for eternality, it suggests a pattern different from the other NICs in Asia such as Korea and Taiwan for example. In 1986 the ratio of GDP was 17.2 percent in Japan, whereas it was 48.1% in Korea and 84.0% in Taiwan. This ratio fell to less than 12% in Japan in 1993. As a mature industrial country the impact of openness in trade on the overall economic growth in Japan is much less than the other NICs in Asia. Another factor may be the existence of strong diminishing returns in the learning by doing process as has been shown by Young (1995) in his empirical studies. Thus in the initial stage the development of new technologies leads to rapid learning by doing. After some time however the productive capability of these new technologies is exhausted and learning by doing slows down.

The estimated results in Table 6.3 are of major significance, since the convergence to the steady state growth of the inputs and output is directly tested here in an econometrically satisfactory manner. First of all, when the externality factor is not introduced, the capital input has faster convergence to its steady state than the skilled female labor but this pattern is reversed when exports is introduced as an explanatory variable. Thus the presence of exports reduces the speed of convergence of capital relative to the major types of labor. Secondly, the unskilled manpower imparts oscillations in the convergence path, which may be directly responsible for the procyclical variations of Solow's productivity residual. Finally, one notes that the skilled manpower variable S has the highest value of $\phi_i = 0.826$ compared

Table 6.4 Two-Step Estimation of the Labor Demand Equation in the Two-Input Model (Backward-Looking Model)

	Dependent Variable	Intercept	$\ln L_{t-1}$	$\ln Y_{t-1}$	$\ln RW_{t-1}$	$\ln V_t$
First Step	$\Delta \ln L_t$	17.913 (3.530)	−0.973 (0.789)	0.186 (0.065)	0.438 (0.149)	-
	$\Delta \ln L_t$	8.931 (2.409)	−0.898 (0.132)	1.859 (0.591)	1.973* (0.614)	−0.859
Second Step	Z_t	−258.27 (0.49)	-	−3.545	−5.496	-
	Z_t	−103.75 (19.72)	- (3.397)	−9.487 (1.694)	−1.527 (1.655)	3.686

		$\hat{a}$	DW	R^2
First Step	$\Delta \ln L_t$	13.94	1.425	0.552
	$\Delta \ln L_t$	7.87	1.761	0.809
Second Step	Z_t	-	1.557	0.608
	Z_t	-	1.749	0.644

Notes: 1. Estimated standard errors are in parentheses.
2. The symbol * indicates that instead of $\ln RW_{t-1}$ a proxy variable $\ln Y_{t-3}$ is used here as an explanatory variable since it had a more significant explanatory power.
3. V_t is used for real exports deflated by the export price index.

Here the production function is $Y = BF(K,L)$ with $B = B(U,V)$, where U is the learning curve effect due to technological learning and skill and V is the externality factor. See Sengupta and Okamura (1996) for details.

to that of capital and female labor, when the export variable is used in the specification. This suggests faster convergence to steady state of skilled manpower. For a mature industrial economy like Japan this may provide strong empirical support to the hypothesis that openness and trade help in the process of rapid development of skilled personnel to its desired target level. The so-called knowledge spillover hypothesis may be still active in the industrial process, although the learning by doing effects may be reaching stages of exhaustion. In this aspect of rapid deployment of skilled personnel in the growth process, Japan may be very similar to the other successful NICs in Asia. There exists some indirect empirical evidence analyzed by Sengupta (1993), which shows that the traditional export items were very dissimilar in pattern across the four countries: Korea, Hong Kong, Japan and Taiwan but similar and homogeneous patterns were found for exports of certain sophisticated R&D intensive products such as electrical machinery, telecommunications and computer equipment, etc.

Finally, the two-step estimation results reported in Table 6.4 provide some interesting insight into the convergence of the optimal labor demand equation for the two-input model. Since the long run level d_t defined in (6.5) and (6.6) may be estimated either by a forward-looking or a backward-looking procedure one could derive two sets of estimates of the labor adjustment equation. The results of the backward looking model are reported in Table 6.4 and this is the conventional method followed by Kennan and others to derive statistically consistent estimates. However for a growing economy interested in sustained growth, the backward and forward looking models need not produce identical results. To test this difference we estimated the forward looking model for labor demand equations as follows:

First Step

$$\Delta \ln L_t = 16.6 - \underset{(0.18)}{0.811 \ln L_{t-1}} + \underset{(0.50)}{1.117 \ln Y_t} - \underset{(0.55)}{1.028 \ln Y_{t+2}}$$

$$+ \underset{(0.21)}{0.447 \ln RW_t} - \underset{(0.202)}{0.368 \ln RW(t+1)}$$

$$R^2 = 0.635; \ DW = 2.18; \ \hat{a} = 3.489$$

Second Step

$$Z_t = -258.3 - \underset{(0.827)}{3.545 \ln Y_{t-1}} - \underset{(2.708)}{5.496 \ln RW_{t-1}}$$

$$R^2 = 0.608; \ DW = 1.557$$

Two points emerge very distinctly. One is that the forward looking estimates are very different in magnitude compared to the backward looking estimates. Furthermore future incomes have strong impact on the current demand for labor. When only the skilled component of the total labor demand equation is considered, this impact is reinforced more strongly. Secondly, the value of $\hat{a}$ as defined in (6.6) by the ratio g_2/h_2 is nearly half that of the backward-looking models thus suggesting an asymmetry in the adjustment process. For the two industrial sectors: durable and nondurable manufacturing in US over 1947–69 Kennan's two-step estimates consistently produced a value of $\hat{a}$ less than 0.14, i.e., 0.134 for the durable and 0.053 for the nondurable sector. This provides a strong evidence that the US producers place much more weight on smoothing out fluctuations in input demand, whereas their Japanese counterparts emphasize their long run goals of an optimal trend. This also explains in part the rationality of Japanese producers in building ahead of demand and concentrating on investment in technology-intensive industries. Japan now spends considerably more as a fraction of GDP on commercial nonbasic research that generates excludable benefits than does the United States and they are better off as a result.

A final comment on the transitional dynamics of Japan (1965–90) may be made in respect of the optimality condition (6.4). The partial adjustment models (6.5) and (6.6) only include the stable characteristic roots. But the other roots implicit in (6.4) can be seen more directly by expressing x_t in (6.4) as a linear function of the past x_{t-1}, x_{t-2} and the future x_{t+1}, x_{t+2}. The following estimates for labor $x_1 = \ln L_t$, capital $x_2 = \ln K_t$ and output $y_t = \ln$ GDP (real) reveal that the future expectations play a much stronger role than the historical past

$$\Delta x_1 = 2.241 - \underset{(t=3.47)}{0.545}\ x_1(t-1) + \underset{(2.53)}{0.432}\,x_1(t+1)$$
$$R^2 = 0.372,\ DW = 3.02$$

$$\Delta x_2 = 0.026 - \underset{(-8.62)}{0.511}\ x_2(t-1) + \underset{(8.00)}{0.512}\,x_2(t+1)$$
$$R^2 = 0.893;\ DW = 2.67$$

$$\Delta y_t = 0.039 - \underset{(-6.47)}{0.505}\ y(t-1) + \underset{(5.45)}{0.500}\,y(t+1)$$
$$R^2 = 0.735;\ DW = 2.728$$

The inclusion of higher order terms like $x(t-2)$ and $x(t+2)$ did not add any statistically significant coefficients. It is clear that in each of the three cases, two inputs and the real output the future variables which embody expectations have a significant positive impact on the growth process. This is a significant characteristic of the industrial learning process in Japan.

6.3 TRADE AND FOREIGN EXCHANGE

The recent trend in globalization of international trade has raised several important policy issues and the international agencies such as IMF and the World Bank have been involved in recent policy discussions relating to growth and stabilization programs of the developing economies. Even for the successful NICs in Asia, the onset of foreign exchange crisis and the rapid decline in the domestic currency values by the end of 1997 have prompted a bail out by IMF of such economies as Korea, Thailand and others, so that the crisis in Asian markets does not continue for very long with a significantly negative impact on the US financial and investment markets. Three types of policy issues will be discussed in this section. The first involves the issue of imbalance in external trade and its impact on growth. The fact that in many of the successful Asian NICs the exports have been used as a conscious policy instrument makes this issue very much relevant. Secondly, there has been increased emphasis by the IMF and World Bank programs on the adjustment of real exchange rates in many Latin American countries suffering foreign debt crisis. An activist policy of real exchange rate depreciation is advocated in these World Bank and Fund programs in order to raise export profitability. Thirdly, the problems of large scale capital flight across the border and the speculator's attack on the currency markets have raised the policy concern as to how one can prevent or reduce the source of such volatility. This third aspect was previously discussed in Chapter 5, where policy coordination issues in respect of exchange markets were discussed in relation to the so-called Tobin tax. Hence we may discuss the first two policy issues in this section.

The policy of outward-oriented or export-promoting strategy, that has been systematically promoted by World Bank programs put forward the following hypothesis: any trade strategy which makes the effective exchange rate for a country's exports (EER_x) lower than for its imports (EER_m) leads to a bias against exports, since it makes exports to be less profitable than the domestic goods. Outward orientation thus implies a trade strategy which reverses this bias or neutralizes it by ensuring an approximate equality of EER_x and EER_m. The use of export promoting strategy as a policy instrument in a dynamic context may be easily specified in an optimal growth theory framework. Thus consider an aggregate production function

$$Y = F(K, AL), \quad A = A(t)$$

with two inputs, K as physical capital and AL as augmented labor, where A depends on the learning by doing effects through international diffusion of technical knowledge. With per capita variables $y = f(k)$, $k = K/AL$ and $y = Y/AL$ and the assumption of constant returns to scale for two inputs K and AL, we can derive the equation of evolution of per capita capital as

$$\dot{k} = \alpha f(k) - (n + g + \delta)k - (c + e) \tag{6.7}$$

where $c = C/AL$, $e = E/AL$, $\alpha = 1+m$, m being the import coefficient, n the exogenous growth rate of labor, g the growth rate of exogeneous skill factor A and δ is the constant rate of depreciation of capital. We assume the social planner or the government to be maximizing the utility functional

$$U = \int_0^\infty \exp(-t(\rho - n))u(z)dt \tag{6.8}$$

where
$$u(z) = (1 - \theta)^{-1}(z^{1-\theta} - 1), \quad \theta > 0$$

$z = (C+X)/L$, X = exports, ρ = constant rate of time preference, subject to the capital growth constraint (6.7), which has the export ratio e as the control variable. The optimal growth path then satisfies the following first order condition

$$\dot{z}/z = (1/\theta)[\alpha f_k - \delta - \rho] = f_k - \delta - \rho \text{ if } \theta = 1$$

where f_k is the marginal productivity of capital. Now if we replace the control variable from z to e in the above optimal growth path, we obtain

$$\dot{e}/e = (1/\theta)[\alpha f_k - \delta - \rho], \quad \alpha = 1 - a + m \tag{6.9}$$

where a is the consumption ratio. It is clear that if the marginal productivity of capital is either constant or declines very slowly, the gap measured by $[\alpha f_k - \delta - \rho]$ would remain positive thus augmenting the export ratio e(t). Thus the link between marginal productivity of capital and export growth is a two-way process, when the former does not decline much due to increasing returns to scale: high marginal productivity generates higher export growth and a greater shift to income-elastic exportable goods and the latter induces more investment in technology-intensive goods exhibiting significant scale economies. For the Korean economy over the period 1967–86 the savings ratio to GDP rose from 11.7 to 44.1% and the investment ratio rose from 20.2 to 37.5%. The export ratio to GDP rose from 8.5 to 48% during the same period. One consequence of this has been that the role of foreign savings $F = I–S$ measured by the investment–savings gap declined over those years as the level of domestic savings rose. This trend of maintaining balance on the external account has prevailed for the other successful NICs in Asia for the same period as follows:

Table 6.5 Evolution of Exports (E), Savings (S) and Investment (I) in Relation to GNP (Y) in %

	1967	1986	Δ(E/Y)	1967	1986	Δ(S/Y)
Korea	8.5	48.1	39.6	11.7	44.1	32.4
Taiwan	24.4	84.0	59.6	18.2	47.0	28.8
Japan	7.6	17.2	9.6	35.7	42.0	6.3
Philippines	24.9	30.4	5.5	22.3	21.9	-0.4
Germany	21.4	34.5	13.1	32.2	29.1	-3.1
	1967	1986	Δ(I/Y)			
Korea	20.2	37.5	17.3			
Taiwan	23.3	25.1	1.8			
Japan	32.1	33.6	1.5			
Philippines	21.5	12.9	-8.6			
Germany	28.3	22.4	-5.9			

Clearly the gains in savings and investment rates were dramatic for Korea. Japan showed a slight increase but not as much as Korea and Taiwan. By contrast Philippines and Germany showed a reduction. The experience of many Latin American countries has been that they developed significant macroeconomic imbalances which manifested themselves in high and unpredictable inflation and periodic balance of payments and debt crisis. As we analyzed before, significant inflation either open or repressed is itself a source of misallocation of resources and impediment to efficiency in the growth process. These policy aspects have been discussed in some detail by

Sachs (1987), who has stressed three important aspects of the export expansion policy of the successful NICs in Asia. First, countries like Korea and Taiwan have maintained nearly balanced government budgets often with large surpluses on the current account. Thus inflation rates have been low and fairly stable. This has helped maintain a stable level of nominal exchange rates without adversely affecting the profitability of exports. Secondly, an incentive system has been generally applied to promote exports with a natural comparative advantage i.e., labor-intensive manufacturing goods initially and then capital-intensive manufacturers. Finally, the active government policy in Korea, Taiwan and Japan has promoted relatively equal income distributions by narrowing the urban–rural differentials and by undertaking fundamental land reforms. By contrast the Latin American countries have failed to secure substantial improvements in income distribution. The major gains from improvements in income distribution have been to stabilize domestic demand and promote stability in the pattern of domestic investment, particularly the infrastructural investment by government in the rural sector. Thus the outward oriented trade strategies have helped reduce distortions in the factor and produce markets, e.g., price controls, credit rationing, etc. and the monetary, fiscal and exchange rate policies have been carefully used in these Asian NICs as major instruments of growth-oriented stabilization policies.

A sound exchange rate policy is essential for maintaining competitiveness in the world markets today. Persistent imbalances or misalignments in the real exchange rates tend to result in substantial divergence of domestic costs and prices from their international levels and thus create balance of payment imbalances. In these circumstances exchange rate adjustments or flexibility in exchange rate management or both can help restore competitiveness and balance to the economy, provided these are supported by appropriate monetary and fiscal policies. One has to emphasize that without appropriate domestic monetary and fiscal strategies to control inflation and the budget deficits, any extent of exchange rate devaluations and export trade promoting strategies cannot stabilize the economies such as Mexico, Colombia and Argentina. In many of these countries of Latin America the governments have attempted to secure a pegged exchange rate by intervening in the foreign exchange markets but without correcting their underlying problems of budget deficits and inflationary pressures but these short term measures invariably fail and the high inflation rates usually return, when the central bank's currency reserve falls to its minimum level. This is the point ripe for speculative attack. In many developing countries today this type of attack has frustrated any role of central bank intervention in the foreign exchange markets. The main lesson from the recent experiences of failure of these intervention policies is that it is unlikely to secure any stability to the real exchange rate unless these are accompanied by fundamental changes in economic policies towards reducing the budget deficit and the inflationary pressures. This is especially true since the trading volume in the foreign exchange market today exceeds $900 billion daily, which is much greater than what the world's central banks can field. The total stock of reserves held by central banks is about $1 trillion and would be exhausted in a single day. When governments cannot signal their commitment to a realistic level of exchange rate, as happened in Fall 1992 in Britain and Italy and again in November–December 1997 in Hong Kong, Thailand, Korea, central banks cannot help but be swept by waves of speculative activity.

6.4   POLICY IMPACT ANALYSIS

The evaluation of impact of any specific economic policy, e.g., increasing the investment rate in the manufacturing sector, devaluation of the domestic currency in relation to US dollar or, imposing an import tariff is most easily done in a general equilibrium framework, where there are several sectors or branches of an economy that are interdependent through demand, supply or technological linkages. From a quantitative standpoint such types of models comprise components which combine in some sense three types of economic relationships. One is the intersectoral interdependence typically specified by a static or dynamic input–output (IO) model based on the Leontief-type fixed input–output coefficients. This is often enlarged by a social accounting matrix (SAM) which imposes the balance condition that for every sectoral income there should be a corresponding outlay or expenditure and also the completeness condition that both the receiver and the sender of every transaction must be identified. Like the IO model the SAM models help to assess the economy-wide effects of an increase in demand in any given sector, e.g., the so-called multiplier effects. The second component provides econometrically estimated relationships for the multimarket or multisector demand and supply components. Thus it encompasses a certain number of macroeconomic components such as investment, savings, balance of payments and government budget. Finally, there is a component which specifies the restrictions or constraints on the policy instruments and also the endogenous variables like sectoral output. The specification of these constraints introduces practical and realistic limits of strategies to be followed in different infrastructures. A linear or nonlinear programming framework allows through the shadow prices the determination of the possible impact of any specific policy constraint on the other sectors.

The framework of the above general equilibrium types of models, usually termed as computable general equilibrium (CGE) models has been widely used by World Bank to study the possible impact of specified types of short and long run policy interventions. Simulation of two or three-tier models has been applied over several countries combining both cross-section and time-series data. Dervis, DeMelo and Robinson (1984) and recently Gunning and Keyser (1993) have discussed for several countries the construction and application of these CGE models. In this section we analyze some of the basic components of these CGE models and consider a new dynamic tool of an innovative activity matrix that has been recently introduced by DeBresson (1996) and his associates.

6.4.1 CGE Models and their Policy Implications

The basic structure of a CGE model may be viewed as a two–stage model, where the first stage is a static model with given values of dynamic variables such as capital and technology and the second stage introduces dynamics either through the savings investment relation or an optimization procedure involving changes in capital stock and technological innovations.

The basic objective of a CGE model for any specific country is to evaluate the quantitative impact of (a) any foreign shocks, e.g., any adverse changes in terms of trade or imbalance in balance of payments, (b) any change in monetary and fiscal policies such as a new tax or subsidy measure or open market policies of the central bank to stabilize the foreign exchange rate, (c) changes in technology in the industrial and agricultural sectors such as the transfer of foreign technology to the domestic economy and finally (d) the change in rates of human capital formation in the form of improved R&D investment and training-cum-education facilities.

In its simplest form the CGE model in equilibrium can be specified as a set of relations as follows. Let X_i be the gross output of sector $i=1,2,...,n$ as in a Leontieff IO model where the aggregate intermediate inputs are

$$R_i = \sum_{j=1}^{n} a_{ik} X_j, \quad \text{where the nonnegative coefficients } a_{ij} \text{ satisfy the standard}$$

IO model assumptions.

$$X_i = F_i(R_i, V_i) = F_i(R_i, L_i, K_i, A_i) \qquad (6.10.1)$$
(production function)

$$L_{ih} = L_{ih}(w_1, w_2, ..., w_m; \hat{p}_i, K_i) \qquad (6.10.2)$$
h=1,2,...,H: different types of labor (labor demand)

$$C_i = C_i(p_1, p_2, ..., p_n; Y) \qquad (6.10.3)$$
(consumption demand)

$$Z_i = \sum_{j=1}^{n} s_{ij} \Delta K_k = Z_i(p_1, p_2, ..., p_n; \Delta Y) \qquad (6.10.4)$$
(investment demand)

$$E_i = E_i(P, p_i, Y_w) \qquad (6.10.5)$$
(export demand)

$$M_i = M_i(P, p_i, Y) \qquad (6.10.6)$$
(import demand)

$$X_i^D = C_i + Z_i + G_i + E_i - M_i \qquad (6.10.7)$$
(demand supply equilibrium)

Here L_i, K_i and A_i are the inputs of labor, capital and technological progress or shift parameter, V_i is value added and $\hat{p}_i = p_i(1 - t_i) - \sum_{j=1}^{n} p_j a_{ji}$ is the net price, t_i being the rate of indirect tax and p_i is the price of good X_i. The sectoral wage rates are w_i and s_{ij} are the shares in the capital composition matrix and Y is total income for the whole economy, with Y_w as the world income which is one of the determinants of export demand (E_i), the other two being the world price level (P) and the dollar price of exports (P_i). Also G_i is the government expenditure which may also be endogeneized by budgetary conditions.

The above model defined by (6.10.1) through (6.10.7) is subject to several practical and institutional constraints, e.g., the labor supply constraint, the capacity constraint, the saving–investment constraint and the foreign exchange constraint, etc. The market clearing conditions may be separately introduced by determining the factor and output prices. For example the familiar condition of wages equalling the value of the marginal products, i.e., $\hat{p}_i \partial X_i / \partial L_{ih} = w_i$ may underlie the labor demand equation (6.10.2). In the short-run the stock of capital K_i and the technological shock variable A_i may be assumed to be given. But in a dynamic setting the sectoral investment demand ΔK_i must be optimally determined. For example the following profit functional may be assumed to be maximized by each sector, when each sector is treated as made up of many similar profit-maximizing and price-taking firms

$$\pi_i = \hat{p}_i X_i - \sum_{h=1}^{H} w_i L_{ih} - \sum_{s=1}^{S} r_i K_{is} - \sum_{s=1}^{S} C(\Delta K_{is})$$
$$\text{Max} \int e^{-\rho t} \pi_i(t) dt$$

where h denotes different types of labor in sector i, s denotes different types of capital and $C(\Delta K_{is})$ denotes adjustment costs due to changing the capital stock over time.

Two central facts of a general equilibrium model are important in the policy impact analysis. One is that the relative prices affect decisions by households and producers and this results in optimal substitution. With respect to production there are two primary ways to allow such substitution. One is to add columns or activities, but keep the coefficient of each activity constant. The second is to allow some or all of the IO coefficients to vary. This is typically done by specifying CES or Cobb–Douglas production functions, e.g.,

$$V_i = A_i L_i^{\alpha_i} K_i^{\beta_i} \tag{6.10.8}$$

where $\dot{A}_i / A_i$ may be interpreted as sectoral Solow residual or sectoral TFP growth.

The second important fact of a CGE model is its dynamic component, where such policy issues as the optimal allocation of total government expenditure $G = \Sigma G_i$ or total new investment by sectors may be specifically discussed. This helps in building up a consistent planning model over a 5 to 8 year horizon, where the various institutional constraints and their shadow prices play critical roles.

Consider for example an application discussed by Dervis et al. (1984) where they write the sectoral demand–supply equilibrium as

$$X_i = d_i(F_i + R_i) + E_i \tag{6.10.9}$$

or

$$X = (I - \hat{D}A)^{-1}(\hat{D}F + E)$$

in vector matrix terms, where d_i is the domestic use ratio denoted by the diagonal matrix $\hat{D}$, F_i is the total final demand ($=C_i + Z_i + G_i$),

$V_i = \sum_{j=1}^{n} a_{ij} X_j$ is the intermediate domestic use demand for sector output X_i

and E_i is the net export demand. Then the time rate of change of X_i can be decomposed as follows:

$$\Delta X = X(t+1) - X(t) = H\hat{D}(\Delta F) + H\Delta E + H(\Delta \hat{D})(F + R)$$

$$\text{with } H = (I - \hat{D}A)^{-1}$$

where the three terms on the right hand side are the effect of domestic demand expansion, the effect of export expansion and the impact of import substitution. Their estimates of the sources of growth of total gross production (%) for some countries are reported in Table 6.6.

When this scenario is projected to the period 1978–85 the role of export expansion in Korea dominates the other sources even more.

Thus the CGE model may complement the econometric analysis in that a model using independently obtained econometric estimates of production, consumption, investment and the pattern of import and export demands may have to pass the consistency requirement when these demand and supply estimates are decomposed by sectors. Here many technical problems arise particularly in the dynamic setup when the sectoral estimates of capital stock are not always easily obtainable in a reliable form.

6.4.2 Innovation Linkages: A New Tool

Following the two–way interdependence of the Leontief type IO matrix, DeBresson (1996) and his associates have empirically estimated an innovative-interaction matrix (IIM) between sectors which are suppliers of innovative activity and the sectors which are users. The IIM is a square matrix in which the supplier industries make up the rows and the user industries make up the columns. Empirical applications have been reported for several countries such as UK, France, Italy, Greece, Canada and also

China. Of these the Italian application is noteworthy, since it is based on the statistical data on technological behavior of 8220 innovating firms which are manufacturing business units surveyed in 1988 by the Italian Statistical Office. Table 6.7 presents the relative importance of different types of innovative businesses. It is clear that Types A, C and F are the predominant forms of innovative business units. In type A firms investment goods coupled with intermediate goods are the main forms of innovative output and they account for about 16% of employment for the total sample.

Table 6.6 Sources of Growth

		Average annual growth rate	Domestic demand expansion	Export expansion	Import substi- tution
Korea	1955–63	5.8	74.5	10.0	21.4
	1963–70	15.7	81.8	21.9	−1.8
	1970–73	16.0	51.9	55.7	−3.2
Mexico	1950–60	6.2	85.5	1.0	5.4
	1960–70	7.2	94.1	3.1	6.0
	1970–75	6.1	89.8	5.9	−1.3
Colombia					
	1953–66	5.8	76.1	10.0	6.9
	1966–70	5.9	69.5	21.8	6.6

Table 6.7 Taxonomy of Innovative Business in Italy (1981–85)

Type of business	% of firms	Main source of innovation	Destination of inno- vation	Per Capita invest- ment (1985)	Exports pro- portion (1985)
A. Design based	19.3	Design	Capital goods	Low	High
B. R&D based	2.3	Design R&D	Capital goods & industrial services	Very Low	High
C. Investment based	29.7	Investment	Intermediate goods	Average	Average
D. Complex innovation	5.7	R&D	Mixed (investment & consumer goods)	Very high	Above average
E. Marketing oriented	12.6	R&D, design, marketing	Mixed	Below average	Low
F. Cost oriented	22.6	Investment	Consumer goods	Below average	Below average
G. Misc	7.8	Mixed	Mixed	-	-
Total	100				

Source: DeBresson (1996).

The major industries here comprise electronics, automobile parts, mechanical engineering and other precision instruments. Type C firms are mainly in intermediate goods such as textiles, leather, rubber, plastics and chemicals, etc. Type B and D are very small in proportion. Type E firms have their basic sources of innovation in marketing coupled with research and development and design; these are mainly oriented towards consumption and intermediate goods such as basic food, drinks, textiles and home appliances. Finally, Type F comprises business units with fixed investment as the main channel for innovative activity, with very low R&D. Process and incremental product innovations are the most important components here embodied mainly in consumption goods. One striking feature of Table 6.7 is the relative insignificant role of R&D based innovation. It only comprises 2.3% of the sample number of firms. This result is consistent with the low levels of industrial research and development expenditure in Italy: only 300 of 2700 innovative businesses claimed that the innovative output had any basic relationships with scientific discoveries. This result is however a contrast with the experience of France or Great Britain. For Japan and Korea the role of commercial R&D expenditure is much more significant and it is increasing over the years.

Two types of hypotheses have been put forward about the trend of innovative output in different sectors of an economy. One is by Schumpeter who postulated that the innovations tend to concentrate in certain sectors rather than evenly distributed over the entire economic space at random. This is because the efforts aimed at improving the new technology-based innovation derive substantial scale economies by concentration. DeBresson (1996) finds substantial evidence of such innovation clusters in Italy, Greece, UK and other countries. The experience of Japan also illustrates this tendency. A second trend is the close interdependence between the innovative activity and the sectoral linkages. DeBresson (1996) estimated a linear regression equation for Italy over the period 1980–84, with innovative activity or output (I) as the dependent variable and the following three independent variables: economic linkages (L), an index (T) of linkage with the available world technology and the R&D expenditure.

$$I = -136.9 + 8.91L + 0.02 \, R\&D + 29.67T \; ; \quad R^2 = 0.71$$

The economic linkages index L includes both forward (demand by end users) and backward (demand for inputs from other sectors) linkages as defined by Hirschman in relation to IO tables. Clearly this shows that the impact of foreign technical know-how is very important. For Japan and Korea this type of international diffusion of innovative knowledge has played an important catalyctic role in their rapid growth episodes. As Dahlman and Nelson (1995) have shown that the four East Asian high performers such as Singapore, Taiwan, Hong Kong and Korea have consistently used the following strategies to capture the international diffusion of technical know-how, e.g., extensive use of technology licensing and link with foreign subsidiary firms, large scale contact with foreign buyers and the development of strong local capital goods industries, where new capital goods embody the latest technical know-how from abroad. On writing the relationship of innovation output (I) with the index of total economic linkage (L) as a loglinear function

$$I_t = AL_t^\beta$$

one can derive the rate of growth of the residual innovative output as

$$\dot{A}/A = (\dot{I}_t/I_t) - \beta(\dot{L}_t/L_t)$$

This may serve as a complementary characterization of the growth of Solow residual. By viewing the above growth equations in terms of sectoral outputs, one could easily derive the estimate of $(\dot{A}_i/A_i)$ for sector i output. This type of characterization would be immensely helpful in tracking down the effects of economic linkages on the growth of innovative output. Even at the aggregate level of total manufacturing the empirical estimates by Norsworthy and Jang (1992) showed a stronger performance of output growth in Japan over US, where the TFP growth contribution is much higher for Japan e.g.

		Output growth	Contribution of Labor	Contribution of Capital	TFP
1965–73					
	Japan	12.46	0.15	4.27	0.91
	US	3.76	0.35	0.37	0.59
1973–78					
	Japan	2.85	–0.32	0.46	1.64
	US	1.08	–0.18	0.14	0.38

This pattern persisted for the high-technology industries of the manufacturing sector, e.g., semiconductor, computer industry and telecommunication services. It may safely be inferred that a large part of this stronger performance of Japan over US may be due to innovation diffusion and transmission.

Recently Kraemer and Dedrick (1994) analyzed the pattern of investment in IT (information technology) industries of 11 countries of the

Asian–Pacific region over the years 1984–90, where the spending on computer hardware and software services was used as a measure of IT investment. They found the average growth in IT investment over 1984–90 has been very high for Korea (24.49), Taiwan (21.64), Singapore (18.06) and Hong Kong (15.22), whereas for slower growth countries it has been much lower, e.g., Malaysia (10.77) or Philippines (12.21). The favorable infrastructure has helped considerably the growth of IT investment in the higher performer countries of Asia.

7. Evolutionary Dynamics in Economic Growth

'Economic growth' is distinguished from 'economic development' by Schumpeter in two key aspects. While economic growth takes place more or less continuously as a result of interactive forces in the market economy, economic development is a more or less discontinuous process activated by the spark of innovations in technology and organizational dynamics. Second, evolution and diversity characterize economic development in a significant sense, whereas economic growth tends to emphasize the steady state, where the forces of economic growth tend to converge.

In this chapter we would discuss these two central features of Schumpeterian economic development but in a more generalized form. However we would not use the term economic development, instead the concept of evolutionary dynamics or, simply evolutionary growth would be adopted.

Recent times have seen a spectacular growth in information technology and this challenge of new technology has spread far and wide across international markets. Characteristics of this new technology and its dynamic effects on evolutionary growth are not yet fully understood. The reasons are several. First of all, economic modelling of the birth of new technology and the decline (or death) of the old has not been very satisfactory; it has been either exogenous or ad hoc. Second, even when new innovations (or technology) have been made endogenous by hypothesizing the incentives and dynamic profit motives of investors and entrepreneurs, their intersectoral impact and diffusion have not been explained. Third, the stochastic uncertainty in future developments in the so-called 'knowledge capital' has transformed the old technological setup in manufacturing to what is now known as flexible manufacturing systems (FMS). The flexibility refers to the ease of adaptivity and adjustment to market conditions and competitive forces, which are changing so rapidly. In this framework economic modelling cannot be restricted only to the linear and convergent dynamics. One has to explore the sources of complexity and chaos in evolutionary economic systems.

7.1   SCHUMPETERIAN DYNAMICS

Two aspects of evolutionary dynamics have prominently featured in recent discussions of Schumpeterian dynamics. One is the dynamic process of 'creative destruction'. Aghion and Howitt (1992, 1996, 1997) have developed this aspect in a model of endogenous growth, where the prospect of more future R&D expenditure discourages current research by creating a potential threat to destroy the monopoly rents from current research. The second is the process of impulse and diffusion in the propagation of new technology. In his *Theory of Economic Development*, Schumpeter (1961) considers six sets of innovations of which the introduction of a new method of production or technology and the opening of a new market through the introduction of new goods are the most important. According to him traditional Walrasian or Marshallian theory is helpful in explaining the steady state growth process, where convergence is the dominant characteristic. Diffusion of new innovations require a different type of theory, where non steady-state and nonequilibrium systems are important. Thus Schumpeter considers a two-part approach. Traditional theory is useful in studying the responses to innovations by those firms which are not innovating themselves, whereas a modern theory is needed to characterize the behavior of innovating firms.

We consider the model of 'creative destruction' first and then analyze the behavior of innovating firms. A simplified version of the model of 'creative destruction' due to Aghion and Howitt (1996) has three essential components: a single final output produced by a continuum of intermediate goods (y_i), each of which is produced by a constant-returns production function, a new version of the intermediate good for the leading-edge variety produced in the innovative sector according to the production function

$$\lambda\mu(K^r / A, H) \equiv \lambda\phi(k^r) \qquad (7.1)$$

with $\quad k^r = K^r / A, \quad \phi' > 0, \quad \phi'' < 0$

where $\mu(\bullet)$ is a regular constant returns production function with λ as the Poisson arrival rate of productivity of new innovation, K^r is the input of capital into R&D, A is the productivity parameter as in the Solow residual and H is the fixed supply of skilled labor allocated to R&D. The prime denotes derivatives. Finally, the growth in the leading-edge sector occurs from the stream of new innovation as follows:

$$\dot{A} = A\lambda\phi(k^r) \tag{7.2}$$

This equation indicates the research spillover effect of the Schumpeterian model, where each innovator's discoveries contribute marginally to the increase in general research knowledge available to every other innovator in future.

Since this model assumes constant returns a steady-state equilibrium condition can be easily derived, when capital, gross output, consumption and the leading edge sector output all grow at the same constant rate g where

$$g = \lambda\phi(k^r) \tag{7.3}$$

The optimal level of R&D research capital is determined by equating the cost of capital to a research firm to the marginal expected return, i.e.,

$$r + \delta_k = \lambda\phi'(k^r)V_t / A_t \tag{7.4}$$

where V_t is the value of an innovation at date t, r the rate of interest and δ_k is the constant rate of depreciation. The value of an innovation V_t at date t can also be written as the expected present value of rents that will accrue until the producer is replaced i.e.

$$V_t = \int_0^\infty e^{-(r+\lambda\phi(k^r))\tau} A_t \pi_\tau d\tau \tag{7.5}$$

where π_τ is the profit function. For closing the model Aghion and Howitt introduce the assumption that the representative household maximizes the life time utility functional

$$U = \int_0^\infty e^{-\rho t} \left(\frac{c_t^{1-\sigma} - 1}{1 - \sigma} \right) dt, \ \sigma > 0, \ \sigma \neq 1 \tag{7.6}$$

where ρ is the common rate of time preference and σ the common elasticity of marginal utility. It then follows from the usual conditions of intertemporal utility maximization that in the steady state when consumption (c_t) grows at the rate g, the rate of interest must satisfy the condition

$$r = \rho + \sigma g \qquad (7.7)$$

Note that the concept of creative destruction underlies the equation (7.4) as follows. A successful innovator produces the newly invented good and protected by the infinitely lived patent right he drives out the previous incumbent by undercutting his price and enjoys monopoly rents until driven out by the next innovation. Thus the success in driving out the previous incumbent depends on his ability to reduce costs by the new innovation and creating a local monopoly. So long as the stream of new innovations do not satisfy these two conditions the process of creative destruction or scrapping old obsolete capital and technology would not work.

Three important propositions about the steady state behavior have been derived from the equation (7.1) through (7.6) as follows:

1. The long run growth rate g can be written as

$$g = g(\rho, \sigma, \delta_k, \pi, \lambda, H) \qquad (7.8)$$

where the function is increasing in λ, H and π and decreasing in ρ, σ, δ_k.

2. The productivity adjusted level of R&D capital k^r is a similar function

$$k^r = k^r(\rho, \sigma, \delta_k, \pi, \lambda, H) \qquad (7.9)$$

where it is increasing in λ, H and π and decreasing in the rest.

3. The long run rate of growth g is positively correlated with the flow of patents of new innovations (ΔP_t), the flow of entry of new firms (ΔN_t), the flow of new products (Δy_t) and the rate of obsolescence of existing capital (d_k):

$$g = g(\Delta P_t, \Delta N_t, \Delta y_t, d_k) \qquad (7.10)$$

The interesting thing about these propositions is that these are empirically testable and by taking a loglinear approximation these can be econometrically estimated over panel data comprising both cross-section and time series observations. Some comments on these propositions may be useful for policy purposes. First of all, one notes with Aghion and Howitt

185

that both the productivity parameter λ, the profits expected π and the supply of skilled worker H have a positive effect on the steady state growth rate g, but the effect of H is not always very significant over cross-country data, since it is more of a proxy for human capital. Second, the correlation of growth rate with the level of R&D in (7.9) is not always positive, since an increase in growth may sometimes reduce the value of innovations and hence of R&D investment. Finally, the hypothesis of Schumpeterian creative destruction may be empirically tested by investigating if the correlation of growth and the other variables like the entry and exit of firms and the obsolescence of capital in specific industries like semiconductor, microelectronics and other industries are positive or not.

Some indirect evidence is available from the empirical measurement of the effect of technological change on productivity by Norsworthy and Jang (1992), who studied three technology-intensive industries e.g., microelectronics (SIC Code: 367), computers (SIC Code: 357) and manufacturing. The trend of total factor productivity (FP) growth for these industries in US was as follows.

	SIC 367	SIC 357	Manufacturing
1959–67	4.32	31.23	0.58
1967–73	5.62	19.26	0.87
1973–81	4.97	26.69	1.39
Average	4.91	26.31	0.91

FP growth can be thought of as the growth in the productivity of all factors combined. Clearly in terms of TFP growth the US computer industry grew much more rapidly than the manufacturing sector as a whole. Much of this rapid TFP growth in the computer industry in US has come from significant economies of scale and learning curve effects and it has been associated with a high rate of obsolescence of capital. In a separate estimate of the translog variable cost function over the period 1960–80 for the microelectronics industry they found that the high rate of technical change due to learning by doing are positively correlated with the higher rates of obsolescence of capital.

The market framework for private investment in R&D expenditure assumed by Aghion and Howitt is that of a monopoly firm with a temporary market power due to patent rights on the new innovation. Yet in this framework the limit pricing model suggests a trend towards cost reduction over time, as has been the trend in the computer industry. This can be formalized through a learning curve model generating significant economies of scale. In this setup it is important to distinguish between current output ($\dot{y} = dy / dt$) and cumulative output $y(t)$ in the production function $\dot{y} = F(y(t), x(t))$ where $x(t)$ denotes the variable inputs, e.g., the functional form

$$\dot{y}(t) = Ay^{\delta} x(t)^{1/\gamma}$$

summarizes the dynamic process of producing the joint products of learning and output from resources and experiences. Assume now a duopolistic framework with two producers producing outputs $\dot{y}_1(t), \dot{y}_2(t)$ at prices $p_1(t)$, $p_2(t)$. The NICs may represent one producer and the rest of the world as the second producer. The dynamic optimization model for the first producer may then take the form

$$\text{Max} J_1 = \int_0^{\infty} e^{-rt}(p_1(t) - c_1(t))\dot{y}_1 dt \qquad (7.11)$$

$$\text{subject to} \quad \dot{y}_i(t) = F_i(y_1(t), y_2(t), p_1(t), p_2(t)); i = 1, 2$$

On using the current value Hamiltonian $H = e^{-rt}\{(p_1 - c_1 + \lambda_1)F_1 + (p_2 - c_2 + \lambda_2)F_2\}$ and assuming the regularity conditions for the existence of an optimal trajectory the Pontryagin maximum principle specifies the following necessary conditions for optimality (for i=1,2):

$$\dot{\lambda}_i = r\lambda_i - \frac{\partial H}{\partial y_i}$$

$$\dot{y}_i = F_i(y_1, y_2, p_1, p_2) \qquad (7.12)$$

$$\partial H / \partial p_i = 0 \text{ for all } t$$

and $\quad \lim_{t \to \infty} e^{-rt} \lambda_i(t) = 0$ (transversality).

By using $\mu_{ii} = (\partial F_i / \partial p_i)(p_i / F_i)$ and $\mu_{ji} = (\partial F_j / \partial p_i)(p_i / F_j)$ when $i \neq j$

187

as the own price elasticity and cross elasticity of demand, the optimal price rule can be written as

$$p_1 = (1 + \mu_{11})^{-1} [\mu_{11}(c_1 - \lambda_1) - \lambda_2 \mu_{21}] \qquad (7.13)$$

with the optimal trajectory for $\lambda_1(t)$ as

$$\dot{\lambda}_1 = r\lambda_1 + (c_1 - \lambda_1)F_{1y_1} - p_1 F_{1y_1} + c_{1y} F_1 \ .$$

i.e. $\qquad \lambda(t) = \int_t^\infty e^{-r(\tau - t)} \left[\left(\frac{p_1}{\mu_{11}} + \frac{\lambda_2 \mu_{21}}{\mu_{11}} \right) F_{1y_1} + c_{1y_1} F \right] d\tau \qquad (7.14)$

where $\quad F_{1y_1} = \partial F_1 / \partial y_1$

$\qquad c_{1y_1} = \partial c_1 / \partial y_1 < 0$, i.e., future cost decline

$\qquad \mu_{11} < 0, \mu_{21} > 0 .$

Clearly the optimal pricing rules involve the trajectories of both the current price $p_1(t)$ and the shadow prices $\lambda_1(t)$. The current pricing rule (7.14) shows the price to be much lower than the monopoly price $(1 + \mu_{11})^{-1}$ $\mu_{11}(c_1 - \lambda_1)$ since λ_2 is usually negative, since more competition hurts the market position of y_1 more. Secondly, the extent of future cost declines $(-c_{1y_1} > 0)$ tends to reduce the dynamic shadow price $\lambda_1(t)$. Thirdly, if the demand function in (7.12) is a function of prices alone, i.e., $\dot{y}_i = F(p_1, p_2)$ then the sign of $\dot{p} = dp / dt$ may be shown as

$$\text{sign}(\dot{p}) = \text{sign}(-r\lambda_1 + c_{1t} - \lambda_2 \mu_{21})$$

where $c_{1t} = \partial c_1 / \partial t$ is the decline of cost over time due to learning and experience since $c_{y_1} < 0$. This shows a strong pressure for price declines over time. This has happened exactly in the semiconductor and R&D intensive industries such as electronics, telecommunications and personal computers.

A simpler form of the decision model (7.11) results when we assume one average market price $p(t)$ for a homogeneous product and a dynamic

Cournot model with two outputs $\dot{y}_1$ and $\dot{y}_2$ as decision variables. In this case we reformulate the model as

$$\text{MaxJ}_1 = \int_0^\infty e^{-rt}(p(t) - c_1(t))\dot{y}_1 dt$$

$$\text{s.t.} \quad \dot{p}(t) = k(\tilde{p} - p), \tilde{p} = a - b(\dot{y}_1 + \dot{y}_2) \tag{7.15}$$

where $\tilde{p} = \tilde{p}(t)$ is the demand price expected and p is the market price. Assuming quadratic cost functions, i.e., $c_1\dot{y}_1 = wu_1 + 1/2u_1^2$ where $u_1 = \dot{y}_1$ and the parameter w declines over time due to learning and experience, the above is a linear quadratic control model and hence the optimal feedback strategies $u_i^*(t)$ can be easily calculated as

$$u_i^*(t) = [1 - bkh(t)]p(t) + bkm(t) - w \tag{7.16}$$

with

$$h(t) = (6k^2b^2)^{-1}[r + 4bk + 2k - \{(r + 4bk + 2k)^2 \\ -12k^2b^2)\}^{1/2}]$$

$$m(t) = (r - 3b^2k^2h(t) + k + 2bk)^{-1}[2 - as\ h(t) - 2bkw\ h(t)]$$

Here zero conjectural variation on the part of each player is assumed. Clearly this linear feedback form of the conjectural equilibrium output path in (7.14) yields a steady state price level p^* as

$$p^* = [2b(1 - bkh^* + 1]^{-1}[a + 2b(w - bkm^*)]$$

where h^*, m^* are the steady state values of $h(t)$ and $m(t)$ respectively. However the zero conjectural variation assumption that $\partial u_i / \partial u_j = 0$, for $i \neq j$ may not hold in the market demand equation. In this case there may be instability in the convergence process and the steady state p^*, u_i^* may not be stable. In such cases the duopolists may see implicit cooperation. For example, Ohyama and Fukushima (1995) have recently shown that in dualistic market structures of the NICs in Asia, the Asian producers adopt a two-tier policy. In the domestic front they act more like a monopoly and tend to exploit all scale economies due to learning and experience, whereas in the international market they attempt to build up implicit cooperation with the US producers, since they do not have a large base in R&D investment.

7.2   DIMENSIONS AND DIFFUSION OF NEW TECHNOLOGY

In the Schumpeterian theory of creative destruction spillover effects of new technology are positive for subsequent adopters, but are likely to be negative for the older firms with prior investments in capital made obsolete by more recent innovations. However, these predictions depend on the shape and form the new innovations take, since there are several dimensions to new technology. As the empirical studies of the computer industry by Norsworthy and Jang (1992) showed that the rapid growth of productivity in this sector has been due to economies of scale and the learning curve effects. The microelectronics and semiconductor industry tend to show a similar trend. Recently Brynjolfsson and Hitt (1993) and Dewan and Min (1997) analyzed the IDG/*Computer World* annual survey data on spending by larger US firms for the period 1988 to 1992 toward information technology (IT) and found that IT is displacing other inputs in the production of goods and services. By 1994, IT accounted for over 15% of fixed investment by the US private sector and the quality adjusted price of computer assets has decreased at the average annual rate of 20% relative to the price of other capital goods over the period 1960–92. The fact that IT capital is a net substitute for both ordinary capital and labor allows it to grow to more significant levels over time. Thus over the 1988–92 sample period and the IDG data the ratio of IT capital to labor rose from 0.113 to 0.287. Furthermore, in 1994 the ratio of new IT investments to labor cost came to about 5% for the US private sector on the 1990 dollar basis.

The spillover effects of new technology is not limited however to the domestic economy alone. Given the worldwide transmissibility of research knowledge and openness in trade and foreign investment, the spillover effects are bound to have international characteristics. Since more than 90% of the world's research is done in a handful of industrial countries, it is natural to expect that the spillover will flow from these few countries to the rest of the world rather than in the reverse direction. In two empirical studies Coe and Helpman (1995) and Coe, Helpman and Hoffmaister (1997) studied the quantitative impact of international R&D spillovers on the improvement of domestic rates of return and the total factor productivity (TFP) growth. They concluded their analysis of 77 developing countries and also G7 industrial countries over a 20 year period 1971–90, by noting that a country's TFP depends not only on how much research and development it does domestically, but also on how much R&D is done in other countries linked by international trade. The more a country is exposed to the international economy, the more it gains from R&D spillover from other countries. Thus they found the elasticity of TFP with respect to R&D stocks as follows

	Domestic	Foreign
G7 countries	0.234	0.294M
Small Industrial	0.078	0.294M
Developing	-	0.837N

Note: M and N are the ratio to GDP of total imports and machinery imports respectively.

Clearly the benefits to TFP growth by foreign R&D in the small industrial and the developing countries are found to be substantial and it is most likely to increase over time as the globalization of trade and investment increase.

In a more specific study of bilateral trade between US and Japan, Bernstein and Mohnen (1994) evaluate the productivity impact of international R&D spillovers between the R&D intensive sectors of the two economies. The data used in their study relate to a common set of industries over the sample period 1962–88. This common set comprises 11 industries such as food and kindred products, paper and allied products, chemicals, petroleum and coal, primary and fabricated metals, electrical machinery, transportation equipment and scientific instruments, etc. The industries for each country, i.e. US and Japan, are aggregated by Fisher index into a single sector. The estimated results for short run and long run elasticities are given in Table 7.1 While the short run elasticities are derived from the short-run demand for capital, assuming that variable factor prices and real discount rate do not change over time, the long run elasticities are derived from the long run capital input demands, when all capital inputs can vary. Several important points clearly emerge from this table. First of all, the short run elasticities show that in the short run a 1% increase in the US R&D capital reduces Japanese direct average variable cost by 0.63%. The long run reduction is −1.057%. This is the direct effect on average variable cost holding fixed the factor intensities. Since one can interpret the increase in

R&D spillovers as technological change, this cost reduction for Japan provides a direct measure of the rate of technological change. Secondly, the international R&D spillovers reduce the labor output and physical capital output ratios for both US and Japanese sectors, though much more for the Japanese sectors. Also the international spillovers cause the Japanese R&D intensive sector to increase its R&D intensity by more than twice the effect found in the US. Finally, in the long run the elasticities for Japan are relatively more elastic than the US. Thus in the long run a 1% increase in US R&D capital leads to a 1.057% decrease in direct average variable cost in Japan. This is the direct effect of the spillover before Japan adjusts its production process in the light of new knowledge received through the spillover. An interesting feature of the long run effects, as stressed by Bernstein and Mohnen (1994) is that as new knowledge is transmitted from the US to Japan, the latter reduces its own R&D intensity. Indirectly this supports the Schumpeterian theory of creative destruction, whereby the spillover effects may be positive for subsequent adopters but are likely to be negative for those with prior investments in capital made obsolete by more recent innovations. Note that the US does not reduce its R&D intensity, e.g., the short and the long run R&D intensity increases by 0.026% and 0.242% respectively with the spillover from Japan.

Table 7.1 Short-Run and Long-Run Spillover Effects

	Short run		Long run	
	US	Japan	US	Japan
Direct ave. variable cost	−0.054	−0.633	−0.069	−1.057
Average variable cost	0.241	−0.426	0.136	−0.430
Labor/Output	−0.014	−3.546	−0.762	−2.058
R&D capital/output	0.026	0.053	0.242	−0.261
Physical capital/output	−0.015	−0.130	0.021	−0.546

The spillover effects may also be characterized in terms of the interaction between two domestic sectors of an economy. Some of these interactions in growth process were analyzed previously in Chapter 2 for the Asian NICs, where the growth of the export sector had strong positive impact on the non export sector. This may be modelled directly in terms of the evolutionary dynamics of a two-sector growth process. Assume that there are two sectors with outputs x and n, where the first may be the R&D innovation-intensive sector like the modern export sector and let $p_{x,n}(t)$ be the transition probability of respective outputs taking specific values at time t and following a birth and death process.

Then the system of differential equations for the transition probability $p_{x,n}(t)$ at time t can be written as

$$dp_{x,n}(t) = -(\lambda_x + \mu_x + \lambda_n + \mu_n)p_{x,n}(t) + \lambda_{x-1}p_{x-1,n}(t)$$

$$+ \mu_{x+1}p_{x+1,n}(t) + \lambda_{n-1}p_{x,n-1}(t) + \mu_{n+1}p_{x,n+1}(t) \qquad (7.17)$$

for x,n=0,1,2,... We now consider the application of the above system of differential equations to two special cases. The first case occurs when there is no death rate, i.e., $\mu_x = 0 = \mu_n$ and the deterministic system in x(t) and n(t) follows one way interdependence as follows

$$dx(t)/dt = \dot{x}(t) = b_1 vx(t)$$
$$dn(t)/dt = \dot{n}(t) = a_2 n(t) + b_2(1 - v)x(t); \quad 0 < v < 1.$$

Here n(t) depends on x(t) for its growth, whereas x(t) grows due to the high proportion of total output x(t) + n(t) devoted to human capital, i.e., high level of v which implies a low level allocated for the growth of the n(t) sector. The means (M_x, M_n) and variances (V_x, V_n) may then be calculated as

$$M_x(t) = \exp(b_1 vt)$$
$$V_x(t) = v(2 - v)^{-1} \exp(b_1 vt)[\exp(b_1 vt) - 1]$$

where the initial value x(0) is set equal to one. However the non export sector output follows a different mean variance structure. The mean is

$$M_n(t) = b_2(1 - v)(b_1 v - a_2)^{-1} \exp(b_1 vt) + \exp(a_2 t)$$

but the variance is a more complicated function with a dominant term proportional to $\exp(2a_2 t)$. It is clear from these mean variance relationships that

$$\partial M_x(t) / \partial V_x(t) < 0 \text{ as } M_x(t) < 1.0$$

i.e., countries with a higher volatility of export output would tend to have a lower mean export level; otherwise $\partial M_x / \partial V_x > 0$ as $M_x(t) > 1.0$. Secondly, the allocation ratio v can be used directly by public policy favoring the export sector. The national governments in NICs in Asia have always stressed these policy measures. For example the government planners in Japan and Korea have consistently allocated a growing share of domestic and foreign resources through credit rationing and other export subsidy measures to capital-intensive industries and also consumer electronics. Finally, at $t \to \infty$, the coefficient of variation (CV) measuring the relative level of fluctuations tends to settle down in both sectors, e.g., $CV_x \sim (v/2 - v)^{1/2}$. This implies that the CV_x ratio increases as v rises.

A second case of the stochastic process model (7.17) occurs when the sectoral interdependence takes the following form

$$\lambda_x = \lambda_1 x, \mu_x = xf(x, n) = x(\mu_{11}x + \mu_{12}n)$$
$$\lambda_n = \lambda_2 n, \mu_n = nf(x, n) = n(\mu_{21}x + \mu_{22}n)$$

where $f(x,n) = \alpha_1 x + \alpha_2 x$ denoting the interaction term. This form allows various types of interaction effects through the functions $f(\bullet)$ and $g(\bullet)$. One could derive from this system differential equations involving the first two moments of the stochastic process as follows:

$$\dot{m}_{11}(t) = \lambda_1 m_{11}(t) - \mu_{11} m_{12}(t) - \mu_{12}\overline{m}_{11}(t)$$

$$\text{(7.18)}$$

$$\dot{m}_{21}(t) = \lambda_2 m_{21}(t) - \mu_{21}\overline{m}_{11}(t) - \mu_{22} m_{22}(t)$$

Here $m_{11}(t) = E\{X(t)\}, m_{12}(t) = E\{X^2(t)\}, m_{21}(t) = E\{N(t)\}$, $m_{22}(t) = E\{N^2(t)$ and $\overline{m}_{11}(t) = E\{X(t)N(t)\}$ and the dot over a variable denotes its time derivative. Clearly if there is no interaction between the sectors, then the two sectoral outputs $m_{11}(t)$ and $m_{21}(t)$ grow at the exponential rates λ_1 and λ_2 respectively. But if $\mu_{12} = 0 = \mu_{21}$ and both μ_{11} and μ_{22} are negative, then both sectoral outputs tend to grow exponentially. The deterministic system corresponding to (7.18) may be specified as

$$\dot{X}(t) = \lambda_1 X(t) - \mu_1 \alpha_1 X^2(t) - \mu_1 \alpha_2 X(t)N(t)$$
$$\dot{N}(t) = \lambda_2 X(t) - \mu_2 \alpha_1 X(t)N(t) - \mu_2 \alpha_2 N^2(t)$$

Note that this system has a logistic time profile for the export sector output if $\mu_1\alpha_2$ is negligibly small, i.e.,

$$\dot{X}(t) = \lambda_1 X(t) - \mu_1 \alpha_1 X^2(t)$$

with steady state values

$$X^* = \lambda_1 /(\mu_1\alpha_1), \ N^* = \frac{\lambda_2}{\alpha_2\mu_2} - \frac{\lambda_1}{\alpha_2\mu_1}$$

The stability of these steady state values depends of course on the underlying characteristic roots. However the stability of the steady state values m_{11}^*, m_{21}^* of the stochastic system (7.17) depends on much more restrictive conditions. As May (1973) has shown that the probability of unstable steady states is much higher and there exist biological systems where this type of instability phenomenon is persistent.

From an applied perspective two remarks may be made about this bivariate growth process. One is that the proportion of innovative output (i.e., x-output) in the total may provide an estimate of the transition probability $p_x(t)$ at time t.

The steady state version of the differential equation model (7.17), in case of linear birth and death processes may then be written as

$$(\lambda + \mu)p_x = \lambda p_{x-1} + \mu p_{x+1}$$

which yields

$$p_x = (1-\rho)\rho^x, \quad \rho = \lambda/\mu \tag{7.18}$$
$$E[x(t)] = \lambda(\mu - \lambda)^{-1}$$

where the birth and death rate parameters are assumed to be positive constants. In the nonsteady state the mean M(t) and variance V(t) of x(t) take the following form

$$M(t) = e^{(\lambda - \mu)t}$$

$$V(t) = (\lambda + \mu / \lambda - \mu)e^{(\lambda - \mu)t}[e^{(\lambda - \mu)t} - 1]$$

(7.19)

where the value of x(t) at time zero is set equal to one as a normalization condition. It is clear from the steady state conditions (7.18) that $\partial Ex(t)/\partial\lambda > 0$ and $\partial Ex(t)/\partial\mu < 0$ i.e., the birth rate parameter has a positive impact on average growth of innovative output, whereas the death rate parameter has a negative impact. Hence any policy which increases λ would tend to increase the innovative output and the reverse holds for μ. Secondly, the nonsteady version of the mean and variance processes in (7.19) clearly shows that even when the birth rate exceeds the death rate ($\lambda > \mu$) and both the mean M(t) and variance V(t) functions tend to be unbounded, the coefficient of variation C(t) always remains bounded

$$C^2(t) = V(t)/M^2(t) = \frac{\lambda + \mu}{\lambda - \mu}\left[1 - e^{(\mu - \lambda)t}\right]$$

(7.19)

Since the endogenous growth models predict sustained growth, this type of linear stochastic growth processes is quite consistent with it.

One important type of innovation was characterized by Schumpeter (1939) as a change in the form of production function. But modern technology based on sophisticated forms of what is commonly called 'knowledge capital' has acquired several new dimensions, where multiple outputs and different ways of organizing multiple inputs have made the very concept of production function inappropriate if now obsolete, particularly in R&D intensive industries such as microelectronics, computer industry and semiconductors. Over the last decade increased competition from innovative firms have forced many firms to adopt higher degrees of automation involving computer-aided design (CAD) and computer–aided manufacturing (CAM). According to the estimates of the Economic Commission of Europe the world market for industrial automation which includes CAD and CAM exceeds 100 billion dollars in 1994. All these massive investments are in one form or other investments in flexible manufacturing systems (FMS). Recently Miller (1985) estimated by regression methods the productivity effects of robotics and FMS technologies for 22 manufacturing establishments in the US and found that a flexible automated batch production plant has on the average a substantial cost advantage over a conventional plant.

Two main reasons may be given why the FMS technology is spreading so fast in the modern technology sector. The first is the productivity effect of flexibility, where the flexibility of a production system is a measure of its capability to adapt to changing market environments and streams of new innovations. The second reason is the *economies of scope* argument in output expansion. Whereas the economies of scale refers to cost advantages due to increases in size, volume or scale, the economies of scope refers to cost savings due to increasing complexity from the variety of technologies, processes or products. If Y is the vector of n outputs $(y_1, y_2, ..., y_n)$ and $C(Y)$ denotes the cost function, then the cost function satisfying $C(\lambda Y) \leq \lambda C(Y)$ for any scalar $\lambda \geq 1$ exhibits economies of scale. But for any two nonnegative output vectors Y_1, Y_2 the cost function displays economies of scope if

$$C(Y_1 + Y_2) \leq C(Y_1) + C(Y_2)$$

Recently Cohen and Lee (1985) and Filippini and Rovetta (1989) have emphasized through empirical case studies that CAD–CAM and robotic FMS are the most economic because they exploit significant economies of scope, scale and flexibility.

The dynamic impact of FMS investments on modern technology is yet to be clearly analyzed in new economic growth theory. Data envelopment analysis is an alternative tool which can be applied here. This tool is more general than the traditional concept of a production function which can only handle the case of a single output. See Sengupta (1995) for some recent applications of this tool in industrial efficiency measurement and analysis.

7.3   MODELS OF EVOLUTION AND DIVERSITY

Recently Saviotti and Metcalfe (1991) stressed in their survey of recent trends in evolutionary economics four key research traditions that have influenced and are still influencing the shape of evolutionary economics today. The first is Schumpeter's model of creative destruction, which involves a nonequilibrium type of qualitative change in the capitalist economy. The second is the biological research tradition on evolution, which emphasizes adaptivity, selection and diversity in the pattern of evolution of different species in different environments. The third influence comes from nonequilibrium thermodynamics and systems theory which emphasize irreversibility of behavior and chaotic instability of certain systems when subjected to strong external constraints. This type of process can be visualized by plotting some output variable y representing the system behavior against some control parameter u. For values of u less than or equal to a level u_0, the system behavior may be stable or convergent. But for some critical value of the control parameter $u > u_0$, the system may become unstable and several new solutions may emerge. This is a bifurcation point and the system has a multiplicity of choice between the different branches of the bifurcation diagram. Finally, the fourth key research tradition is the new organization theories of firm and their interactions. This tradition emphasizes the adoption of decision rules by firms under imperfect knowledge and uncertainty, satisfying rather than optimizing behavior by firms and the role of bargaining and conflict in the evolution of organizations. This tradition has been developed by a number of authors, e.g., Simon (1957), Cyert and March (1963), Nelson and Winter (1982). This research tradition views the evolutionary role of a firm in terms of its capacity to learn how to change its internal decision rules, when the environment changes and its profit and managerial goals go unfulfilled.

Since the implications of nonequilibrium systems and chaotic dynamics would be discussed in the next section, we analyze here briefly two key concepts from the ecological models of evolution of species in competitive environments. One is the concept of diversity and variety in an aggregate population: how to measure it in an operational way and what are its implications for new growth theory in economies? The second is the concept of evolutionary competition, where only those species grow and dominate in the aggregation, which maximize the fitness in the natural selection processes. This type of fitness model may be easily correlated with the rapid growth of those industries which have a higher proportion of innovation or R&D intensive firms. Also these innovative firms may follow certain strategies which are analogous to the evolutionary stable strategies (ESS) of noncooperative game theory model as developed by Smith (1982) in the context of ecological competition.

The ecological concept of diversity may be related to two key concepts in economic growth theory. One is to describe how the concentration of firms within an industry changes, when the industry undergoes a growth process. Like the ecological distribution of species in ecological environments, the concept of 'a representative firm' was used in Marshallian theory to model the evolution of an industry. Shannon's concept of entropy has been often used by economists as an inverse measure of concentration to analyze the size distribution of firms. For example Theil (1992) applied the entropy measure

$$H(y) = \sum_{i=1}^{n} y_i \log(1 / y_i) \qquad (7.20)$$

to analyze the dispersal pattern of firms, where y_i is the market share of total output of the ith firm. The minimum entropy occurs when $H(y) = 0$, i.e., $y_i = 1$ for only one i. This corresponds to maximum concentration or minimal dispersal. The other extreme is $H(y) = \log n$ which is the maximum entropy given n and this corresponds to the minimum degree of concentration or maximal dispersal. If we interpret y_i as the share of sectoral output in total GNP, then one can analyze how entropy $H(y)$ changes over time, as GNP rises due to technology shocks or opening up in international trade.

The second concept is one of expanding product variety and improving product quality associated with process or product innovation due to R&D investments. This aspect has been analyzed in some detail by Grossman and Helpman (1991) in the context of endogenous models of economic growth. In this model the households' tastes for diversity in consumption provide the key motivation for innovations that serve to expand the set of available varieties. Thus the representative household maximizes utility over an infinite horizon

$$U = \int_{t}^{\infty} e^{-\rho(\tau-t)} \log D(\tau) d\tau \qquad (7.21)$$

where

$$D = \left[\int_{0}^{n} x(j)^{\alpha} dj \right]^{1/\alpha}, \quad 0 < \alpha < 1 \qquad (7.22)$$

denotes an index of diversity in consumption, ρ is the subjective discount rate and $x(j)$ denotes consumption of brand j, where there are n brands. The specification of D in this form due to Dixit and Stiglitz (1977) imposes a constant and equal elasticity of substitution between every pair of goods. It is then easy to show that with these preferences, the elasticity of substitution between any two products is $\varepsilon = 1/(1-\alpha)$ which exceeds unity and a household spending an amount M maximizes instantaneous utility by demanding an amount $x(j)$ of brand $j \in [0,n]$

$$x(j) = M \, p(j)^{-\varepsilon} / \int_{0}^{n} p(\tilde{j})^{1-\varepsilon} d\tilde{j}$$

where $p(j)$ is the price of brand j. These can be aggregated across consumers to obtain aggregate demands with exactly the same form u_t but with M then representing the aggregate spending by all households. Two features of this approach have been stressed by Grossman and Helpman (1991). One is that this model allows increasing diversity in consumption. Secondly, the CES form of (7.22) allows a single parameter α to characterize different tastes for variety. The production function (7.22) implies that total factor productivity (TFP) increases with the number of available varieties. To see this assume a symmetric equilibrium with equal quantities $x(j) = x$ for each brand (or each intermediate service). Then $D = n^{1/\alpha} x$. The final output per unit of primary input (i.e., TFP) is then $D/X = n^{(1-\alpha)/\alpha}$, where $X = nx$. This shows that as n grows the TFP rises. Ethier (1982) has related this property of the technology production function (7.22) to the increasing degree of specialization in production.

In case of rising product quality Grossman and Helpman replace the instantaneous utility function (7.22) by

$$\log D(t) = \int_{0}^{1} \log \left[\sum_{m} q_m(j) x_{mt}(j) \right] dj$$

where $x_{mt}(j)$ denotes consumption of quality m in product line j at time t. This model allows quality ladder, where one firm is the leader and the others are followers. The diversity in the distribution of firms then results under the equilibrium solution of monopolistic competition. Recently Barro and Martin (1994) have extended this formulation, where technological progress occurs in the form of improvements in quality in an array of intermediate inputs to production. Here they show that if industry leaders have lower costs of R&D output, then the leaders act as a monopoly with the prices of leading-edge good set above the competition level. But if the cost advantage is not very large, then the equilibrium research intensity and overall growth rate depend on the existence of the competitive fringe as in the dynamic limit pricing model.

Thus the property of TFP growth due to increasing n may be related to changes in market structure and hence changes in entropy $H = H(y)$ defined in (7.20). Thus one can specify an empirical specification

$$TFP_t = f(H_{t-1}, u_{t-1}) \tag{7.23}$$

where u_t is a vector of shocks due to the stream of innovations and H_t is the entropy measure of diversity in the industrial sector. The marginal impact on TFP_t is positive for any increase in entropy H_{t-1} and this may be intensified by the innovations shock term u_t, provided it leads to expanding variety of new processes or new products.

The concept of evolutionary competition has been applied by Metcalfe (1985) and Saviotti and Metcalfe (1991) to model the dynamic evolution of technologies. The key point in their approach is that it is not only the average representative firm or technology that matters but also their distribution in the whole population. They obtain the interesting result that the rate of change of average unit cost (dh/dt) is proportional to the weighted variance in unit costs in the industry, i.e.

$$dh / dt = [r\theta / (\theta + r)[v_0 C(h, \alpha) - V(h)] \tag{7.24}$$

where h is unit costs, $V(h, \alpha)$ is the covariance of unit cost and the product quality denoted by α, r and θ are parameters describing the environment in which firms operate and the type of market competition and v_0 is a constant relating quality adjusted price to product quality. In the special case in which all products are of the same quality, this fitness model equation (7.24) reduces to

$$dh / dt = [r\theta / (\theta + r)]v(h)$$

which means that the average practice unit cost declines at a rate proportional to the variance of unit costs within the industry. This assumes a negative value for the market competition parameter θ, which implies the existence of cost-efficient firms in the industry enjoying monopoly rents in the short run for their innovative outputs. If one assumes that the variance of unit costs is higher in the initial phase of evolution of a new technology and falls as technology (or product) matures, then this would generate a pattern of firm growth, where mature technologies would show a slower rate of productivity growth than the new technologies. But as competition proceeds and some competing firms are eliminated by new designs, the surviving firms are likely to have not only a higher average productivity but a lower productivity variance. But this may lead to a switch to a new technology paradigm, as the new streams of innovations follow. Clearly this provides a dynamic characterization of industry growth, which captures the essence of the concept of 'creative destruction' in Schumpeterian dynamics.

Finally, we consider the dynamic limit pricing model of firm growth, where one firm is dominant in view of its position as a leader in leading-edge technology and the others are in the competitive fringe with less superior technology. This framework is typically one of Nash equilibrium in noncooperative game theory. The dominant player in this two-person noncooperative game may follow predatory pricing strategy in the short run so as to reduce or eliminate the existing firms. The success of this strategy depends of course on the strategic behavior of the other players. This type of predator–prey behavior underlies the well known hawk–dove game example considered by Smith (1982). In this game the two animals (hawk and the dove) are contesting a resource of value v, which increases the Darwinian fitness of an individual. Thus v is the gain in fitness to the winner, while c is the cost of an injury which reduces fitness. The payoff matrix in terms of changes in fitness is:

				v=2, c=4	
	H	D		H	D
H	(v–c)/2	v	H	−1	2
D	0	v/2	D	0	1

Three assumptions behind the payoff matrix of the symmetric game above are: (1) hawk vs. hawk: each contestant has a 50% chance of injuring its opponent and obtaining the resource v and a 50% chance of being injured; (ii) hawk vs. dove: hawk obtains the resource and dove retreats before being injured; (iii) dove vs. dove: the resource is shared equally by the two contestants.

Now consider an infinite population of individuals, each adopting the strategy H or D at random. In this model behaviors with higher fitness have an advantage in reproducing. Thus if the population consists only of doves, then this will continue in the next generation but if there is a mutation that introduces a hawk into the population, then over time the fraction of doves in the population will decrease and the fraction of hawks will increase. Similarly if the population consists entirely of hawks, a mutant dove can successfully invade the population. The only stable population is thus evenly divided between hawks and doves; here mutation would not disturb the population distribution. As Mailath (1992) has discussed, the idea underlying ESS is that a stable pattern of behavior in a population should be able to eliminate any invasion by a 'mutant'. Thus if a population pattern of behavior is to eliminate invading mutations, it must have a higher fitness (i.e. higher payoff) than the mutant in the population that results from the invasion. Suppose then that a population is playing a mixed strategy vector p and there is an invasion by a q-group with a mixed strategy vector q. The population strategy is then perturbed from p to $(1-\varepsilon)p + \varepsilon q$, where ε with $0 \leq \varepsilon \leq 1$ specifies the size of the influx. We can now compare the fitness of the p-player (or p-group) in this population with that of the q-player. The strategy q will not succeed in invading a population playing p if p is fitter (i.e., obtains a greater payoff) than q. This gives

$$E(p,(1-\varepsilon)p + \varepsilon q) > E(q,(1-\varepsilon)p + \varepsilon q) \qquad (7.25)$$

where $E(\bullet)$ is the payoff to the mixed strategies of the two players. Now this condition (7.25) will hold for sufficiently small ε if and only if

$$E(p,p) \geq E(q,p)$$

and $\qquad\qquad\qquad\qquad\qquad\qquad\qquad\qquad\qquad\qquad\qquad$ (7.26)

$$\text{If } E(p,p) = E(q,p), \text{ then } E(p,q) > E(q,q)$$

The two parts of the condition (7.26) have a simple interpretation. The first part says that if p is to resist invasion, it must do so at least as well as q against the p-group. The second part says that if p does exactly as well as q, then we have to look at the much less frequent encounters with the q-group. Thus the mixed strategy vector p is an ESS in Maynard Smith's definition if for all $q \neq p$, the condition (7.26) holds. Since the conditions (7.25) and (7.26) are equivalent, an alternative definition is that p is an ESS if for any other $q \neq p$ there exists some $\varepsilon_0(q) > 0$ such that for all ε with $0 < \varepsilon < e_0(q)$ we have

$$E(p, (1-\varepsilon)p + \varepsilon q) > E(q, (1-\varepsilon)p + \varepsilon q)$$

If we denote the matrix of fitness or payoff by $A = (a_{ij})$, then the fitness of the mixed strategy p can be written as $\sum_i \sum_j p_i a_{ij} q_i = p \bullet Aq$. Then the mixed strategy vector is an ESS strategy if for all $q \in I_n = \{1,2,...,n\}$ we have

$$p \bullet Ap \geq q \bullet Ap \qquad (7.27)$$

and if

$$p \bullet Ap = q \bullet Ap, \text{ then } p \bullet Aq > q \bullet Aq \ .$$

ESS strategies can be viewed as a refinement of Nash equilibrium, since not all symmetric Nash equilibria are ESS.

ESS is basically a static notion. We follow Mailath (1992) in describing its dynamic implication. Suppose individuals now choose only pure strategies and let p_i^t denote the proportion of population choosing strategy $i \in I_n = \{1,2,...,n\}$ in period t. Since a_{ij} is the fitness of i against j, it can be interpreted as the number of offspring that i has after playing j. In the replicator dynamics, the fraction playing strategy i is determined by how well i faces, relative to the population average fitness $(p^t \bullet Ap^t)$. The dynamics of evolution is then

$$p_i^{t+1} - p_i^t = p_i^t \frac{(e_i \bullet Ap^t - p^t \bullet Ap^t)}{p^t \bullet Ap^t} \qquad (7.28)$$

where e_i is unity for each i. In continuous time this becomes

$$dp_i / dt = p_i(e_i \bullet Ap - p \bullet Ap) \qquad (7.29)$$

This replicator dynamics is useful in testing for stability of the evolution process. However we have to note that this type of dynamics does not fulfill the market dynamics of the limit pricing model discussed in economic theory. There are two reasons for this. One is that the dynamics in (7.28) or (7.29) is not a best reply dynamics. Secondly, this does not capture stability against continual small stochastic shocks.

The ESS strategies however play two useful roles in evolutionary growth theory in economics. One is that it provides a rational framework for the fitness model (7.24) for the evolution of a leading-edge innovative firm. The second is that the equilibrium distribution of products under monopolistic competition may be viewed as a process analogous to the replicator dynamics as above. Parker and Hammerstein (1985) have shown that the second part of the ESS condition (7.26) or (7.27) has important consequences in games of interspecies interactions. Here solutions must be combinations of ESSs, one for each species (i.e., each firm in an industry model). An ESS for one of these species must be a pure strategy if there is no intraspecific frequency dependence of fitness in this population. These interactions are for example host/parasite, or predator/prey interactions. The implications of these interactions in dynamic market models in the form of differential games are of great importance in the dynamic models of industry growth.

7.4   CHAOTIC DYNAMICS IN ECONOMIC GROWTH

Chaotic dynamics is an important part of the study of evolutionary dynamics in economic growth because of several reasons. First of all, the Schumpeterian model of innovations contains the seed of nonlinearity in dynamics. As Goodwin (1990) pointed out, Schumpeter maintained that at the end of an innovatory burst, a new one will commence because of the exponential growth of new ideas. Thus a second boom and collapse is initiated and so on. Thus Goodwin modelled the introduction of a successful innovation by a logistic function

$$\dot{x} = dx \, / \, dt = bx(1 - \bar{x})$$
or $\quad x_{t+1} = a \, x_t(1 - x_t \, / \, \bar{x})$ $\hfill (7.30)$

where the parameter a is positive and $\bar{x}$ is the maximum level for the innovation. Normalization with $\bar{x} = 1$ yields the result

$$x_{t+1} = a \, x_t(1 - x_t) = a \, x_t - a \, x_t^2 \hfill (7.31)$$

The logistic function has a fixed point $\hat{x}$ at $\hat{x} = 1 - (1/a)$. For $1 < a < 3$ the fixed point of (7.31) is stable. But as the hump mapped out by (7.31) steepens, the fixed point becomes unstable, giving rise to a cascade of stable cycles with periods $2, 4, 8, ..., 2^n$. This is called the period doubling phenomenon. But for values of a in the interval $3.57 < a \le 4$ we encounter a chaotic regime. As the value of a increases beyond 3.57, very high odd period cycles appear. Here there occur chaotic attractors for which there is neither a fixed point nor a fixed motion. Hence this tends to almost destroy the notion of equilibrium of an economic system, since the system never repeats itself and remains very sensitive to initial conditions. Brock (1990),

Puu (1993), Lorenz (1993) and others have explored the econometric and other applied aspects of logistic chaos.

Secondly, the innovation process when modelled through accumulated knowledge or experience could introduce significant nonlinear dynamics into the production process, if we assume a stochastic process generating this R&D learning and investment. For example assume a birth and death process model previously considered with λ and μ as the constant birth and death rates respectively and let $X(t)$ denote the experience at time t and $Z(t) = \int_0^t X(u)du$ as the cumulative experience. It is assumed that $X(t)$ follows a homogeneous birth and death process. With $X(0)=m$ and $Z(0)=0$ the mean $M(t)$ and variance $V(t)$ of the $Z(t)$ process can be derived as

$$M(t) = \frac{m}{\lambda - \mu}\left[e^{(\lambda-\mu)t} - 1\right]$$

$$V(t) = m\left[\frac{\lambda + \mu}{(\lambda - \mu)}(e^{2(\lambda-\mu)t} - 1) - \frac{2t(\lambda + \mu)}{(\lambda - \mu)^2}e^{(\lambda-\mu)t}\right]$$

$$cov[x(t), Z(t)] = m\left(\frac{\lambda + \mu}{\lambda - \mu}\right)e^{(\lambda-\mu)t}\left[\frac{1}{\lambda - \mu}\left\{e^{(\lambda-\mu)t} - 1\right\} - t\right]$$

Note that the underlying difference–differential equation in transition probability shows evidence of nonlinear instability and when the parameters λ, μ change logistically, this map generates chaotic instability. Note that if $\lambda > \mu$ for different bursts of knowledge innovations, both mean and variance tend to explode and the correlation coefficient $\rho(X,Z)$ tends to 1.0 as $t \to \infty$. Thus the stochastics of the learning by doing model can generate a type of chaotic instability which is not easily distinguishable from deterministic instability.

Finally, the model of expanding variety of products which we considered before may easily give rise to chaotic dynamics, when the leader (or dominant innovator) follows certain types of strategy in duopoly games. For example, Dana and Montrucchio (1993) have considered such a dynamic duopoly game model, where the two players strategy sets are X and Y and their instantaneous profit functions are $U^1(x,y)$ and $U^2(x,y)$. Their inter-temporal profit functions are $\sum_{t=1}^{\infty} U^i(x_t, y_t)\delta^{t-1}$, i=1,2 where $0 < \delta < 1$ is their discount factor. They assume that in odd numbered periods (t=1,3,...)

player 1 chooses an action that is maintained for two periods. Similarly player 2 moves in even number periods (t = 0,2,...). Let $x_t = r_1(x_{t-1}, y_{t-1})$ and $y_t = r_2(y_{t-1}, x_{t-1})$ be the reaction functions of the two players, where the pair (r_1, r_2) is said to be a *reaction function equilibrium* (RFE) if

$$r_1(x,y) = \arg \max_{x_1 \in X}\left[U^1(x_1, r_2(x,y)) + \delta V^1_{r_2}(x_1, r_2(x,y)) \right]$$

$$r_2(x,y) = \arg \max_{y_1 \in Y}\left[U^2(r_1(x,y), y_1) + \delta V^2_{r_1}(r_1(x,y), y) \right]$$

where $V^1_{r_2}(x,y)$ is the unique value function of player 1 as defined by Bellman's principle

$$V^1_{r_2}(x,y) = \max_{x \in X}\left[U^1(x_1, r_2(x,y)) + \delta f(x_1, r_2(x,y)) \right]$$

The other value function $V^2_{r_1}(x,y)$ is defined symmetrically.

Now assume for this symmetric game on the unit square that the payoff functions are

$$U^1 = -y(1/10)\, x(1-x)$$

$$U^2 = -x + (1/10)\, y(1-y)$$

This yields the unique static equilibrium: $x = y = 1/2$. Hence $r_1(x,y) = r_2(x,y) = 1/2$ is a RFE for all discount factors. But there exists another equilibrium: $r_{1\delta} = (10\delta)^{-1} y(1-y)$, $r_{2\delta} = (10\delta)^{-1} x(1-x)$ for discount factors $1/40 \le \delta \le 1.0$. As the discount factor δ decreases, the dynamical complexity increases. For instance when δ assumes the value $1/40$, the dynamic strategies become

$$x_{t+1} = 4y_t(1 - y_t)$$

$$y_{t+1} = 4x_t(1 - x_t)$$

On comparing this system with (7.31) it is clear that this yields chaotic instability for the family of RFE over time.

In concluding we may note with Brock (1990) that some kind of *positive feedback* behavior has to exist for chaotic type of unstable dynamics. Much of economic adjustment however involves negative feedback mechanisms such as when price goes up demand goes down but supply goes up leading to a fall in price in the future. This leads to equilibrating adjustment. However expectations about price rise in future may lead to positive feedback, e.g., hyperinflation. Other sources of positive feedback are changes in fashion or tastes, the spread of rumors in exchange markets. The presence of chaotic dynamics makes the conventional methods of econometric estimation totally useless.

8. Infrastructure and Economic Growth

Infrastructure services (IS) are usually classified into two groups: economic infrastructure (EIS) and social infrastructure (SIS). EIS generally includes power, transport, telecommunications, provision of water and sanitation and safe disposal of wastes and other pollutants. The *World Development Report* 1994: *Infrastructure for Development* published by the World Bank stressed several important links of EI to economic growth in both developed and developing economies. In terms of value added share of GDP by the use of EIS services, the transport and communication accounts for 5.34, 6.78 and 9.46% respectively for the low-income, middle-income and high-income countries. Gas, electricity and water account for 1.29, 2.24 and 1.87% respectively. This World Bank Report cites several empirical country-specific and time series studies which show a significant link of EIS expenditure to the growth of GDP. Public investment in transport and communications which includes roads, railways and telephones is found to be positively and significantly correlated with growth in developing countries. An analysis of the value of EIS stocks in recent years shows that their composition changes significantly as per capita income rises. In the first stage more basic infrastructure such as water supply, irrigation and basic roads become the dominant component for low income countries. Then in the second stage as the economy matures into the middle income stage, the share of agriculture declines and more transport infrastructure is developed. Finally, in the high income stage the share of power and telecommunications becomes most important.

The SIS services often termed as the social overhead capital include education, health care and the process of urbanization. Social indicators are sometimes used as a proxy measure for these SIS services. Clearly the human capital and intersectoral knowledge spillover and diffusion of innovation are all interlinked with the SIS services. In economic theory they have the public goods characteristics of externalities.

Development of the export sector, which is so critical in the new growth theory depends very significantly on the high quality EI and SI services. Over the last two decades the major advances in transport and communications have accelerated the pace of increased globalization of world trade. From a policy viewpoint both EIS and SIS have been dominated by the public sector. This is due to a number of reasons: the economic and social importance of infrastructure in overall growth, the element of scale economies in EI investment and a forward looking view of the long run growth process where the government can play a catalytic role. The central emphasis of this chapter is to analyze the role of the public sector capital expenditure in infrastructure in general or, EI in particular in relating to the models of endogenous economic growth. Recently Holtz-Eakin and Schwartz (1994) have examined this issue empirically. This is then followed by a brief discussion of the following three issues: the role of institutions and appropriate organizational structures, impact of externalities of public goods and finally the issue of environmental quality and sustained economic growth.

8.1   PRODUCTIVITY OF PUBLIC CAPITAL

Not all government expenditure can be viewed as investment. Government consumption services either directly through military and law and order expenditure, or indirectly through welfare services which enter into households' utility functions are not investment oriented.

Landau (1983) analyzed 104 countries on a cross-sectional basis using data on government consumption and other variables from Summers and Heston (1984). His measure of government 'consumption expenditure' excludes public investment and transfers but includes most expenditures on defense and education. He found significantly negative relations between the growth rate of GDP per capita and the ratio of government consumption expenditure to GDP. However, Landau's regressions held constant a measure of investment in education which generates human capital. Recently Barro (1989) adjusted the Summers–Heston data on government consumption by subtracting the ratios to GDP of government spending (h/y) on defense and education from the ratios reported by Summers and Heston. This was denoted by g^c/y and used as a proxy for the government spending ratio h/y. He also measured the ratio of real public gross investment to real GDP and denoted by g^i/y. This public investment corresponds to a stock of public capital which generates productive services and takes the form of water, power, transportation, etc. as included by EIS. For the 97 countries Barro performed a regression of the average annual growth rate of real GDP per capita from 1960 to 1985 on a set of explanatory variables, which yielded the estimated coefficient on g^c/y to be -0.13 with a standard error of 0.03. The estimated coefficient on g^i/y becomes 0.16 with a standard error of 0.08. If the ratio g^i/y is replaced by

g^i/i, where i is the sum of private and public investment, then the estimated coefficient on g^i/i turns out to be 0.020 with a standard error of 0.020. Thus there is a strong indication that an increase in government consumption expenditure tends to lower per capita growth, whereas public investment contributes positively to growth.

We concentrate now on the productive side of public capital investment, viewing it as an input into the production function. Let the aggregate production function be in the Solow form:

$$Y_t = K_t^\alpha G_t^\beta (A_t L_t)^{1-\alpha-\beta} \tag{8.1}$$

where K_t, G_t are private and public capital, L_t is labor growing at the exponential rate n and A_t is the labor-augmenting variety of technical progress which is assumed to grow at the exponential rate of λ. Expressing each variable in efficiency units of $A_t L_t$ and using lower case letters to denote per capita values one can derive the production function as

$$y_t = k_t^\alpha g_g^\beta = f(k_t, g_t) \tag{8.2}$$

where the growth of g_t and k_t are as follows:

$$\dot{g}_t = uy_t - hg_t, \quad h = \lambda + n + v \tag{8.3}$$

$$\dot{k}_t = f(k_t, g_t) - c_t - g_t - (\lambda + n)k_t \tag{8.4}$$

The equation of motion (8.3) for the growth of public capital assumes that a fraction (u) of total GDP is spent to augment public productive capital but this growth–inducing effect declines as more and more public capital is accumulated, i.e., $\dot{G}_t = uY_t - vG_t$. The equation of motion (8.4) for private capital stock embodies the equilibrium of savings and investment.

An optimal growth trajectory can now be specified by assuming that each household maximizes a discounted stream of utilities:

$$\text{Max} \int_0^\infty e^{-\rho t} U(c_t) dt$$

where $\tag{8.5}$

211

$$U(c_t) = (1/\theta)c_t^\theta$$

By Pontryagin's maximum principle the optimal trajectories can then be easily determined by the following conditions:

$$U_c = \partial U / \partial c_t = q_t$$
$$\dot p_t = (h - uf_g)p_t + (1 - f_g)q_t \qquad (8.6)$$
$$\dot q_t = (h - v - f_k)q_t - uf_k p_t$$

where f_g, f_k denote the marginal product of g and k and $h = \rho + \lambda + n + v$. The variables p_t and q_t are the Lagrange multipliers associated with (8.3) and (8.4) respectively. The optimality conditions (8.6) have the usual economic interpretations. For example, the first condition of (8.6) says that at every instant t the marginal utility of consumption should equal the optimal shadow price of the private capital investment. The other two equations imply that as u increases, the incremental shadow prices tend to fall, i.e., $\partial \dot p_t / \partial u < 0$, $\partial \dot q_t / du < 0$. Finally, the steady state levels imply the following:

$$\bar q / \bar p = U_c / \bar p = (1 - f_g)^{-1}[uf_g - h]$$
$$\bar q / \bar p = uf_k / (h - v - f_k) \qquad (8.7)$$
$$f_k = [(h - v)U_c / \bar p] / (u + U_c / \bar p)$$
$$f_g = [h + U_c / \bar p] / \{u + U_c / \bar p\}$$

Several implications follow from these steady state equations. First of all, as the proportion u of public investment rises, it tends to lower both the marginal products of private and public capital. Secondly, an increase in the marginal productivity of public capital augments the marginal productivity of private capital if $f_g < 1$, otherwise it reduces f_k. Thirdly, if $f_g = f_k$ i.e., both capital stocks have identical marginal products, then the ratio g/y denoting the share of public capital in output rises as β rises. Thus the higher the output elasticity of public capital in the production function (8.1), the greater the ratio of public capital to output. Finally, for any given u the two growth equations (8.3) and (8.4) can be combined in the steady state to yield

$$\bar{y} = \left(\frac{u}{n + \lambda - v}\right)^{\beta/(1-\beta)} (\bar{k})^{\alpha/(1-\beta)}$$

$$\bar{g} = \left(\frac{u}{n + \lambda - v}\right)^{1/(1-\beta)} (\bar{k})^{\alpha/(1-\beta)}$$

This shows that the long run differences in per capita output and EIS will depend very significantly on the level of u, the proportion of output allocated to EIS. Thus the correlation between $\bar{g}$ and $\bar{y}$ is greatly influenced by the ratio u.

For the US economy, Aschauer (1989) estimated an output elasticity for public capital of 0.39 in time series regressions using post war data (1949–85). This finding suggests that public capital in the form of EIS is very important for output and growth but the magnitude of the output elasticity seems very large. Recently Hamilton (1996) tested Aschauer's results for the existence of unit roots and endogeneity and found them to be robust. Thus public capital not only explains the variation in output over time but persistence as well. However the large magnitude of public capital productivity is found to be due to omitted variable bias, e.g., human capital is an omitted variable in Aschauer's model. Inclusion of this relevant omitted variable reduces the public capital elasticity from 0.54 to 0.19 over the extended data set from 1948 to 1993 analyzed by Hamilton. He also found that the marginal product of public capital does not greatly exceed that of private capital, e.g., in 1987 dollars with NIPA data set his estimates are 0.47 and 0.40 for public and private capital. This is consistent with the implications of the results (8.7) analyzed before.

For developing economies however the infrastructure investment by public expenditure is not always sufficient on its own to generate sustained increases in economic growth. Reasons are several. First of all, the economic impact of IS investment varies not only by sector but also by its implementation, efficiency and location. Secondly, inadequate maintenance and inefficiency of operations account for a significant loss of productivity. According to the *World Development Report* 1994 of the World Bank about one-quarter of the power utilities in developing countries in 1987 had suffered losses of electricity in the transmission and distribution network that were twice those in efficiently operated systems.

8.2   SOCIAL OVERHEAD CAPITAL

Social infrastructure services are largely 'public goods' and hence these are neither 'rival' (consumption by one user does not reduce the supply to other users), nor 'excludable' (a user cannot be prevented from consuming them). Competition in market framework work best in providing pure private goods or services which are mostly 'rival' and excludable. However many infrastructure services like the community health care system have the characteristics of private goods but they produce spillovers or externalities which can be both positive and negative. Positive externalities contribute to intersectoral growth through diffusion of knowledge and the extension of the network system. Negative externalities have their negative impact on the growth of output in other sectors. For example if one ignores the negative externality of emissions from fossil fuel, then a program of rapid generation of power may adversely affect the environment and also the quality of life in general. Recently Grossman and Krueger (1994) have empirically estimated the reduced-form relationship between national GDP and various indicators of local environmental conditions such as water and air quality using panel data from the Global Environmental Monitoring System. They found that for most indicators of environmental quality, the economic growth process brings an initial phase of deterioration followed by a subsequent phase of improvement. Most probably higher income levels bring an increased demand for better protection of environmental quality.

To the extent that social infrastructure services are not like private goods subject to market competition, two types of economic inefficiency have thrived under the public provision of SIS. One is the cost inefficiency due to inadequate utilization of available capacity. Sometimes this takes the form of dead weight loss. The second is the loss due to in optimal capacity expansion in the face of expected increase in demand due to population growth and urbanization. These inefficiencies are prevalent for example in the public outlays for schools, health care facilities, roads and other IS. Several types of policy measures have been suggested as possible remedies: privatizing the provision of social infrastructure services, public ownership with operation contracted to the private sector, and community approaches in supplying sustainable services using e.g., intermediate technologies in rural areas and in the low income settlements which often develop outside the existing urban service network.

In endogenous growth theory one could suggest two different ways of incorporating externalities of SIS. One is to rewrite the instantaneous utility function in (8.5) as $U(c_t, \tilde{g}_t)$ dependent on both consumption and government expenditure allocated towards social infrastructure. Arrow and Kurz (1970) used this formalization to analyze the impact of public SIS investments on the potential direct consumption benefits and social welfare. By contrasting this case with the situation where $\tilde{g}_t$ is absent, one could characterize the divergence of the two optimal growth paths, one based on private optimization and the other on the public criterion. In order to counter such divergence between private decisions and social objectives, the government may have to introduce specific instruments such as tax and monetary policies. A second approach due to Caballero and Lyons (1992) relates the externality effects to the Solow residual and applies it to the US manufacturing sector. Thus one writes the rate of growth (i.e., log change) of manufacturing value added (y) as a cost-weighted input measure (x) and a residual (ε):

$$y = \phi x + \varepsilon, \, x = \alpha \ell + (1 - \alpha)k \tag{8.8}$$

where α is the share of labor in total factor costs, ℓ and k are the growth in labor and capital input and ε is the rate of technological progress. If there were no externalities so that the technologies used were similar across firms, then the parameter ϕ represents the returns to scale. In the presence of externality at the industry level i, one obtains the production function

$$y_i = \gamma x_i + \beta y + v_i \tag{8.9}$$

On summing over all industries one obtains (8.8) where $\phi = \gamma(1 - \beta)^{-1}$ and $\varepsilon = v(1 - \beta)^{-1}$. Caballero and Lyons then estimate the equations (8.8) and (8.9) on the basis of the industry means denoted by a bar by using the data of US manufacturing expanded to correct for possible structural changes due to oil shocks. The estimating equations are as follows:

$$\bar{y} = \bar{\phi}\,\bar{x} + h_1\bar{p}$$
$$\bar{y}_i = \bar{\gamma}\,\bar{x}_i + \bar{\beta}\bar{y} + h_2\bar{p}_i \tag{8.10}$$

where $\bar{p}$ is the growth rate of the price of oil. The resulting estimates obtained through three stage least squares are as follows:

$$\bar{\phi} = 1.33, \bar{\theta} = 1.15, \bar{\gamma} = 0.98, \bar{\beta} = 0.18$$
$$(0.07) \quad (0.06) \quad (0.05) \quad (0.04)$$

with standard errors in parentheses. Here $\bar{\theta}$ is the coefficient of $\bar{x}_i$ with no externalities. It is clear that the estimated values satisfy the inequality

$$\bar{\phi} > \bar{\theta} > \bar{\gamma} .$$

Note that the externality parameter $\bar{\beta}$ estimate is positive and statistically significant. Its magnitude 0.18 implies that when other manufacturing industries expand their output by 10%, a given industry's total output is raised by about 1.8 percent. Note also that $\bar{\phi}$ is significantly greater than one, thus suggesting significant economies of scale.

8.3   HUMAN DEVELOPMENT AND GROWTH

The impact of social overhead capital is only partially measurable in terms of GDP and its growth, since the concept of GDP does not adequately measure the environment of human behavior. Two applied approaches have been attempted here to develop a more representative index of human and social behavior as it relates to development. One is the eco-behavioral approach developed by Barker (1968) and extended by Fox (1985). This approach uses behavior setting concepts and time allocation matrices to relate to the OECD list of social indicators originally published in 1982. This OECD list includes 33 specific indicators grouped under eight major headings: health, education and learning, employment and quality of working life, time and leisure, command over goods and services, physical environment, social environment and personal safety. The OECD list, recommended for implementation by OECD member countries includes systematically selected statistical measures of individual well being which can be influenced by social policies and community actions.

The second approach developed by the United Nations Development Program (UNDP) has introduced a new way of measuring human development by combining indicators of life expectancy, educational attainment and income into a composite index, called the human development index (HDI). The first *Human Development Report* (1990) of the UNDP introduced this index and it has been improved since then in several ways. One way the index has been improved is through disaggregation e.g., by different regions, different ethnic groups and different genders. Another way of improvement is by reducing a country's overall HDI in proportion to its internal disparities e.g., between black and white communities, etc. Since 1991, these *Human Development Reports* have published two disparity-adjusted HDIs — one for gender and one for income distribution. Thus in the income-distribution adjusted HDI, more egalitarian countries rise in the rankings, while others fall. A further possibility for adjusting the HDI would be to reflect a country's environmental performance.

Thus HDI offers an alternative to GDP or GNP for measuring the relative socio-economic progress of nations. Judging by the UNDP and World Bank policy recommendations, it may be safely said that the published series of HDI have enabled many governments to evaluate the overall record of progress of human development over time and to determine priorities for social goals and policy intervention. A comparison of HDI ranking with the GNP per capita ranking based on 1994 values is interesting

	HDI value	HDI rank	GNP per capita rank	GNP per capita rank minus HDI rank
Industrial countries:				
1. Canada	0.932	1	11	10
2. France	0.927	6	13	7
3. Japan	0.929	3	3	0
4. USA	0.925	8	9	1
Developing countries:				
5. S. Korea	0.859	32	36	4
6. Singapore	0.836	43	21	−22
7. Colombia	0.813	50	91	41
8. Mexico	0.804	52	51	−1
9. China	0.644	94	143	49

Source: Human Development Report 1994 (UNDP)

One innovative feature of the HDI stressed by the UNDP Report is the way its components are combined. Each indicator is measured in different units: life expectancy in years of life, schooling in mean years of schooling, income in constant dollars and adult literacy as a percentage. To combine these indicators the range of values of each component is put into a scale of 0 to 1, where zero is the minimum and one is the maximum. Hence if the minimum life expectancy is 25 years and the maximum 85 and the actual value for a country is 55 years, then its index value for life expectancy is 0.50. On an overall basis HDI measures a country's relative position in relation to a final target expressed as a value between zero and one. Countries with an HDI below 0.5 are considered to have a low level of human development, those between 0.5 and 0.8 a medium level and those above 0.8 a high level. Over the years 1960–92 all countries have made substantial progress in human development e.g., the overall HDI for the developing countries increased from 0.260 to 0.541. In East Asia, the region with the largest increase in HDI, the HDI value increased from 0.255 to 0.653, i.e., two and a half times.

It would be quite challenging to incorporate these aspects of human development into the main corpus of new growth theory.

8.4 INSTITUTIONAL CHANGE AND ORGANIZA-TIONAL DEVELOPMENT

Economic growth is a process involving the various agents, who are consumers, producers, innovators and risk takers. But they all have to operate in the framework of a given institution, its structure and organization. Economic historians who study the empirical experiences of what is called 'overall social development' find in the current economic growth theory several basic weaknesses. First of all, the technology of physical and human capital and their evolution comprise only a very superficial aspect of the whole process of growth as development. It is the structure of incentives and disincentives that make up the institutional structure and organizational change, which constitute the basic foundation of the whole development process. Olson (1982) and North (1990) have analyzed the roles of institutional change and organizational reforms in the historical context. Recently Greif (1993) has argued on the basis of historical case studies that it is the belief systems of societies and their value systems and the way they evolve that is the key underlying determinant of institutional change and overall development. Secondly, economic growth dependent as it is on a stable system of political and economic institutions requires the continuous interaction between institutions and organizations. As North (1996) has argued convincingly that it is this interaction which is the key to institutional change and it occurs in the economic setting of scarcity and market competition. In this view the institutions are the rules of the game, whereas organizations are the players, e.g., firms, households, corporate bodies, government and other political and educational organizations. To substantiate his view, North refers to the successful growth experiences of NICs in Asia, where the active participation of the government and other political and corporate organizations played a decisive role in bringing about competitive market framework and an openness in world trade. Finally, the experiences of the World Bank in initiating and implementing a large number of specific development projects related to infrastructure services have found the organizational problems as the key stumbling blocks to growth and development. Thus the *World Development Report* 1994 mentions a survey of 44 countries over the period 1980–92 which had initiated World Bank-financed projects designed to improve infrastructure performance. The survey results revealed that the most common problems are managerial: unclear goals, lack of managerial autonomy and accountability and labor problems. The political will to initiate organizational reforms and introduce managerial efficiency also seems to be lacking in many developing societies that did not have success stories of rapid economic growth of the Asian NICs.

Innovations need not be only in R&D. They must occur in organizational structure also, since the organizational structure is not about reporting lines but about making room for processes of change and evolution. History shows the three key elements of organizational development as an innovative process: learn, coordinate and integrate. Learn the new knowledge about the new technology, then coordinate the different facets of the learning game across the managers and organization leaders in different divisions and areas and finally, integrate and improve the innovative process. Much like Schumpeter we have to initiate the innovative process, stay with it and improve on it continually. This is as much in product-oriented research as in organizational and institutional development. Past history in the sense of endowment and the institution–organization complex is as much important as future expectations in a forward-looking view of economic growth as an overall process of development.

References

Aghion, P. and Howitt, P. (1977), 'A Schumpeterian perspective on growth and competition', in D.M. Kreps and K.F. Wallis (eds.), *Advances in Economics and Econometrics: Theory and Applications*, New York: Cambridge University Press.

Aghion, P. and Howitt, P. (1992), 'A model of growth through creative destruction', *Econometrica*, **60**: 323–351.

Aghion, P. and Howitt, P. (1996), 'The observational implications of Schumpeterian growth theory', in S. Durlauf, J.F. Helliwell and B. Raj (eds.), *Long-Run Economic Growth*, Heidelberg: Physica-Verlag.

Amsden, A.H. (1989), *Asia's Next Giant*, Oxford: Oxford University Press.

Arrow, K.J. (1962), 'The economic implications of learning by doing', *Review of Economic Studies*, **29**: 155–174.

Arrow, K.J. and Kurz, M. (1970), *Public Investment, The Rate of Return and Optimal Fiscal Policy*, Baltimore: Johns Hopkins Press.

Aschauer, D.A. (1989), 'Public investment and productivity, growth in the group of seven', *Economic Perspectives*, **13**: 17–25.

Aumann, R.J. (1974), 'Subjectivity and correlation in randomized strategies', *Journal of Mathematical Economics*, **1**: 67–96.

Bacha, E.L. (1984), 'Growth with limited supplies of foreign exchange: a reappraisal of the two-gag model', in M. Syrquin, L. Taylor and W. Westphal (eds.), *Economic Structure and Performance*, New York: Academic Press.

Balassa, B. (1983), 'Outward vs. inward orientation once again', *World Development*, **11**: 215–218.

Barker, G. (1968), *Ecological Psychology: Concepts and Methods for Studying the Environment of Human Behavior*, Stanford: Stanford University Press.

Barro, R.J. (1989), 'Government spending in a simple model of endogenous growth', Working Paper No. 186, Washington, D.C.: National Bureau of Economic Research.

Barro, R.J. and Martin, X. (1994), 'Quality improvements in models of growth', Working Paper, Washington, D.C: National Bureau of Economic Research.

Basu, S. and Fernald, J.G. (1995), 'Are apparent productive spillovers a figment of specific error?', *Journal of Monetary Economics*, **36**: 165–188.

Basu, S. (1996), 'Procyclical productivity: increasing returns on cyclical utilization', *Quarterly Journal of Economics*, **111**: 719–752.

Benassy, J. (1982), *The Economics of Market Disequilibrium*, New York: Academic Press.

Bernstein, J. and Mohnen, P. (1994), 'International R&D spillovers between US and Japanese R&D intensive sectors', National Bureau of Economic Reesarch Working Paper No. 4682, Cambridge, Massachusetts.

Bhagwati, J.N. (1988), 'Export promoting trade strategy: issues and evidence', *World Bank Research Observer*, **3**: 27–58.

Bharucha-Reid, A.T. (1960), *Elements of the Theory of Markov Processes and Their Applications*, New York: McGraw Hill.

Binder, M. and Pesaran, M.H. (1996), 'Stochastic growth', Working Paper No. 96-18, University of Maryland, Department of Economics.

Brock, W.A., Dechert, W.D. and Scheinkman, J. (1986) 'A test for independence based on the correlation dimension', Working Paper, Department of Economics, University of Wisconsin, Madison.

Brock, W.A. (1990), 'Chaos and complexity in economic and financial science', in G.M. von Furstenbreg (ed.), *Acting Under Uncertainty*, Dordrecht: Kluwer Academic Publishers.

Bradford, C.I. (1987), 'Trade and structural change: NICs and next-tier NICs as transitional economies', *World Development*, **15**: 299–316.

Brynjdfsson, E. and Hitt, L. (1993), 'Is information systems spending productive? new evidence', *Proceedings of the 14th International Conference on Information Systems*, Orlando, Florida.

Caballero, R. and Lyons, R. (1992), 'The case for external economies', in A. Cukierman, Z. Hercowitz and L. Leiderman (eds.), *Political Economy, Growth and Business Cycles*, Cambridgem Massachusetts: MIT Press.

Caballero, R.J. and Lyons, R.K. (1992), *Political Economy, Growth and Business Cycles*, in A. Cukierman, Z. Hercowitz and L. Leidermann (eds.), Cambridge, Massachusetts: MIT Press.

Caballero, R. and Lyons, R. (1992), 'External effects in U.S. procyclical productivity', *Journal of Monetary Economics*, **29**: 209–226.

Caves, R.E. and Barton, D.R. (1989), 'Efficiency, productivity growth and international trade', in D. Audretsch, L. Sleuwaegen and H. Yamawaki (eds.), *The Convergence of International and Domestic Markets*, Amsterdam: North Holland.

Cheung, Y. and Lai, K.S. (1977), 'On cross-country differences in the persistence of real exchange rates', Working Paper No. 372, Department of Economics, University of California Santa Cruz.

Cho, Y.J. (1990), 'The financial policy and the financial sector developments in Korea and Taiwan,' in J.W. Kwon (ed.), *Korean Economic Development*, New York: Greenwood Press.

Chow, P.C. (1967), 'Causality between export growth and industrial development', *Journal of Development Economics*, **26**: 55–62.

Coe, D. and Helpman, E. (1995), 'International R&D spillovers', *European Economic Review*, **39**, 859–887.

Coe, D., Helpman, E. and Hoffmaister, A. (1997), 'North-South R&D spillovers', *Economic Journal*, **107**, 134–149.

Cohen, M.A. and Lee, H.L. (1985), 'Manufacturing strategy: concepts and methods', in P. Kleindorfer (ed.) *The Management of Productivity and Technology in Manufacturing*, New York: Plenum Press.

Cohen, W.M. and Levinthal, D.A. (1989), 'Innovation and learning: the two faces of R&D', *Economic Journal*, **99**: 569–596.

Creedy, J. and Martin, V.L. (1994), *Chaos and Nonlinear Models in Economics*, Cheltenham, U.K.: Edward Elgar Publishing.

Cyert, R.M. and March, J.G. (1963), *A Behavioral Theory of the Firm*, Englewood Cliffs, New Jersey, Prentice Hall.

Dadkhah, K.M. and Zahedi, F. (1986), 'Simultaneous estimation of production function and capital stocks for developing countries', *Review of Economics and Statistics*, **68**, 75–82.

Dahlman, C. and Nelson, R. (1995), 'Social absorption capability, national innovation systems and economic development,' in B. Koo and D.H. Perkins (eds.), *Social Capability and Long-Term Economic Growth*, New York: St. Martin's Press.

Dana, R. and Montrucchio, L. (1993), 'Stationary Markovian strategies in dynamic games', in R. Becker, M. Boldrin, R. Jones and W. Thompson (eds.), *General Equilibrium, Growth and Trade*, New York: Academic Press.

Day, R.H. and Chen, P. (1993), *Nonlinear Dynamics and Evolutionary Economics*, New York: Oxford University Press.

DeBresson, C. (1996), *Economic Interdependence and Innovative Activity: An Input-Output Analysis*, Cheltenham, U.K.: Edward Elgar.

Delong, J. and Summers, L. (1991), 'Equipment investment and economic growth', *Quarterly Journal of Economics*, **106**, 445–502.

Dervis, K., DeMelo, J. and Robinson, S. (1984), *General Equilibrium Models for Development Policy*, Cambridge: Cambridge University Press.

Dewan, K. and Min, M. (1997), 'Information technology and its impact', *World Development*, **25**, 143–164.

Dixit, A. and Stiglitz, J.E. (1977), 'Monopolistic competition and optimum product diversity', *American Economic Review*, **67**: 297–308.

Dixit, A. and Norman, V. (1980), *Theory of International Trade: A Dual General Equilibrium Approach*, New York: Cambridge University Press.

Duysters, G. (1996), *The Dynamics of Technical Innovation*, Cheltenham, U.K.: Edward Elgar Publishing.

Eaton, J. and Kortum, S. (1995), 'International patenting and technology diffusion', Working paper, Boston University, Boston.

Edwards, S. (1989), 'Openness, outward orientation, trade liberalization and economic performance in developing countries', Working Paper No. 2908, Cambridge, Massachusetts: National Bureau of Economic Research.

Edwards, S. (1997), 'Openness productivity and growth: what do we really know?', National Bureau of Economic Research, Working paper.

England, R.W. (1994), *Evolutionary Concepts in Contemporary Economics*, Ann Arbor, Michigan: University of Michigan Press.

Engle, R.F. and Granger, C.W.J. (1987), 'Cointegration and error correction: representation, estimation and testing', *Econometrica*, **56**: 251–276.

Enos, J.L. and Park, W.H. (1988), *The Adoption and Diffusion of Imported Technology*, London: Crom Helm.

Ethier, W.J. (1982), 'National and international returns to scale in the modern theory of international trade', *American Economic Review*, **72**: 389–405.

Feder, G. (1982), 'On exports and economic growth', *Journal of Development Economics*, **12**: 59–73.

Filippini, L. and Rovetta, A. (1989), 'Economic aspects of factory automation and system flexibility', in F. Archetti (ed.), *Operations Research Models in Flexible Manufacturing Systems*, New York: Springer Verlag.

Fischer, S. (1993), 'The role of macroeconomic factors in growth', National Bureau of Economic Research Working Paper No. 4565, Cambridge, Massachusetts.

Fox, K.A., Sengupta, J.K. and Thorbecke, E. (1973), *The Theory of Quantitative Economic Policy with Applications to Economic Growth, Stabilization and Planning*, Amsterdam: North Holland.

Fox, K.A. (1985), *Social System Accounts*, Dordrecht: Reidel Publishing Company.

Frankel, J. and Froot, K. (1986), 'Understanding the US Dollar in the 80s: the expectations of chartists and fundamentalists', *Economics Record*, **62**: 24–38.

Frankel, J.A. (1991), 'The collapse of purchasing power parities during the 1970s', in G. Menil and R.J. Gordon (eds.), *International Volatility and Economic Growth*, Amsterdam: North Holland.

Goodwin, R.M. (1990), *Chaotic Economic Dynamics*, Oxford: Clarendon Press.

Granger, C.W.J. (1969), 'Investigating causal relations by econometric models and cross-spectral methods', *Econometrica*, **37**: 85–94.

Grassberger, P. and Procaccia, I. (1983), 'Estimation of the Kolmogorov entropy from the chaotic signal', *Physical Review*, **28**: 2591–2593.

Gregory, A.W., Pagan, A.R. and Smith, G.W. (1993), 'Estimating linear quadratic models with integrated processes', in P.C.B. Phillips (ed.), *Models, Methods and Applications in Econometrics,* Cambridge: Blackwell Publishers.

Greif, A. (1993), 'Cultural beliefs and the organization of society', *Journal of Political Economy*, **101**: 912–950.

Grossman, G.M. and Helpman, E. (1991), *Innovations and Growth in the Global Economy*, Cambridge, Massachusetts: MIT Press.

Grossman, G.M. and Helpman, E. (1994), 'Endogenous innovation in the theory of growth', *Journal of Economic Perspectives*, **8**: 23–44.

Grossman, G.M. and Helpman, E. (1990), 'Trade innovations and growth', *American Economic Review*, **80**: 86–91.

Grossman, G.M. and Helpman, E. (1991), *Innovation and Growth in the Global Economy*, Cambridge, Massachusetts: MIT Press.

Grossman, G.M. and Krueger, A.B. (1994), 'Economic growth and the environment', National Bureau of Economic Research Working Paper No. 4634, Washington, D.C.

Gunning, J.W. and Keyser, M. (1993), 'Applied general equilibrium models in policy analysis', in T.N. Srinivasan and J. Behrman (eds.), *Handbook of Development Economics*, Vol. 3, Amsterdam: Elsevier Science Publishers.

Hall, R.E. (1990), 'Invariance properties of Solow's productivity residual', in P. Diamond (ed.), *Growth, Productivity and Unemployment*, Cambridge, Massachusetts: MIT Press.

Hall, S.G. and Henry, S.G. (1988), *Macroeconomic Modelling*, Amsterdam: North Holland.

Hamilton, D.E. (1996), 'How productive are public, private and human capital in the U.S?', unpublished paper.

Havrylyshyn, O. (1990), 'Trade policy and productivity gains in developing countries: a survey of literature', *World Bank Research Observer*, **5**: 1–24.

Holtz-Eakin, D. and Schwartz, A.E. (1994), 'Infrastructure in a structural model of economic growth', National Bureau of Economic Research Working Paper No. 4824, Washington, D.C.

Jovanovic, B. (1997), 'Learning and growth', in D.M. Kreps and K.F. Wallis (eds.), *Advances in Economics and Econometrics: Theory and Applications*, Cambridge: Cambridge University Press.

Kearns, P. and Pagan, A.R. (1990), 'Australian stock market volatility', Working Paper No. 248, Rochester Center for Economic Research, University of Rochester.

Kellman, M. and Chow, P.C. (1989), 'The comparative homogeneity of the East Asian NIC exports of similar manufacturers', *World Development*, **17**: 65–74.

Kennan, J. (1979), 'The estimation of partial adjustment models with rational expectations', *Econometrica*, **47**: 1441–1457.

Kennedy, C. (1964), 'Induced bias in innovation and the theory of distribution', *Economic Journal*, **74**: 150–162.

Kerman, J. (1979), 'The estimation of partial adjustment models with rational expectations', *Econometrica*, **47**: 1441–1457.

Kim, L. (1995), 'Absorptive capacity and industrial growth: a conceptual framework and Korea's experience', in B. Koo and D.H. Perkins (eds.), *Social Capability and Long-Term Economic Growth*, New York: St. Martin's Press.

Kraemer, K.L. and Dedrick, J. (1994), 'Payoffs from investment in information technology: lessons from the Asia–Pacific Region', *World Development*, **22**, 1921–1931.

Krugman, P.R. (1991), 'Target zones and exchange rate dynamics', *Quarterly Journal of Economics*, **56**: 669–682.

Kwon, J.K. (1986), 'Capital utilization, economies of scale and technical change in the growth of total factor productivity: an explanation of South Korean manufacturing growth', *Journal of Development Economics*, **24**: 75–89.

Landau, D. (1983), 'Government expenditure and economic growth: a cross-country study', *Southern Economic Journal*, **49**: 783–792.

Lau, L.J. (1996), 'The sources of long term economic growth: observations from the experience of developed and devloping countries', in R. Landau, T. Taylor and G. Wright (eds.), *The Mosaic of Economic Growth*, Stanford: Stanford University Press.

Lee, J. (1990), 'Government spending and economic growth', in J.K. Kwon, (ed.), *Korean Economic Development*, New York: Greenwood Press.

Lee, S.C. (1991), 'The heavy and chemical industries promotion plan (1973-79)', in L. Cho and Y. Kim (eds.), *Economic Development in the Republic of Korea*, Honolulu: University of Hawaii Press.

Levine, R., Klevorick, A., Nelson, R. and Winter, S. (1987), 'Appropriating the returns from industrial R&D', *Brookings Papers on Economic Activity*, **35**: 783–820.

Levine, R. and Reinelt, D. (1982), 'A sensitivity analysis of cross-country growth regressions', *American Economic Review*, **82**: 942–963.

Levine, R. and Reinelt, D. (1990), 'A sensitivity analysis of cross-country growth regressions', Working Paper, Harvard University.

Levine, A. and Raut, L.K. (1992), 'Complementarities between exports and human capital in economic growth: evidence from the semi-industrialized countries', Working Paper, University of California, San Diego.

Lin, D. (1996), *Explaining Economic Growth: A New Analytical Framework*, Cheltenham, U.K.: Edward Elgar Publishing.

Lombardini, S. and Donati, F. (1996), 'Selection, innovation and economic development: computational economic analysis', in S. Lombardini (ed.), *Growth and Economic Development*, Cheltenham, UK: Edward Elgar Publishing.

Lorenz, E. (1963), 'Deterministic nonperiodic flow', *Journal of the Atmospheric Sciences*, **20**: 130–141.

Lorenz, H. (1993), *Nonlinear Dynamical Economics and Chaotic Motion*, Berlin: Springer-Verlag.

Lucas, R.E. (1988), 'On the mechanics of economic development', *Journal of Monetary Economics*, **22**: 3–22.

Lucas, R.E. (1990), 'Why does not capital flow from rich to poor countries?', *American Economic Review*, **80**: 92–96.

Lucas, R.E. (1993), 'Making a miracle', *Econometrica*, **61**: 251–272.

Mailath, G.J. (1992), 'Introduction symposium on evolutionary game theory', *Journal of Economic Theory*, **57**: 259–277.

Mairesse, J. and Sassenou, M. (1991), 'R&D and productivity: a survey of econometric studies at the firm level', National Bureau of Economic Research Working Paper No. 3666, Washington D.C.

Mankiew, N., Romer, D. and Weil, D. (1992), 'A contribution to the empirics of economic growth', *Quarterly Journal of Economics ,* **107**: 407–437.

May, R.M. (1973), *Stability and Complexity in Model Ecosystems*, Princeton, N.J.: Princeton University Press.

McCallum, B.T. (1996), 'Neoclassical vs. endogenous growth analysis: an overview', National Bureau of Economic Research Working Paper No. 5844, Washington D.C.

Medio, A. (1992), *Chaotic Dynamics: Theory and Applications to Economics*, Cambridge: Cambridge University Press.

Metcalfe, J.S. (1985), 'On the diffusion of innovation and the evolution of technology', in B. Williams, J. Bryan and G. Brown (eds.), *Knowns and Unknowns in Technical Change*, London: Technical Change Centre.

Miller, S.M. (1985), 'Impacts of robotics and flexible manufacturing technologies on manufacturing costs and employment', in P.R. Kleindorfer (ed.), *The Management of Productivity and Technology in Manufacturing*, New York: Plenum Press.

Morrison, C.J. and Berndt, E.R. (1981), 'Short-run labor productivity in a dynamic model', *Journal of Econometrics*, **16**: 339–365.

Nadiri, M.I. and Kim, S. (1996), 'R&D, production structure and productivity growth: a comparison of the US, Japanese and Korean manufacturing sectors', National Bureau of Economic Research Working

Paper No. 5506, Cambridge, Massachusetts.

Nelson, D.B. (1991), 'Conditional heteroscedasticity in asset returns: a new approach', *Econometrica*, **59**: 347–370.

Nelson, R. and Winter, S. (1982), *An Evolutionary Theory of Economic Change*, Cambridge, Massachusetts, Harvard University Press.

Nordhaus, W.D. (1967), 'The optimal rate and direction of technical change', in K. Shell (ed.), *Essays on the Theory of Optimum Economic Growth*, Cambridge, Massachusetts: MIT Press.

Norsworthy, J.R. and Jang, S.L. (1992), *Empirical Measurement and Analysis of Productivity and Technological Change*, Amsterdam: North Holland.

North, D. (1990), *Institutions, Institutional Change and Economic Performance*, Cambridge: Cambridge University Press.

North, D. (1996), 'Some fundamental puzzles in economic history and development', unpublished paper, Washington University, St. Louis.

Ohyama, M. and Fukushima, Y. (1995), 'Endogenous dualistic structure, Marshallian externalities and industrialization', in S. Chang and S. Katayama (eds.), *Imperfect Competition in International Trade*, Dordrecht: Kluwer Academic Publishers.

Olson, M. (1982), *The Rise and Decline of Nations*, New Haven: Yale University Press.

Parente, S. and Prescott, E. (1994), 'Barriers to technology adoption and development', *Journal of Political Economy*, **102**: 298–321.

Parker, G.A. and Hammerstein, P. (1985), 'Game theory and animal behavior', in P.J. Greenwood, P. Harvey and M. Slatkin (eds.), *Evolution: Essays in Honour of John Maynard Smith*, Cambridge: Cambridge University Press.

Phillips, P.C. and Durlauf, S.N. (1986), 'Multiple time series regressions with integrated processes', *Review of Economic Studies*, **53**: 473–495.

Puu, T: (1993), *Nonlinear Economic Dynamics*, Berlin: Springer-Verlag.

Quah, D. and Rauch, J.E. (1990), 'Openness and the rate of economic growth', seminar paper presented in University of California, Santa Barbara.

Renis, G. (1990), 'Contrasts in the political economy of development and policy change', in G. Gereffi and D.L. Wyman (eds.), *Manufacturing Miracles: Paths of Industrialization in Latin America and East Asia*, Princeton: Princeton University Press.

Romer, P.M. (1986), 'Increasing returns and long-run growth', *Journal of Political Economy*, **94**: 1002–1037.

Romer, P.M. (1990), 'Are non convexities important for understanding growth?', *American Economic Review*, **80**: 97–103.

Romer, P.M. (1990), 'Endogenous technological change', *Journal of Political Economy*, **98**: S71–S102.

Romer, P. (1991), 'Increasing returns and new developments in the theory of growth', in W.A. Barnett (ed.), *Equilibrium Theory and Applications*, Cambridge: Cambridge University Press.

Rosenberg, N. (1996), 'Uncertainty and technological change', in R. Landau, T. Taylor and G. Wright (eds.), *The Mosaic of Economic Growth*, Stanford: Stanford University Press.

Sachs, J.D. (1987), 'Trade and exchange rate policies in growth-oriented adjustment programs', in V. Corbo, M. Goldstein and M. Khan (eds.), *Growth-Oriented Adjustment Programs*, Washington, D.C.: IMF and the World Bank.

Saviotti, P.O. and Metcalfe, J.S. (1991), *Evolutionary Theories of Economic and Technological Change*, Chur: Harwood Academic Publishers.

Scherer, F.M. (1996), 'Learning by doing and international trade in semiconductors', in E. Helmstadter and M. Perlman (eds.), *Behavioral Norms, Technological Progress and Economic Dynamics: Studies in Schumpeterian Economics*, Ann Arbor: University of Michigan Press.

Schive, C. (1990), 'The next stage of industrialization in Taiwan and South Korea,' in G. Gereffi and D.L. Wyman (eds.), *Manufacturing Miracles: Paths of Industrialization in Latin America and East Asia*, Princeton: Princeton University Press.

Schumpeter, J.A. (1934), *The Theory of Economic Development*, Cambridge, Massachusetts: Harvard University Press.

Schumpeter, J.A. (1961), *The Theory of Economic Development*, New York: Oxford University Press.

Schumpeter, J.A. (1939), *Business Cycles*, New York: McGraw Hill.

Sengupta, J.K. (1991), 'Rapid growth in NICs in Asia: tests of new growth theory for Korea', *Kyklos*, **44**: 561–579.

Sengupta, J.K. and Espana, J.R. (1992), 'Exports and economic growth in Asian NICs', Working Paper, University of California, Santa Barbara.

Sengupta, J.K. (1993), 'Growth in NICs in Asia', *Journal of Development Studies*, **29**: 342–357.

Sengupta, J.K. (1993), 'Growth in NICs in Asia: some tests of new growth theory', *Journal of Development Studies*, **29**: 342–357.

Sengupta, J.K. and Espana, J.R. (1994), 'Exports and economic growth in Asian NICs: an econometric analysis for Korea', *Applied Economics* , **26**: 41–51.

Sengupta, J.K. (1994), 'Empirical tests of new growth theory: openness and growth', *Journal of Economic Integration*, **9**: 393–415.

Sengupta, J.K. (1995), *Dynamics of Data Envelopment Analysis*, Dordrecht: Kluwer Academic Publishers.

Sengupta, J.K. (1995), *Dynamics of Data Envelopment Analysis: Theory of Systems Efficiency*, Dordrecht: Kluwer Academic Publishers.

Sengupta, J.K. and Zheng, Y. (1995), 'Empirical tests of chaotic dynamics in market volatility', *Applied Financial Economics*, **5**: 291–300.

Sengupta, J.K. and Okamura, K. (1996), 'Learning by doing and openness in Japanese growth: a new approach', *Japan and the World Economy*, **8**: 43–64.

Sengupta, J.K. and Fanchon, P. (1997), *Control Theory Methods in Economics*, Dordrecht: Kluwer Academic Publishers.

Sengupta, J.K. and Sfeir, R.E. (1997a), 'Modelling exchange rate volatility', *International Journal of Systems Science*, **28**: 617–624.

Sengupta, J.K. and Sfeir, R.E. (1997b), 'Exchange rate instability: some empirical tests of temporal dynamics', *Applied Economics Letters*, **4**: 547–550.

Shafer, D.M. (1994), *Winners and Losers: How Sectors Shape the Development Prospects of States*, Ithaca: Cornell University Press.

Simon, H.A. (1957), *Models of Man: Social and Rational*, New York: John Wiley.

Sims, C. (1972), 'Money, income and causality', *American Economic Review*, **62**: 540–552.

Smith, J.M. (1982), *Evolution and the Theory of Games*, Cambridge: Cambridge University Press.

Solow, R.M. (1956), 'A contribution to the theory of economic growth', *Quarterly Journal of Economics*, **70**: 65–94.

Solow, R.M. (1957), 'Technical change and the aggregate production function', *Review of Economics and Statistics*, **39**: 312–320.

Solow, R.M. (1994), 'Perspectives on growth theory', *Journal of Economic Perspectives*, **8**: 45–54.

Solow, R.M. (1997), *Learning from Learning by Doing*, Stanford: Stanford University Press.

Song, B. (1994), *The Rise of the Korean Economy*, New York: Oxford University Press.

Stokey, N.L. (1991), 'Human capital, product quality and growth', *Quarterly Journal of Economics*, **106**: 587–616.

Summers, R. and Heston, A. (1984), 'Improved international comparisons of real product and its composition: 1950–80', *Review of Income and Wealth*, **30**: 207–262.

Sylos-Labini, P. (1984), *The Forces of Economic Growth and Decline*, Cambridge, Massachusetts: MIT Press.

Tallman, E. and Wang, P. (1993), 'Educational achievement and economic growth: evidence from Taiwan', Working Paper, Federal Reserve Bank of Atlanta.

Theil, H. (1992), *Consumer Demand Analysis and Information Theory*, Boston: Kluwer Academic Publishers.

Tintner, G. (1969), 'An application of the variate difference method to permanent income hypothesis', unpublished paper.

Tintner, G. and Sengupta, J.K. (1972), *Stochastic Economics*, New York: Academic Press.

Tobin, J. (1994), 'A tax on international currency transactions', *Human Development Report 1994*, Oxford: Oxford University Press.

Treadway, A.B. (1974), 'The globally optimal flexible accelerator', *Journal of Economic Theory*, **7**: 17–39.

Verbiest, J.P. (1989), 'Exchange rate experience in the Asian–Pacific region in the 1980s', *Econometric Modelling and Forecasting in Asia, Development Papers No. 9*, New York: United Nations.

Wen, K. (1996), 'Continuous-time chaos in stock market dynamics', in W.A. Barnett, A.P. Kirman and M. Salmon (eds.), *Nonlinear Dynamics and Economics*, New York: Cambridge University Press.

Young, A. (1991), 'Learning by doing and the dynamic effects of international trade', *Quarterly Journal of Economics*, **106**: 369–406.

Young, A. (1995), 'The tyranny of numbers: confronting the statistical realities of the East Asian growth experience', *Quarterly Journal of Economics*, **110**: 641–680.

Yu, X. (1996), 'Controlling Lorenz chaos', *International Journal of Systems Science*, **27**: 355–360.

Index

accumulation of capital 16–18, 210
adaptive system 61–65
adjustment costs 86
agents' expectations 86
Arrow, K. 41
Asian NIC 66–73

balance of payments 122–124
birth and death process 57–60
Bharucha-Reid, A.T. 47

capital accumulation 41–44
  and learning 52–56
  in Romer model 55
cointegration 68–70
commodity market 174
  and general equilibrium 172–178
comparative advantage 122–124
competitive market structure 9–11
complementarities in
  production 13–15, 17–20
computable equilibrium 174–176
computer industry
  and CAD 189–191, 195
  and CAM 194–196
conditional convergence 21
convergence 20–26
creative destruction 183–191

Darwinian evolution 194–196
death of firms 57, 193–197
developing countries 209–213
development models 9–12

econometric decision rules 86–92
economies of scale 16–20, 84–87
education
  and knowledge capital 18–20, 113
  and R&D 113–115, 178–180
efficiency 17–20
evolution
  after Schumpeter 183–187
  biological 197–198
evolutionary processes 201–203
evolutionary stable equilibrium
  202–205
ESS theory 202–206
exchange rate fluctuations 122–127
externalities in growth 67–82

financial markets instability 133–
  138
foreign investment
  and economic growth 84, 94
  and R&D expenditure 174–179
free trade and openness 18–21, 74–
  76

growth theory
  and human capital 17–23
  and learning by doing 41–46
  and productivity growth 22–26

human capital and economic
  growth 17–21
human development index 216–
  218

inflation and exchange rates 122–125

information technology and knowledge spillover 190–195
and R&D investment 195

infrastructure and development 209–213

innovations in Schumpeterian model 183-186

instability in chaotic systems 51–52
in exchange markets 124, 133

interdependence
between innovations 57–60
between sectors 18–22

inventions and R&D investment 183–186

investment
in human capital 17–19, 81–82
in physical capital 15–20
in R&D expenditure 190–193

labor allocation in research 55

learning
and evolution 197–198
by doing 40–48, 187
process 182–185

Lucas, R.E. 17

manufacturing industry and flexible manufacturing 196–197

market power and growth 61

model of creative destruction 183

monopolistic competition 159–161

Nash equilibrium and ESS theory 200–205

new growth theory 2–6, 12–18

newly industrializing country (NIC) 66–74

nonstationary 7

oligopoly 61, 84–88

optimal growth and market equilibrium 86–88

optimal path of growth
in Lucas model 17–20
in Solow model 21–22, 83–84

price changes and technological progress 62–64

price system in equilibrium path 64

privatization 213

product innovations 198–200

production (externalities) 215

production function and technical change 13–14, 62–63
in Lucas model 15–18

productivity and economic growth 42–45, 209
and infrastructure investment 209
of human capital 17

propensity to innovate 183–187

public goods
and capital productivity 210–214
and externalities 215
and infrastructure investment 214

rate of technical progress 41–43

rational expectations and optimal adjustment 155–163

research and development
and economic growth 190–191
in Schumpeterian model 183–187

returns to scale 3–5, 17–20

risk and research activity 195–197

Romer, P.M. 17

Schumpeterian models 183–186

social overhead capital 214–217

Solow models 3–6, 15, 70–72

species evolution 197–200

speculators' role 119–121

stationary state and optimal
  growth 14–16, 21

stochastic process
  in birth and death process model 57
  in diffusion 60–62
  in logistic model 205–207

technological progress and
  investment 13–16

telecommunications industry 187

trade balance 122

transmission of knowledge 18, 113,
  115

uncertainty in decision
  models 44–49

utility functional 43, 56, 169

variety of products 198

Walrasian equilibrium 172